Mathematics
for Elementary Teachers
ACTIVITIES MANUAL

THIRD EDITION

SYBILLA BECKMANN
UNIVERSITY OF GEORGIA

Addison-Wesley

Boston   Columbus   Indianapolis   New York   San Francisco   Upper Saddle River
Amsterdam   Cape Town   Dubai   London   Madrid   Milan   Munich   Paris   Montreal   Toronto
Delhi   Mexico City   Sao Paulo   Sydney   Hong Kong   Seoul   Singapore   Taipei   Tokyo

Acquisitions Editor: Marnie Greenhut
Executive Project Manager: Christine O'Brien
Editorial Assistant: Elle Driska
Senior Managing Editor: Karen Wernholm
Associate Managing Editor: Tamela Ambush
Senior Production Project Manager: Sheila Spinney
Designer Supervisor: Andrea Nix
Senior Design Specialist: Heather Scott
Digital Assets Manager: Marianne Groth
Media Producer: Christine Stavrou
Executive Marketing Manager: Roxanne McCarley
Marketing Assistant: Kendra Bassi
Senior Author Support/Technology: Joe Vetere
Senior Prepress Supervisor: Caroline Fell
Rights and Permissions Advisor: Michael Joyce
Manufacturing Manager: Evelyn Beaton
Senior Manufacturing Buyer: Carol Melville
Senior Media Buyer: Ginny Michaud
Text Design Studio: Montage
Production Coordination, Composition, and Illustrations: Aptara Corporation

Cover photo: Butterflies, Shutterstock, stylized by Tamara Newman.

Photo credits: p. 255 U.S. Air Force, all others courtesy of the author.

Many of the designations used by manufacturers and sellers to distinguish their products are claimed as trademarks. Where those designations appear in this book, and Pearson was aware of a trademark claim, the designations have been printed in initial caps or all caps.

1 2 3 4 5—CRW—11 10

Addison-Wesley
is an imprint of

www.pearsonhighered.com

ISBN-10:   0-321-64696-7
ISBN-13: 978-0-321-64696-5

To Will, Joey, and Arianna

CONTENTS

PREFACE

The activities in this book are designed to help prospective elementary school teachers develop a deep understanding of elementary school mathematics.

I wrote these activities because I wanted my students to be actively engaged in mathematics in class. Few students seem to get much out of long lectures, and every teacher of math knows that math is not a spectator sport: To learn math, you have to *do* math, and you have to *think deeply* about math. Every teacher also knows that when you explain something to someone else, you deepen your own understanding—or you uncover a gap in your understanding. So when students explain their mathematical ideas to each other in class, it helps develop their own thinking.

I have tried to strike a good balance between structure and guidance on the one hand, and leaving room for students to put their own thinking into the activities on the other hand.

Although the activities are designed for college-educated adults, many can be adapted easily for use in elementary school. Indeed, I have used a number of them with children myself, and my students have too. Therefore, I hope prospective teachers will keep these activities in mind for their own teaching.

Sybilla Beckmann

Athens, Georgia

Numbers and the Decimal System

1.1 The Counting Numbers

Class Activity 1A: The Counting Numbers as a List

One way to think about the counting numbers is as a list. What are the characteristics of this list?

1. To help us think about the characteristics of the list of counting numbers, let's examine errors that very young children commonly make when they are first learning to say the list of counting numbers. Examples of some of these errors follow.

    a. Child 1 says: "1, 2, 3, 4, 5, 8, 9, 4, 5, 2, 6, …"

    b. Child 2 says: "1, 2, 3, 1, 2, 3, …"

    Identify the nature of the errors. What are characteristics of the correct list of counting numbers?

2. Children usually learn the list of counting numbers at around the same time they learn the alphabet. Compare and contrast the alphabet and the counting numbers. In particular, why is the order of the list of counting numbers more important than the order of the letters of the alphabet?

Class Activity 1B:
Connecting Counting Numbers as a List with Cardinality

To determine the number of objects in a set, we generally count the objects one by one. The process of counting the objects in a set connects the list view of the counting numbers with cardinality. Surprisingly, this connection is more subtle and intricate than we might think.

1. Spend a moment thinking about this question: If a child can correctly say the first five counting numbers—"one, two, three, four, five"—will the child necessarily be able to determine how many blocks are in a collection of 5 blocks? Why or why not? Return to this question after completing parts 2 and 3.

2. To help us think about the nature of the connection between the list view of the counting numbers and cardinality, let's examine some errors that very young children commonly make when they are first learning to count the number of objects in a set. Examples of errors follow. The picture of a pointing hand indicates a child pointing to the object. A number indicates a child saying the number.

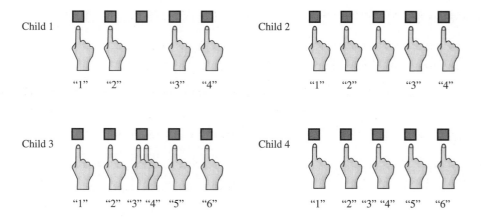

What are characteristics of correctly counting a set of objects and how does this process connect the counting numbers as a list with cardinality?

3. Compare the responses of the following two children to a teacher's request to determine how many blocks there are. Even though both children make a one-to-one correspondence between the 5 blocks and the list 1, 2, 3, 4, 5, do both children appear to understand counting equally well? If not, what is the difference?

Teacher: "How many blocks are there?"

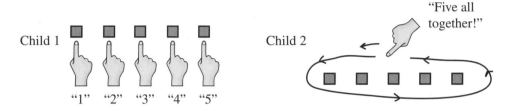

Teacher: "So how many blocks are there?"

"Five all together!"

4. Return to the question in part 1 of this activity.

5. What do children need to understand about the connection between the counting numbers as a list and for cardinality to answer the question posed by the teacher in the next scenario?

The teacher shows a child some toy bears:

The child counts that there are 6 bears. Then the teacher covers the bears and puts one more bear to the side:

The teacher says: "Now how many bears are there in all?"

a. Child 1 is unable to answer.

b. Child 2 says "1, 2, 3, 4, 5, 6" while pointing to the covered bears, then points at the new bear and says "7," and finally says "there are 7 bears."

   c. Child 3 says "6" while pointing to the covered bears, then points at the new bear and says "7," and finally says "there are 7 bears."

6. Compare these different responses to the question in part 5:

Class Activity 1C:
How Many Are There?

Each person participating in this activity needs a bunch of toothpicks (fewer than 100) or other small objects, such as coffee stirrers. Each person also needs several small plastic snack bags, some rubber bands, or both.

The purpose of this activity is to help you understand the development of our way of writing numbers.

1. Arrange your toothpicks so that you can *visually see* how many toothpicks you have. Use your plastic snack bags or rubber bands to help you organize your toothpicks. Describe how you arranged your toothpicks.

2. Does the way you arranged your toothpicks in part 1 correspond to the way you write the number that represents how many toothpicks you have? If so, explain how. If not, try to arrange your toothpicks so that you can visually see how many toothpicks you have and so that this way of arranging the toothpicks corresponds to the way we write the number that stands for how many toothpicks you have.

3. Put your toothpicks together with the toothpicks of several other people. Once again, arrange the toothpicks so that you can visually see how many toothpicks there are and so that your way of arranging the toothpicks corresponds to the way we write the number that stands for how many toothpicks there are. Use snack bags or rubber bands to help organize the toothpicks. Describe how you arranged the toothpicks.

4. Repeat the steps in part 3 but now with the toothpicks from everyone in the class. How many toothpicks are there in all?

5. If you give a child in kindergarten a bunch of counting chips and ask the child to show you what the 2 in 23 stands for, the child might show you 2 of the counting chips. You might be tempted to respond that the 2 really stands for "twenty" and not 2. It's true that the 2 does stand for twenty, but is there a better way you can respond so as to draw attention to the decimal system?

6. Draw rough pictures showing how to bundle 137 toothpicks so that the way the toothpicks are organized corresponds to the way we write the number 137.

7. Explain why the way the bagged and loose toothpicks pictured here are organized does not correspond to the way we write that number of toothpicks. Show how to reorganize these bagged and loose toothpicks so as to correspond to the way we write the number that stands for how many toothpicks there are.

Class Activity 1D: Showing the Values of Places in the Decimal System

Mrs. Kubrick wants her students to get a feel for the values of the places in the decimal system. She decides to use small stars printed on paper for this purpose, as shown in the next set of figures. One star, 10 stars, 100 stars, and 1000 stars all fit on one piece of paper. Even 10,000 stars fit on a piece of ordinary $8\frac{1}{2}$-by-11-inch paper, as on the next page.

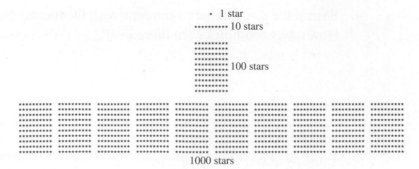

1. How many pieces of paper will Mrs. Kubrick need to show 100,000 stars? How many pieces of paper will Mrs. Kubrick need to show 1,000,000 stars?

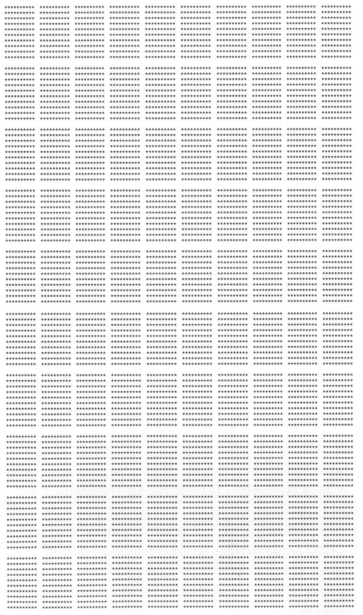

2. Mrs. Kubrick's students really want to see a billion stars. How many pieces of paper would Mrs. Kubrick need to show one billion stars?

A standard package of paper contains 500 sheets. How many packages of paper would Mrs. Kubrick need to show one billion stars? Realistically, can Mrs. Kubrick show one billion stars?

1.2 Decimals and Negative Numbers

Class Activity 1E:
Representing Decimals with Bundled Objects

1. It is not a strange idea to use 1 object to represent an amount less than 1. After all, 1 penny stands for $0.01, or one hundredth of a dollar.

   Let's make 1 paperclip stand for 0.001, or one thousandth. Show simple drawings of bundled paperclips so that the way of organizing the paperclips corresponds to the way we write the following decimals:

   0.034

   0.134

   0.13

2. Let's let 1 small bead stand for 0.0001, or one ten-thousandth. Show simple drawings of bundled beads so that the way of organizing the beads corresponds to the way we write the following decimals:

   0.0028

   0.012

3. List at least three different decimals that the toothpicks pictured here could represent. In each case, state the value of the single toothpick.

Class Activity 1F:
Representing Decimals as Lengths

A good way to represent positive decimal numbers is as lengths. Cut out the 5 long strips in Figure A.1 on page 403 and tape them end-to-end without overlaps to make one long strip. The length of this long strip is 1 unit. Cut out the ten 0.1-unit-long strips.

1. By placing strips end-to-end without gaps or overlaps, verify the following:

   a. The 1-unit-long strip is as long as 10 of the 0.1-unit-long strips.

   b. A 0.1-unit-long strip is as long as 10 of the 0.01-unit-long strips.

   c. A 0.01-unit-long strip is as long as 10 of the 0.001-unit-long strips.

   d. Now cut apart the 0.01- and 0.001-unit-long strips.

   Represent the following decimals as lengths by placing appropriate strips end-to-end without gaps or overlaps (as best you can). In each case, draw a rough sketch (which need not be to scale) to show how you represented the decimal as a length.

2. 1.234

3. 0.605

4. 1.07

5. 1.007

6. 0.089

7. Use the strips to represent some other decimals as lengths.

Class Activity 1G:
Zooming In on Number Lines

1. Label the tick marks on the number lines that follow with appropriate decimals. The second, third, and fourth number lines should be labeled as if they are "zoomed in" on the indicated portion of the previous number line.

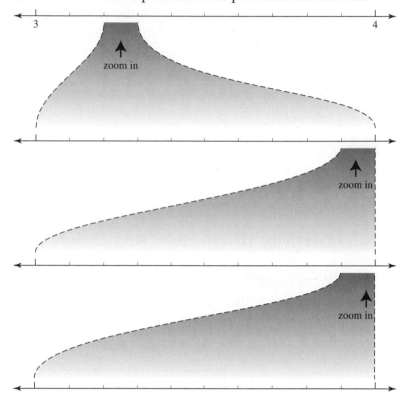

2. Now plot 3.2996 on each of the number lines in part 1 (it's easiest to start at the last number line and work backwards). Use the number lines to answer the following questions:

   a. Which whole numbers does 3.2996 lie between?

   b. Which tenths does 3.2996 lie between?

   c. Which hundredths does 3.2996 lie between?

3. Label the tick marks on the next three number lines in three different ways. In each case, your labeling should fit with the structure of the decimal system and the fact that the tick marks at the ends of the number lines are longer than the other tick marks. You may further lengthen the tick marks at either end as needed. It may help you to think about zooming in on the number line.

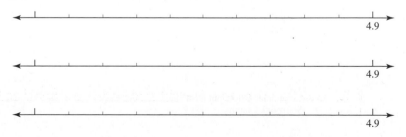

4. Why does the labeling on the next number line not fit with the structure of the decimal system?

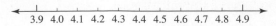

3.9 4.0 4.1 4.2 4.3 4.4 4.5 4.6 4.7 4.8 4.9

5. Label the tick marks on the next three number lines in three different ways. In each case, your labeling should fit with the structure of the decimal system and the fact that the tick marks at the ends of the number lines are longer than the other tick marks. You may further lengthen the tick marks at either end as needed. It may help you to think about zooming in on the number line.

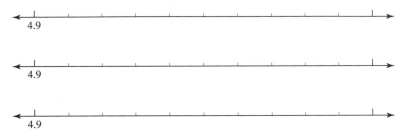

4.9

4.9

4.9

Class Activity 1H: Numbers Plotted on Number Lines

1. What number could the point labeled A on the next number line be? Among the numbers in this list, which ones could A possibly be? Which ones could A definitely not be? Why?

1.18, 1.8, 1.861, 1.4, 1.4263, 1.43, 1.6

1   A   2

2. Label the tick marks on the following number lines so that the tick marks fit with the structure of the decimal system, are as specified, and so that the given number can be plotted on the number line. The number need not land on a tick mark.

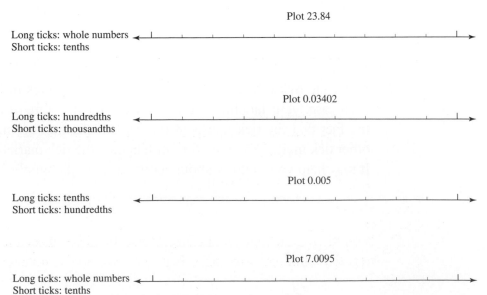

Plot 23.84

Long ticks: whole numbers
Short ticks: tenths

Plot 0.03402

Long ticks: hundredths
Short ticks: thousandths

Plot 0.005

Long ticks: tenths
Short ticks: hundredths

Plot 7.0095

Long ticks: whole numbers
Short ticks: tenths

3. Label the tick marks on the next number lines appropriately (so that the long and short tick marks fit with the structure of the decimal system) and explain why you labeled them that way.

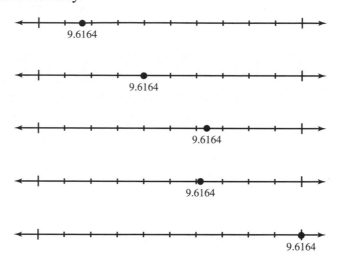

Class Activity 1I: Negative Numbers on Number Lines

1. Katie, Matt, and Parna were asked to label the tick marks on a number line on which one tick mark was already labeled as −7. What's wrong with their work? Show how to label the number line appropriately. Is there more than one way to label it appropriately?

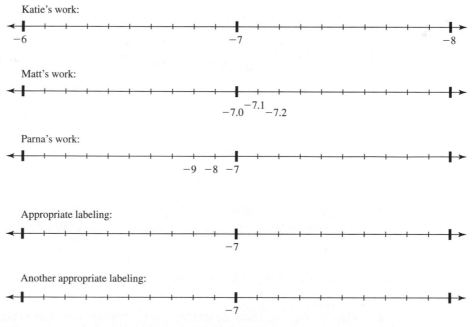

2. Sometimes students get confused about the relative locations of certain decimals, negative numbers, and zero. Plot −1 on the next number line. Then give a few

examples of numbers that lie between 0 and 1, including some that land *between* tick marks, and give a few examples of numbers that lie between 0 and −1.

1.3 Comparing Numbers in the Decimal System

Class Activity 1J: Places of Larger Value Count More Than Lower Places Combined

1. Think for a moment about how you compare two numbers to decide which one is greater. For example, how do you know that 1023 is greater than 789? Why can we compare numbers the way we do? Contemplate these questions for a few moments before moving on to the rest of the activity. Then return to these questions.

2. What is the largest number you can make that has nonzero digits only in the tens and ones places?

    make the largest ⟶ ____ ____

    What is the smallest number you can make that has a nonzero digit in the hundreds place?

    make the smallest ⟶ ____ ____ ____

    Draw *rough* pictures of bundled objects to compare these two numbers. Which is larger? How can we see this?

3. What is the largest number you can make that has nonzero digits only in the hundreds, tens, and ones places?

    make the largest ⟶ ____ ____ ____

    What is the smallest number you can make that has a nonzero digit in the thousands place?

    make the smallest ⟶ ____ ____ ____ ____

    Draw *rough* pictures of bundled objects to compare these two numbers. Which is larger? How can we see this?

4. To compare two numbers, we first look at the place of largest value in which at least one of the numbers has a nonzero entry. Why does this make sense?

Class Activity 1K: Misconceptions in Comparing Decimals

1. The list that follows describes some common errors students make when comparing decimals. For each error, think about why students might make that error.

Error 1: $2.352 > 2.4$

Error 2: $2.34 > 2.5$ (but identify correctly that $2.5 > 2.06$)

Error 3: $5.47 > 5.632$

Error 4: $1.8 = 1.08$

The next list describes some of the misconceptions students can develop about comparing decimals (See [13] and [14] for further information, including additional misconceptions and advice on instruction.)

Whole number thinking: Students with this misconception treat the portion of the number to the right of the decimal point as a whole number, thus thinking that $2.352 > 2.4$ because $352 > 4$. These students think that longer decimals are always larger than shorter ones.

Column overflow thinking: Students with this misconception name decimals incorrectly by focusing on the first nonzero digit to the right of the decimal point. For example, they say that 2.34 is "two and thirty-four tenths." These students think that $2.34 > 2.5$ because 34 tenths is more than 5 tenths. These students usually identify longer decimals as larger; they will, however, correctly identify 2.5 as greater than 2.06 because 5 tenths is more than 6 hundredths.

Denominator-focused thinking: Students with this misconception think that any number of tenths is greater than any number of hundredths and that any number of hundredths is greater than any number of thousandths, and so on. These students identify 5.47 as greater than 5.632, reasoning that 47 hundredths is greater than 632 thousandths because hundredths are greater than thousandths. Students with this misconception identify shorter decimal numbers as larger.

Reciprocal thinking: Students with this misconception view the portion of a decimal to the right of the decimal point as something like the fraction formed by taking the reciprocal. For example, they view 0.3 as something like $\frac{1}{3}$ and thus identify 2.3 as greater than 2.4 because $\frac{1}{3} > \frac{1}{4}$. These students usually identify shorter decimal numbers as larger, except in cases of intervening zeros. For example, they may say that $0.03 > 0.4$ because $\frac{1}{3} > \frac{1}{4}$.

Money thinking: Students with this difficulty truncate decimals after the hundredths place and view decimals in terms of money. If two decimals agree to the hundredths place, these students simply guess which one is greater—sometimes guessing correctly, sometimes guessing incorrectly. Most of these students recognize that 1.8 is like $1.80, although some view 1.8 incorrectly as $1.08.

2. Put the set of decimals that follow in order from least to greatest. Then show how students with the misconceptions just described would probably put the numbers in order.

3.3   3.4   3.05   3.25   3.251

Correct order (least to greatest):	
Whole number thinking:	
Column overflow:	
Denominator focused:	
Reciprocal thinking:	
Money thinking:	

3. Make up a decimal comparison quiz that provides ten pairs of decimals and asks students to circle the larger decimal in each pair. Try to pick the ten pairs so that students with the different misconceptions previously described will not give exactly the same answers for all ten pairs. For each misconception, show how students with that misconception would probably answer the quiz.

Class Activity 1L: Finding Smaller and Smaller Decimals

1. Contemplate the questions in the next paragraph for a few minutes before you continue with the rest of the activity. Then return to these questions at the end.

   The number 3 is the smallest whole number that is greater than 2. But is there a smallest *decimal* that is greater than 2? If so, what is it? If not, why not?

2. Work with a partner and take turns listing decimals, each of which is greater than 2 but less than the previous decimal that was listed. For example, if you list 2.3, your partner could list 2.2, and then you could list 2.1. You and your partner should each list six decimals.

3. Now try to stump your partner; that is, try to find a decimal such that your partner won't be able to find a decimal that is smaller than yours but is still greater than 2. Continue taking turns until one of you has stumped the other or you both agree that neither of you will be able to stump the other.

4. Does the following describe a valid decimal?

   the number 2 followed by a decimal point and infinitely many zeros and then a 1.

5. Return to the questions in part 1.

Class Activity 1M: Finding Decimals Between Decimals

1. Contemplate the questions in the following paragraph for a few minutes before you continue with the rest of the activity. Then return to these questions at the end.

   There aren't any whole numbers between 2 and 3, but there are plenty of decimals in between 2 and 3. If you are given two decimals, will there always be another decimal in between the two? Are there some decimals that don't have any other decimals in between them?

2. Work with a partner and take turns giving your partner a pair of decimals and challenging him or her to find a decimal in between your pair. For example, you could give your partner the pair 1.2, 1.4; your partner could respond with 1.3. Try to stump your partner! Continue taking turns until one of you has stumped the other or you both agree that neither of you will be able to stump the other.

3. Return to the questions in part 1.

Class Activity 1N: Decimals Between Decimals on Number Lines

For each of the pairs of numbers that follow, find a number in between the two numbers. Label the longer tick marks on the number line so that all three numbers can be plotted visibly and distinctly. The labeling should fit with the structure of the decimal system. Plot all three numbers. The numbers need not land on tick marks.

1. The numbers 1.6 and 1.7

Now, describe how to use money to find a number between 1.6 and 1.7.

2. The numbers 12.54 and 12.541

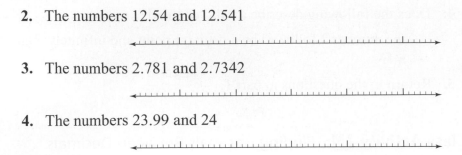

3. The numbers 2.781 and 2.7342

4. The numbers 23.99 and 24

Class Activity 1O: "Greater Than" and "Less Than" with Negative Numbers

1. Explain in two different ways why a negative number is always less than a positive number.

2. Johnny says that $-5 > -2$. Describe two different ways to explain to Johnny why this is not correct.

1.4 Rounding Numbers

Class Activity 1P: Why Do We Round?

Why do we round numbers? Write down several reasons.

Class Activity 1Q: Explaining Rounding by Zooming Out

1. Label the next number lines so that each number line is zoomed out from the previous one and so that 34,617 can be plotted on each number line. Plot 34,617 on each number line.

2. Use the same number lines to help you explain how to round 34,617 to the nearest ten, the nearest hundred, the nearest thousand, and the nearest ten-thousand.

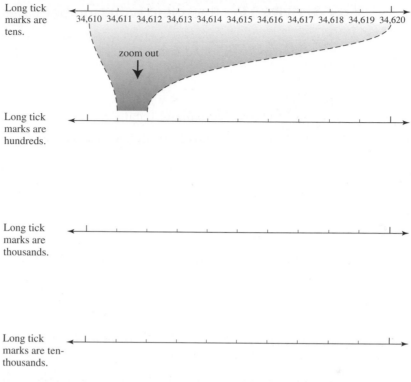

Long tick marks are tens.

34,610 34,611 34,612 34,613 34,614 34,615 34,616 34,617 34,618 34,619 34,620

zoom out

Long tick marks are hundreds.

Long tick marks are thousands.

Long tick marks are ten-thousands.

Rounding 34,617

3. Label the next number lines so that each number line is zoomed out from the previous one and so that 99.253 can be plotted on each number line. Plot 99.253 on each number line.

4. Use the same number lines as in part 3 to help you explain how to round 99.253 to the nearest hundredth, the nearest tenth, the nearest one (i.e., to the nearest whole number), and the nearest ten.

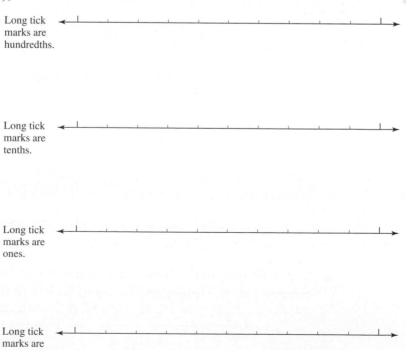

Long tick marks are hundredths.

Long tick marks are tenths.

Long tick marks are ones.

Long tick marks are tens.

Rounding 99,253

Class Activity 1R: Rounding with Number Lines

Using number lines to round can help us focus on the decimal system and understand its structure better.

a. The tick marks on the following number line are labeled with hundreds. Plot 3872 in its approximate location on this number line. Then use the number line to explain how to round 3872 to the nearest hundred.

b. Label the unlabeled tick marks on the following number line with appropriate tens so that you can plot 3872 in its approximate location on this number line. Then use the number line to explain how to round 3872 to the nearest ten.

c. The tick marks on the following number line are labeled with hundredths. Plot 2.349 in its approximate location on this number line. Then use the number line to explain how to round 2.349 to the nearest hundredth.

d. Label the unlabeled tick marks on the following number line with appropriate tenths so that you can plot 2.349 in its approximate location on this number line. Then use the number line to explain how to round 2.349 to the nearest tenth.

e. Label the tick marks on the following number line so that you can use the number line to explain how to round 54,831 to the nearest hundred.

f. Label the tick marks on the following number line so that you can use the number line to explain how to round 16.936 to the nearest hundredth.

g. Label the tick marks on the following number line so that you can use the number line to explain how to round 16.936 to the nearest tenth.

Class Activity 1S: Can We Round This Way?

Maureen has made up her own method of rounding. Starting at the right-most place in a decimal number, she keeps rounding to the value of the next place to the left until she reaches the place to which the decimal number was to be rounded.

For example, Maureen would use the following steps to round 3.2716 to the nearest tenth:

$$3.2716 \rightarrow 3.272 \rightarrow 3.27 \rightarrow 3.3$$

Try Maureen's method on several examples. Is her method valid? That is, does it always round decimal numbers correctly? Or are there examples of decimal numbers where Maureen's method does not give the correct rounding?

Fractions

2.1 The Meaning of Fractions

Class Activity 2A:
Fractions of Objects

1. Take a blank piece of paper and imagine that it is $\frac{4}{5}$ of some larger piece of paper. Fold your piece of paper to show $\frac{3}{5}$ of the larger (imagined) piece of paper. Do this as carefully and precisely as possible without using a ruler or doing any measuring. Explain why your answer is correct. Could two people have different-looking solutions that are both correct?

2. Benton used $\frac{3}{4}$ cup of butter to make a batch of cookie dough. Benton rolled his cookie dough out into a rectangle, as shown in the next figure. Now Benton wants to cut off a piece of the dough so that the portion he cuts off contains $\frac{1}{4}$ cup of butter. How could Benton cut the dough? Explain your answer.

Class Activity 2B: The Whole Associated with a Fraction

1. Maurice says that the next picture shows that $\frac{3}{6}$ is bigger than $\frac{2}{3}$. The shaded portion representing $\frac{3}{6}$ *is* larger than the shaded portion representing $\frac{2}{3}$, so why is Maurice not correct?

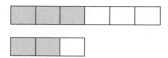

2. Kayla says that the shaded part of the next picture can't represent $\frac{1}{4}$ because there are 3 shaded circles, and 3 is more than 1, but $\frac{1}{4}$ is supposed to be less than 1. What can you tell Kayla about fractions that might help her?

3. When Ted was asked what the 4 in the fraction $\frac{3}{4}$ means, Ted said that the 4 is the whole. Explain why it is not completely correct to say, "4 is the whole." What is a better way to say what the 4 in the fraction $\frac{3}{4}$ means?

Class Activity 2C:
Relating a Fraction to Its Whole

1. At a neighborhood park, $\frac{1}{3}$ of the area of the park is to be used for a new playground. Swings will be placed on $\frac{1}{4}$ of the area of the playground. What fraction of the neighborhood park will the swing area be? Draw a picture to help you solve the problem, and explain your answer. For each fraction in this problem, and in your solution, describe the whole associated with this fraction. In other words, describe what each fraction is *of*. Are all the wholes the same or not?

2. Ben is making a recipe that calls for $\frac{1}{3}$ cup of oil. Ben has a bottle that contains $\frac{2}{3}$ cup of oil. Ben does not have any measuring cups. What fraction of the oil in the bottle should Ben use for his recipe? Draw a picture to help you solve the problem, and explain your answer. For each fraction in this problem, and in your solution, describe the whole associated with this fraction. In other words, describe what each fraction is *of*. Are all the wholes the same or not?

Class Activity 2D: Comparing Quantities with Fractions

In some situations, we can use fractions to compare amounts. Comparative language, such as "3 times as many as" and "$\frac{1}{3}$ as much as," is often difficult for children. This activity will help you practice using clear and accurate language to compare quantities.

1. Fill in the blanks to compare the amount of money Nate and Tyler raised in a fundraiser.

Nate's amount:

Tyler's amount:

Nate raised _____ as much as Tyler. The whole for this fraction is

_____

Tyler raised _____ as much as Nate. The whole for this fraction is

_____

2. Draw a strip diagram (like the one in part 1) showing that Company A sells $\frac{4}{5}$ as many trucks as Company B. Then describe the relationship the other way around, using an appropriate fraction. For each fraction, say what its whole is.

3. Make up your own examples in which you use a fraction to describe the relationship between two quantities. If possible, draw strip diagrams to show the relationships. In each case, describe the relationship the other way around, and for each fraction, say what its whole is. What do you notice about how the fractions are related?

Class Activity 2E: Fractions of Non-Contiguous Wholes

The whole that a fraction refers to need not be a single contiguous object. Instead, the whole can consist of several pieces that need not even be the same size. Working with non-contiguous wholes provides an opportunity to think more deeply about the definition of fraction.

Recall these definitions:

- An amount is $\frac{1}{B}$ of a whole if B copies of it joined together make the whole.
- An amount is $\frac{A}{B}$ of a whole if it can be formed by A parts, each of which is $\frac{1}{B}$ of the whole.

1. *Peter's garden problem:* The diagram below is a map of Peter's garden, which consists of two plots. The two plots have each been divided into 5 pieces of equal area. The shaded parts show where carrots have been planted. What fraction of the area of Peter's garden is planted with carrots?

   Spend a few minutes solving this problem yourself. Then move on to the next parts, which show methods that some students used as they attempted to solve this problem.

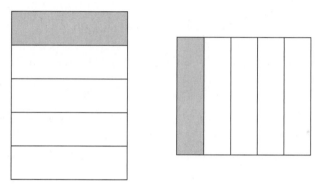

2. Mariah thought about Peter's garden problem this way: "There are 2 parts out of a total of 10 parts, so $\frac{2}{10}$ of the garden is planted with carrots. Since $\frac{2}{10} = \frac{1}{5}$, then $\frac{1}{5}$ of the garden is planted with carrots."

   Is Mariah's reasoning valid? Why or why not?

   What if the two garden plots had been the same size, then would her reasoning be valid?

3. Aysah drew this picture as she was thinking about Peter's garden problem:

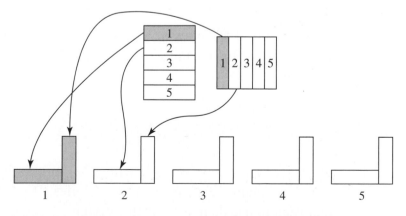

   Can Aysah's picture be used to solve the problem? Explain.

4. Matt said: "$\frac{1}{5}$ of the first plot is shaded and $\frac{1}{5}$ of the second plot is shaded. Because there are two parts shaded, each of which is $\frac{1}{5}$, this means two fifths of Peter's garden are planted with carrots."

   Is Matt's reasoning valid? Why or why not?

   What if the two garden plots were the same size and each plot had an area of 1 acre. Could Matt's reasoning be used to make a correct statement? Explain.

Class Activity 2F: Is the Meaning of Equal Parts Always Clear?

Note: A set of pattern tiles would be useful for part 4.

1. Matteo says that he can't show $\frac{1}{3}$ of these marbles because some of the marbles are big and some are little. What do you think?

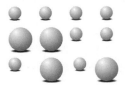

2. A first-grade worksheet asked children to "show 4 equal parts" and showed a picture like the one on the left in the next figure. Arianna's response is on the right. Although Arianna's work is probably not what the authors had in mind, can it still be considered correct?

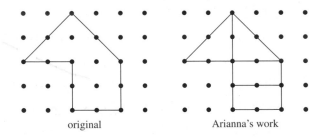

original   Arianna's work

3. The definition of fractions of objects refers to dividing objects into equal parts. Discuss whether the meaning of equal parts is clearly defined in every situation.

4. The design that follows is made with 1 hexagon in the middle, surrounded by 6 rhombuses (diamond shapes) and 6 triangles. If pattern tiles are available, you might want to use them to copy this design.

   a. What fraction of the shapes in the design is made of triangles?

   b. What fraction of the area of the design is made of triangles? Is this the same fraction as in part (a)?

c. To find the fractions in part (a) and part (b), you divided the design into equal parts. Did you interpret "equal parts" the same way in (a) and (b)?

Class Activity 2G: Improper Fractions

1. Suppose you use a picture like the next one to talk about the fraction $\frac{5}{4}$. What kind of confusion could arise about this picture? What must you do in order to interpret the shaded region as $\frac{5}{4}$?

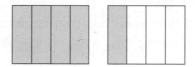

2. Enrico says that it doesn't make sense to talk about $\frac{5}{4}$ of a piece of paper, because if you divide a piece of paper into 4 equal pieces, then you only have 4 pieces and can't show 5 pieces. What can you tell Enrico that might help him?

3. Examine what Meili said as she pointed one-by-one to the fractional pieces (the hand indicates Meili pointing, starting from the left, moving to the right). Why do you think Meili described the pieces that way? What would you ask Meili?

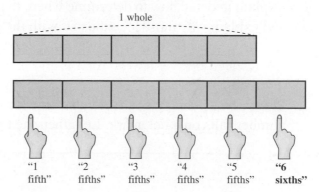

2.2 Interlude: Solving Problems and Explaining Solutions

2.3 Fractions as Numbers

Class Activity 2H: Number Line Errors with Fractions

1. Students were asked to plot the fractions $\frac{1}{4}$, $\frac{2}{4}$, and $\frac{3}{4}$ on a number line on which 0 and 1 were already plotted.

   a. Eric labeled his number line this way:

   What error is Eric making?

   b. Kristin labeled her number line this way:

   Although Kristin's labeling is not incorrect, what might she be misunderstanding about number lines?

   c. Discuss ideas you have for helping students understand number lines. How might you draw their attention to the lengths of intervals and to distance from 0—away from merely counting tick marks without attending to length and distance?

2. When Tyler was asked to plot $\frac{3}{4}$ on a number line showing 0 and 2, he plotted it as shown on the next number line. What might be the source of Tyler's confusion?

Class Activity 2I: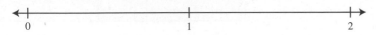
Fractions on Number Lines, Part 1

1. Explain in detail how to determine where to plot $\frac{3}{4}$ and $\frac{5}{4}$ on the number line below, and explain why those locations fit with the definition of fraction.

2. Plot 0, 1, $\frac{1}{4}$, $\frac{7}{4}$, and $\frac{11}{4}$ on the number line for this problem in such a way that each number falls on a tick mark. Lengthen the tick mark of whole numbers.

For each of the following problems, place equally spaced tick marks on the number line so that you can plot the requested fraction on a tick mark. You may place the tick marks "by eye"; precision is not needed. Explain your reasoning.

3. Plot $\frac{5}{4}$.

0 1

4. Plot 1.

0 .... $\frac{3}{2}$

5. Plot 1.

0 .... $\frac{3}{4}$

6. Plot $\frac{3}{5}$.

0 .... $\frac{4}{5}$

2.4 Equivalent Fractions

Class Activity 2J:
Equivalent Fractions

1. Use the meaning of fractions of objects and the pictures below to give a detailed conceptual explanation for why

$$\frac{2}{3}$$

of a ribbon is the same amount of ribbon as

$$\frac{2 \cdot 4}{3 \cdot 4}$$

of the ribbon.

   Discuss how to use the pictures below to explain the process of multiplying both the numerator and denominator of $\frac{2}{3}$ by 4.

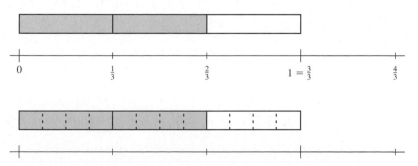

2. When you explain part 1 to students, they may find it confusing that in the picture, the fraction pieces are *divided* into 4 equal pieces, but in the numerical work, we *multiply* the numerator and denominator by 4. Address this confusing point by discussing what happens to the *size* of the pieces and what happens to the *number* of pieces when we create equivalent fractions.

3. Discuss how to modify your explanation and the picture for part 1 to show that $\frac{2}{3}$ of a ribbon is the same amount of ribbon as $\frac{2 \cdot 5}{3 \cdot 5}$ of the ribbon.

4. Suppose A and B are whole numbers and B is not 0. Also suppose that N is any natural number. Explain why $\frac{A}{B}$ of some object is the same amount of that object as $\frac{A \cdot N}{B \cdot N}$ of the object.

Class Activity 2K: Misconceptions about Fraction Equivalence

1. Anna says that

$$\frac{2}{3} = \frac{6}{7}$$

because, starting with $\frac{2}{3}$, you get $\frac{6}{7}$ by adding 4 to the top and the bottom. If you do the same thing to the top and the bottom, the fractions must be equal.

Is Anna right? If not, why not? What should we be careful about when talking about equivalent fractions?

2. Don says that $\frac{11}{12} = \frac{16}{17}$ because both fractions are one part away from a whole. Is Don correct? If not, what is wrong with Don's reasoning?

3. Peter says that $\frac{6}{6}$ is greater than $\frac{5}{5}$ because $\frac{6}{6}$ has more parts. Is Peter correct? If not, what is wrong with Peter's reasoning?

Class Activity 2L: Common Denominators

1. Write $\frac{1}{3}$ and $\frac{3}{4}$ with two different common denominators. Show each on the rectangles in the next figure. In terms of the pictures, what are we doing when we give the two fractions common denominators?

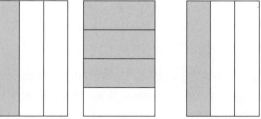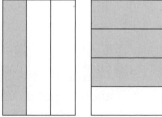

first common denominator   second common denominator

2. Write $\frac{3}{4}$ and $\frac{5}{6}$ with two different common denominators. In terms of the strips and the number lines, what are we doing when we give the two fractions common denominators?

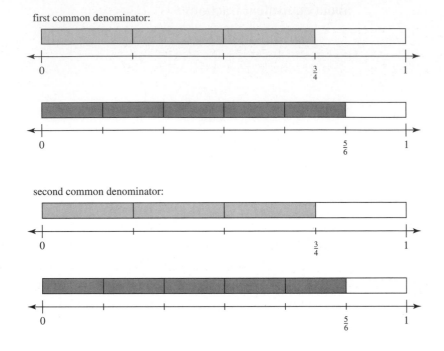

Class Activity 2M:

Solving Problems by Changing Denominators

1. Take a blank piece of paper and imagine that it is $\frac{2}{3}$ of some larger piece of paper. Fold your piece of paper to show $\frac{1}{6}$ of the larger (imagined) piece of paper. Do this as carefully and precisely as possible without using a ruler or doing any measuring. Explain why your answer is correct.

    In solving this problem, how does $\frac{2}{3}$ appear in a different form?

    Could two people have different solutions that are both correct?

2. Jeremy first put $\frac{3}{4}$ cup of butter in the sauce he is making. Then Jeremy added another $\frac{1}{3}$ of a cup of butter. How much butter is in Jeremy's sauce? Draw pictures to help you solve this problem. Explain why your answer is correct.

    In solving the problem, how do $\frac{3}{4}$ and $\frac{1}{3}$ appear in different forms?

    For each fraction in this problem, and in your solution, describe the whole associated with this fraction. In other words, describe what each fraction is *of*.

3. Jeans has a casserole recipe that calls for $\frac{1}{2}$ cup of butter. Jean only has $\frac{1}{3}$ cup of butter. Assuming that Jean has enough of the other ingredients, what fraction of the casserole recipe can Jean make? Draw pictures to help you solve this problem. Explain why your answer is correct.

In solving this problem, how to do $\frac{1}{2}$ and $\frac{1}{3}$ appear in different forms?

For each fraction in this problem, and in your solution, describe the whole associated with this fraction. In other words, describe what each fraction is *of*.

4. One serving of SugarBombs cereal is $\frac{3}{4}$ cup. Joey wants to eat $\frac{1}{2}$ of a serving of SugarBombs cereal. How much of a cup of cereal should Joey eat? Draw pictures to help you solve this problem. Explain why your answer is correct.

In solving the problem, how does $\frac{3}{4}$ appear in a different form?

For each fraction in this problem, and in your solution, describe the whole associated with this fraction. In other words, describe what each fraction is *of*.

Class Activity 2N: Fractions on Number Lines, Part 2

1. Plot 1, $\frac{2}{3}$, and $\frac{5}{2}$ on the number line for this problem in such a way that each number falls on a tick mark. Lengthen the tick marks of whole numbers.

2. Plot 9, $\frac{55}{6}$, and $\frac{33}{4}$ on the number line for this problem in such a way that each number falls on a tick mark. Lengthen the tick marks of whole numbers.

3. Plot 1, 0.7, and $\frac{3}{4}$ on the number line for this problem in such a way that each number falls on a tick mark. Lengthen the tick marks of whole numbers.

For the next two problems, place equally spaced tick marks on the number line so that you can plot the requested fraction on a tick mark. You may place the tick marks "by eye"; precision is not needed.

4. Plot $\frac{3}{4}$.

5. Plot $\frac{3}{5}$.

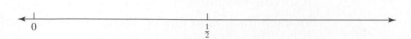

Class Activity 20: Simplifying Fractions

1. Use the next diagram to help you explain why the following equations that put $\frac{6}{15}$ in simplest form make sense:

$$\frac{6}{15} = \frac{2 \cdot 3}{5 \cdot 3} = \frac{2}{5}$$

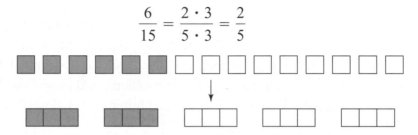

2. Use blocks or snap-together cubes in two different colors, or draw pictures, to help you demonstrate why the following equations that put $\frac{8}{12}$ in simplest form make sense:

$$\frac{8}{12} = \frac{2 \cdot 4}{3 \cdot 4} = \frac{2}{3}$$

3. Show two different ways to write equations that put $\frac{12}{18}$ in simplest form. (One way can take several steps to simplify the fraction.)

4. Use blocks or snap-together cubes in two different colors, or draw pictures, to help you explain why your equations, above (in part 3), make sense.

2.5 Comparing Fractions

Class Activity 2P: Can We Compare Fractions This Way?

You will need a calculator for part 1 of this activity.

One method for comparing fractions is to determine the decimal representation of each fraction and to compare the decimals.

When you are asked to compare two fractions to see whether they are equal, your first inclination might be to use a calculator to divide, converting each fraction to a decimal, so that you can compare the decimals. This usually works well, but watch out, because calculators can display only so many digits.

Compare

$$\frac{111,111,111,111}{1,000,000,000,000} \quad \text{and} \quad \frac{111,111,111,111}{999,999,999,999}$$

by dividing, thereby converting both fractions to decimals. Use a calculator for the second fraction. (If your calculator holds only 8 digits, then work with the fractions $\frac{11,111,111}{100,000,000}$ and $\frac{11,111,111}{99,999,999}$ instead.)

1. According to your calculator's display, do the two fractions appear to be equal?

2. In fact, *are* the two fractions equal? If not, which is bigger, and why? Explain this by reasoning about the fractions.

Class Activity 2Q: What Is Another Way to Compare These Fractions?

For each of the pairs of fractions shown, determine which fraction is greater in a way other than finding common denominators or converting to decimals. Explain your reasoning.

$$\frac{1}{49} \qquad \frac{1}{39}$$

$$\frac{7}{37} \qquad \frac{7}{45}$$

Class Activity 2R:
Comparing Fractions by Reasoning

Use reasoning other than finding common denominators, cross-multiplying, or converting to decimals to compare the sizes (=, <, or >) of the following pairs of fractions:

$$\frac{27}{43} \quad \frac{26}{45}$$

$$\frac{13}{25} \quad \frac{34}{70}$$

$$\frac{17}{18} \quad \frac{19}{20}$$

$$\frac{9}{40} \quad \frac{12}{44}$$

$$\frac{51}{53} \quad \frac{65}{67}$$

$$\frac{13}{25} \quad \frac{5}{8}$$

Class Activity 2S:
Can We Reason This Way?

1. Claire says that

$$\frac{4}{9} > \frac{3}{8}$$

because

$$4 > 3 \quad \text{and} \quad 9 > 8$$

Discuss whether Claire's reasoning is correct.

2. Conrad says that

$$\frac{4}{11} > \frac{3}{8}$$

because

$$4 > 3 \quad \text{and} \quad 11 > 8$$

Discuss whether Conrad's reasoning is correct.

2.6 Percent

Class Activity 2T: Pictures, Percentages, and Fractions

1. For each of diagrams 1 through 5, determine the percent of the diagram that is shaded, explaining your reasoning. Write each percent as a fraction in simplest form, and explain how to see that this fraction of the diagram is shaded. You may assume that portions of each diagram which appear to be the same size really are the same size.

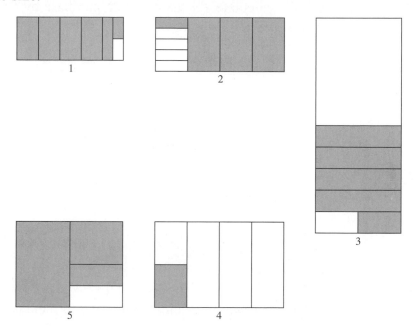

Class Activity 2U: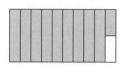
Calculating Percents of Quantities by Using
Benchmark Fractions and Percent Tables

We can make some percentage problems easy to solve mentally by working with a common fraction that is easy to calculate with. Pictures can help you understand this technique. Simple percent tables can help you record and clarify your thinking.

1. Mentally calculate 95% of 80,000 by calculating $\frac{1}{10}$ of 80,000, calculating half of that result, and then taking this last amount away from 80,000. Use the following picture and the percent table to help you explain why this method makes sense and to record your thinking:

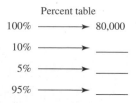

2. Mentally calculate 15% of 6500 by first calculating $\frac{1}{10}$ of 6500. Use the following picture and a percent table to help you explain why this method makes sense and to record your thinking.

Percent table

3. Mentally calculate 7% tax on a $25 purchase by first finding 1%. Use a percent table to record the strategy.

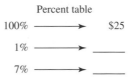

Percent table

100% ⟶ $25

1% ⟶ _____

7% ⟶ _____

4. Mentally calculate 60% of 810 by first calculating $\frac{1}{2}$ of 810. Use the following picture and a percent table to help you explain why this method makes sense.

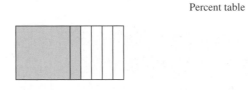

Percent table

5. Find another way to calculate 60% of 810 mentally. Use a percent table to show your method.

6. Mentally calculate 55% of 180. Use a percent table to show your method.

7. Make up a mental percent calculation problem, and explain how to solve it.

Class Activity 2V: Calculating Percentages with Equivalent Fractions

A basic percent problem involves an equation stating that two fractions are equivalent:

$$\frac{P}{100} = \frac{\text{portion}}{\text{whole amount}}$$

Solve the next percent problems by making equivalent fractions. This method could make sense to students who have learned about equivalent fractions but who have not yet learned standard algebraic techniques for solving equations.

When deciding how to set up your equivalent fractions, it may help you to think about a percent table:

$$P\% \rightarrow \text{portion}$$
$$100\% \rightarrow \text{whole amount}$$

1. Show how to determine what percent 60 is of 400 by finding equivalent fractions. Explain why you should look for a fraction that has denominator 100.

$$\frac{60}{400} =$$

2. The number 225 is what percent of 500? Solve by finding equivalent fractions.

3. Show how to determine what percent 6 is of 25 by finding equivalent fractions.

4. Show how to determine what percent 12 is of 75 by using equivalent fractions. *Note:* You may take several steps to get to a fraction with denominator 100.

5. What percent of 60 is 42? Solve by using equivalent fractions.

6. The number 24 is what percent of 16? Solve by using equivalent fractions.

7. The number 16 is what percent of 24? Solve by using equivalent fractions. *Note:* It's ok for a decimal to appear in the numerator (or denominator) of your fractions.

Class Activity 2W: Calculating Percentages with Pictures and Percent Tables

1. In Green Valley, the average daily rainfall is $\frac{5}{8}$ of an inch. Last year, the average daily rainfall in Green Valley was only $\frac{3}{8}$ of an inch. What percent of the average daily rainfall fell last year in Green Valley? Solve this problem with the aid of either a picture or a percent table, or both. Explain your reasoning.

2. If a $\frac{1}{4}$ cup serving of cheese provides your full daily value of calcium, then what percentage of your daily value of calcium is provided by $\frac{1}{3}$ cup of the cheese? Solve this problem with the aid of either a picture or a percent table, or both. Explain your reasoning.

Class Activity 2X:
Calculating a Quantity from a Percentage of It

1. Lenny has received 6 boxes of paper, which is 30% of the paper he ordered. How many boxes of paper did Lenny order? Draw a picture to help you solve this problem. Explain your reasoning.

2. Solve the problem about Lenny's paper in part 1 by completing the next percent table. Explain your reasoning.

$$30\% \rightarrow 6$$

3. Now solve the problem about Lenny's paper in part 1 by making equivalent fractions (without cross-multiplying). Explain your reasoning.

$$\frac{30}{100} = \frac{6}{\quad}$$

4. Ms. Jones paid $2.10 in tax on an item she purchased. The tax was 7% of the price of the item. What was the price of the item (not including the tax)? Solve this problem with the aid of a percent table. Explain your reasoning.

Class Activity 2Y: Percent Problem Solving

1. There are 30 blue marbles in a bag, which is 40% of the marbles in the bag. How many marbles are in the bag? Solve this problem in at least one of three ways: 1) with the aid of a picture, 2) with the aid of a percent table, and 3) by making equivalent fractions (without cross-multiplying). Explain your reasoning.

2. Andrew ran 40% as far as Marcie. How far did Marcie run as a percentage of Andrew's running distance? Draw a picture to help you solve the problem. Use your picture to help explain your answer.

3. In a terrarium, there are 10% more female bugs than male bugs. If there are 8 more female bugs than male bugs, then how many bugs are in the terrarium?

   a. Solve the bug problem and explain your solution.

   b. An easy error to make is to say that there are 80 bugs in all in the terrarium. Why is this not correct and why is it an easy error to make?

4. The animal shelter has only dogs and cats. There are 25% more dogs than cats. What percentage of the animals at the animal shelter are cats? Explain your solution.

Addition and Subtraction

3.1 Interpretations of Addition and Subtraction

Class Activity 3A: Relating Addition and Subtraction—
The Shopkeeper's Method of Making Change

When a patron of a store gives a shopkeeper A for a B purchase, we can think of the change owed to a patron as what is left from A when B are taken away. In contrast, the shopkeeper might make change by starting with B and handing the customer money while adding on the amounts until they reach A.

Explain how the shopkeeper's method links subtraction to addition.

Class Activity 3B:
Types of Addition and Subtraction Story Problems

The basic addition and subtraction equations are of the form

$$A + B = C \quad D - E = F$$

Addition and subtraction problems arise when two out of the three quantities in an addition or subtraction equation are known and the other quantity is to be found.

1. For each of the following equations, write a story problem that is formulated naturally by the equation.

a. $6 + 9 = ?$

b. $6 + ? = 15$

c. $? + 6 = 15$

d. $15 - 6 = ?$

e. $15 - ? = 6$

f. $? - 6 = 9$

For the addition equations (a, b, and c), you
lems; for the subtraction equations (d, e, and f),
(or separate) problems. These are the most common type of
problems. However, there are several other types of addition and subtra
problems that mathematics education researchers have identified (see [9], page
[2], p. 12; or [4], page 70).

Add to or "join" problems. Example for the equation $6 + ? = 15$:

Asia had 6 stickers. After Asia got some more stickers, she had 15 stickers. How many stickers did Asia get?

Take away or "separate" problems. Example for the equation

$$? - 6 = 9:$$

Asia had some stickers. After Asia gave 6 of her stickers away, she had 9 stickers left. How many stickers did Asia have at first?

Add to and take away problems are "change" problems that involve change over time.

Part-part-whole problems. Example for the equation $6 + 9 = ?$:

Asia has 6 small stickers and 9 large stickers (and no other stickers).

How many stickers does Asia have in all?

Part-part-whole problems involve two distinct parts that make a whole. Part-part-whole problems don't involve change over time. Notice that the equations $5 - ? = 6$ and $? - 6 = 9$ don't fit naturally with part-part-whole problems.

Compare problems. Example for the equation $6 + ? = 15$:

Asia has 6 stickers. Taryn has 15 stickers. How many more stickers does Taryn have than Asia?

Example for the equation $? - 6 = 9$:

Asia has some stickers. Taryn has 9 stickers, and that is 6 stickers fewer than Asia has. How many stickers does Asia have?

Compare problems involve comparing two quantities.

2. Write a part-part-whole problem for the equation $6 + ? = 15$. (Your problem will probably fit naturally with the equation $? + 6 = 15$ as well.)

Write a compare problem for the equation $6 + 9 = ?$.

4. Write a compare problem for the equation $? + 6 = 15$.

5. Write a compare problem for the equation $15 - 6 = ?$.

6. Write a compare problem for the equation $15 - ? = 6$.

Class Activity 3C: Why Can't We Rely on Keywords to Solve Story Problems?

In this activity you will see why keywords are not reliable for deciding which operation to use to solve a story problem. When it comes to solving story problems, there is just no substitute for reading and understanding them!

For each of the next story problems

- identify the language that might cause children to solve the problem incorrectly if they rely only on keywords;
- formulate an equation that fits with the language of the story problem;
- identify what type of story problem the problem is (add to, take away, part-part-whole, or compare).

1. Clare had 3 bears. After she got some more bears, Clare had 12 bears. How many bears did Clare get?

2. Clare has 12 bears altogether; 3 of the bears are red and the others are blue. How many blue bears does Clare have?

3. Clare had some bears. After she got 3 more bears, Clare had 12 bears altogether. How many bears did Clare get?

4. Clare has 12 red bears. She has 3 more red bears than blue bears. How many blue bears does Clare have?

5. Clare has 12 red bears and 3 blue bears. How many more red bears does Clare have than blue bears?

6. Matt had some dinosaurs. After he gave away 5 dinosaurs, he had 9 dinosaurs left. How many dinosaurs did Matt have at first?

7. Matt has 5 fewer dinosaurs than bears. Matt has 9 dinosaurs. How many bears does Matt have?

Class Activity 3D: Using Simple Diagrams to Decide Whether to Add or Subtract to Solve a Story Problem

If you did the previous activity, then you saw that keywords are not reliable for determining how to solve a story problem. Very young children from prekindergarten through about first grade often use small objects or their fingers to act out a problem. (You will study young children's solution methods in the activities in the next section.) But children from about third or second grade on can draw and use simple strip diagrams such as the ones shown here to help them understand story problems and determine how to solve the problems.

1. For each of the diagrams (A–F) that follow, determine which of the following equations could fit with the diagram. (Each diagram fits with *more than one* equation. You may also write other equations that fit with the diagrams.)

$$30 + 45 = ? \qquad 30 + ? = 75 \qquad ? + 30 = 75$$
$$75 - 30 = ? \qquad 75 - ? = 30 \qquad ? - 30 = 45 \qquad ? - 45 = 30$$

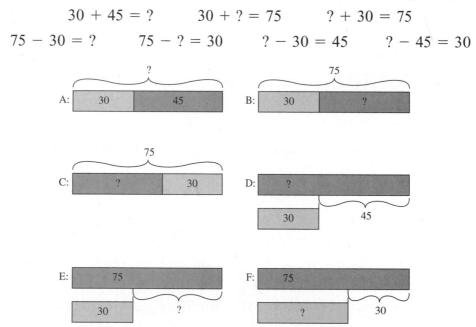

2. For each diagram in part 1, imagine drawing the diagram in order to solve a story problem. Which of the following would you draw the diagram for: an add to problem, a take away problem, a part-part-whole problem, or a compare problem? (You may wish to write a few example problems.)

3. For each diagram in part 1, use the diagram to determine whether to add or subtract to solve for the unknown amount.

3.2 The Commutative and Associative Properties of Addition, Mental Math, and Single-Digit Facts

Class Activity 3E:
Mental Math

Try to find ways to make the problems that follow easy to do *mentally*. In each case, explain your method.

1. $7999 + 857 + 1$

2. $367 + 98 + 2$

3. $153 + 19 + 7$

4. $7.89 + 6.95 + .05$

Class Activity 3F:
Children's Learning Paths for Single-Digit Addition

In order for children to develop fluency with the basic addition facts (from $1 + 1 = 2$ up to $9 + 9 = 18$), they first need extensive experience solving these basic addition problems in ways that make sense to them and become increasingly sophisticated. The next levels describe the increasingly sophisticated methods children learn. (See [2] and [4].)

Level 1: Direct modeling, count all To add $5 + 4$, a child at this level counts out 5 things (or fingers), counts out another 4 things (or fingers), and then counts the total number of things (or fingers).

Level 2: Count on To add 6 + 3, a child at this level imagines 6 things, says "six" (possibly elongating it, as in "siiiiix," while perhaps thinking about pointing along a collection of 6 things). Then the child says the next 3 number words, "seven, eight, nine," usually keeping track on fingers.

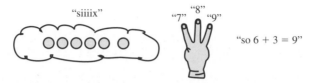

Count on from larger After children can count on from the first addend, they learn to count on from the larger addend. So to add 2 + 7, a child at this level would count on from 7 instead of counting on from 2.

Level 3: Derived fact methods Children at this level use addition facts they already know to find related facts.

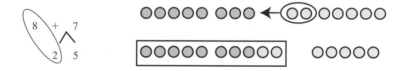

Make-a-ten method To calculate 8 + 7 with this strategy, a child breaks 7 apart into 2 + 5 so that a 10 can be made from the 8 and the 2. So the total is a 10 and 5 ones, which is 15 (as shown above).

Make-a-ten from larger The child makes a 10 with the larger number instead of just with the first addend.

Doubles ±1 Children who know the doubles facts (1 + 1, 2 + 2, up to 9 + 9) can use these facts to find a related fact in which one of the addends is one more or one less than the addends in the double. For example, a child could determine that 6 + 7 is 1 more than 6 + 6.

1. For each method in the three levels, act out a few examples of how a child could use that method to solve a basic addition problem (adding two 1-digit numbers).

2. What property of addition does the count on from larger method rely on? Explain, writing equations to demonstrate how the property is used.

3. Why is the property of addition you discussed in the previous part especially important for lightening the load of learning the table of basic addition facts (from 1 + 1 up to 9 + 9)?

4. What property of addition does the make-a-ten method rely on? Explain, writing equations to demonstrate how the property is used.

5. Why is the make-a-ten method especially important?

6. What property of addition does the doubles +1 method rely on? Explain, writing equations to demonstrate how the property is used.

7. Explain why the following three items are prerequisites for children to be able to understand and use the make-a-ten method fluently:

   a. For each counting number from 1 to 9, know the number to add to it to make 10—the partner to 10.

   b. For each counting number from 11 to 19, know that the number is a 10 and some ones. For example, know that $10 + 3 = 13$ without counting and know that 13 decomposes as $10 + 3$.

   c. For each counting number from 2 to 9, know all the ways to decompose it as a sum of two counting numbers (and know all the basic addition facts with sums up to 9).

Class Activity 3G:
Children's Learning Paths for Single-Digit Subtraction

For each of the subtraction methods listed next, act out a few examples of how a child could use that method to solve a basic subtraction problem.

Level 1: Direct modeling, take away To subtract $9 - 4$, a child at this level counts out 9 things (or fingers), takes away 4 things (or puts down 4 fingers), and then counts the number of things (or fingers) remaining.

Level 2: Count on to find the unknown addend The child views a subtraction problem as an unknown addend problem and counts on from the known addend to the total. So $13 - 9 = ?$ becomes $9 + ? = 13$. The child counts on from 9, using fingers to keep track of how many have been counted on, and stops when the total is said. (This method is easier than counting down, which is difficult for most children. It makes subtraction as easy as addition.)

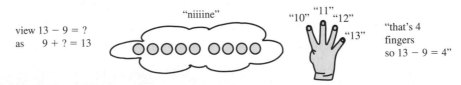

Level 3: Make-a-ten methods

Make-a-ten with the unknown addend $14 - 8 = ?$ becomes $8 + ? = 14$. The child figures that adding 2 to 8 makes 10, then adding another 4 makes 14, so the unknown addend is $2 + 4 = 6$.

Subtract from ten This is like the previous method but the child breaks 14 into 10 and 4 and subtracts 8 from 10, leaving 2, then combines this 2 with the remaining 4 from 14 to make 6.

Subtract down to ten first To solve $12 - 3 = ?$ the child breaks 3 into $2 + 1$, takes 2 away from 12 to get down to 10, then takes the remaining 1 away from 10 to get 9.

Compare and contrast the methods at level 3. When are the first two methods easier than the third? When is the third method easier than the first two?

Class Activity 3H: Solving Addition and Subtraction Story Problems: Easier and Harder Subtypes

In Section 3.1 you studied the broad categories of addition and subtraction story problems: add to and take away problems (which are change problems that involve change over time), part-part-whole problems, and compare problems. In this activity you will examine subcategories of the change problems and another type of part-part-whole problem.

Change Problems (add to and take away problems): For each of the following subtypes, write a story problem of that type. Then model how a young child might solve such a problem and explain why problems of that type are either easier, medium, or harder.

Result unknown (easier) $8 + 5 = ?$, $16 - 9 = ?$

Change unknown (medium) $8 + ? = 13$, $16 - ? = 7$

Start unknown (harder) $? + 5 = 13$, $? - 9 = 7$

Part-Part-Whole Problems As with the change problems, the whole can be unknown (easier) or one of the parts can be unknown (harder).

Both parts unknown $5 = ? + ?$ For example: Patti has 5 turtles and two boxes to put them in. How many turtles can Patti put in each box?

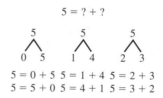

$$5 = ? + ?$$

$$5 = 0 + 5 \quad 5 = 1 + 4 \quad 5 = 2 + 3$$
$$5 = 5 + 0 \quad 5 = 4 + 1 \quad 5 = 3 + 2$$

Explain why this type of problem is especially useful for the level 3 derived fact methods described in the previous two activities (include an example as part of your explanation). Then write and solve a "part-part-whole, both parts unknown" story problem for $7 = ? + ?$.

Class Activity 3I: Using Properties of Addition in Mental Math

For each addition problem in this activity, the equations show how one or more properties of addition have been used to make the problem easier to do mentally. In each case,

- identify the property or properties that have been used;

- describe the strategy that is shown, using groups of marbles, parts of pies, or money.

Example:

$$297 + 35 = 297 + (3 + 32)$$
$$= (297 + 3) + 32$$
$$= 300 + 32$$
$$= 332$$

Solution: The associative property was used at the second equal sign to say that

$$297 + (3 + 32) = (297 + 3) + 32$$

If you had 297 marbles and got 35 more marbles, you could first take 3 of the 35 marbles and put them with 297 marbles to make 300 marbles. Then you could add on the remaining 32 marbles. This shows that you have 332 marbles in all.

1.
$$153 + 19 + 7 = 153 + 7 + 19$$
$$= 160 + 19$$
$$= 179$$

2.
$$687 + 799 = (686 + 1) + 799$$
$$= 686 + (1 + 799)$$
$$= 686 + 800$$
$$= 1486$$

3.
$$2\frac{5}{8} + 6\frac{3}{8} = 2 + \frac{5}{8} + 6 + \frac{3}{8}$$
$$= 2 + 6 + \frac{5}{8} + \frac{3}{8}$$
$$= 8 + 1$$
$$= 9$$

4.
$$3.95 + 2.87 = 3.95 + (.05 + 2.82)$$
$$= (3.95 + .05) + 2.82$$
$$= (4.00 + 2.82)$$
$$= 6.82$$

Class Activity 3J: Writing Correct Equations

The problems that follow are hypothetical examples of student work. In each case, the student has a good idea for how to solve the problem but doesn't use the equal sign correctly. Describe the student's strategy in words, and explain briefly why the strategy makes sense. Then rewrite the student's work, using the same ideas, but using the = sign correctly.

1. The problem: $136 + 57$

Student solution: **Your correction:**
$$136 + 50 = 186 + 7$$
$$= 193$$

2. The problem: $378 - 102$

Student solution:

$$378 - 100 = 278 - 2$$
$$= 276$$

Your correction:

3. The problem: $235 - 65$

Student solution:

$$235 - 5 = 230 - 30$$
$$= 200 - 30$$
$$= 170$$

Your correction:

4. The problem: $416 + 99$

Student solution:

$$416 + 100 = 516 - 1$$
$$= 515$$

Your correction:

5. The problem: $114 - 97$

Student solution:

$$97 + 3 = 100 + 14$$
$$= 114$$

So, the answer is:

$$3 + 14 = 17$$

Your correction:

Class Activity 3K: Writing Equations That Correspond to a Method of Calculation

Write equations which correspond to the solution strategies that follow and that are described in words. In each case, explain briefly why the strategy makes sense. For parts 1 and 2, write your equations in the following form:

$$\text{original problem} = \text{some expression}$$
$$= \text{some expression}$$
$$= \vdots$$
$$= \text{final answer}$$

1. *Problem:* $268 + 496$

Solution: $268 + 500 = 768$, but that's 4 too many, so take away 4. The answer is 764.

2. *Problem:* 123 − 58
   Solution: 120 − 60 = 60, plus 3 is 63. I took away 2 too many, so add on 2 to make 65.

3. *Problem:* 153 − 76
   Solution: 76 and 4 make 80, and 20 make 100, and 53 make 153. So the answer is 4 + 20 + 53, which is 77.

Class Activity 3L: Other Ways to Add and Subtract

1. John and Anne want to solve 253 − 99 by first solving 253 − 100. They calculate
$$253 - 100 = 153$$
   John says that they must now *subtract* 1 from 153, but Anne says that they must *add* 1 to 153.

   a. Draw a number line (which need not be perfectly to scale) to help you explain who is right and why. Do not just say which answer is numerically correct; use the number line to help you explain why the answer must be correct.

   b. Explain in another way who is right and why.

2. Jamarez says that he can solve 253 − 99 by adding 1 to both numbers and solving 254 − 100 instead.

   a. Draw a number line (which need not be perfectly to scale) to help you explain why Jamarez's method is valid.

   b. Explain in another way why Jamarez's method is valid.

      c. Could you adapt Jamarez's method to other subtraction problems, such as to the problem $324 - 298$? Explain, and give several examples.

3. Find ways to solve the addition and subtraction problems that follow *other than* by using the standard addition or subtraction algorithms. In each case, explain your reasoning, and—except for part (g)—write equations that correspond to your line of reasoning.

    a. $183 + 99$

    b. $268 + 52$

    c. $600 - 199$

    d. $164 - 70$

    e. $999 + 9999$

    f. $\$10.00 - \$2.99$

    g.   2.99   (No equations are needed.)
$$\begin{array}{r} 2.99 \\ 3.99 \\ 1.99 \\ + \ 4.99 \\ \hline \end{array}$$

3.3 Why the Common Algorithms for Adding and Subtracting Numbers in the Decimal System Work

Class Activity 3M: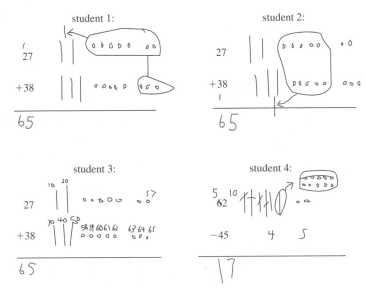
Adding and Subtracting with Ten-Structured Pictures

The hypothetical student work below is similar to actual work of urban Latino first-graders whose performance on 2-digit addition and subtraction tasks with regrouping was substantially above the performance of first-graders of higher socioeconomic status and of older children. (See [5].)

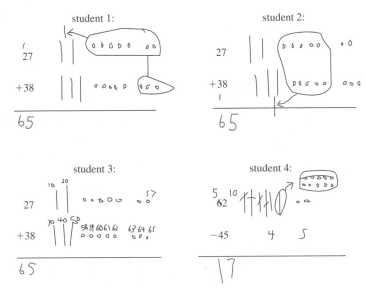

1. Examine and discuss the students' work. Compare the work of students 1, 2, and 3. In particular, compare the methods of student 1 and student 2 for adding 7 + 8. What mental method for subtracting 12 − 5 does the work of student 4 suggest?

2. Show how students 1, 2, and 3 might solve the addition problem 36 + 27 and how student 4 might solve the subtraction problem 43 − 18.

Class Activity 3N:
Understanding the Common Addition Algorithm

Bundled toothpicks (or other small objects) would be useful for this activity.

1. Add the numbers, using the standard paper-and-pencil method. Notice that regrouping is involved.

$$\begin{array}{r} 147 \\ + \ 195 \\ \hline \end{array}$$

2. If available, use bundles of toothpicks (or other objects) to solve the addition problem 147 + 195. Draw rough pictures to indicate the process you used.

3. If available, use bundles of toothpicks (or other objects) to solve the addition problem 147 + 195 *in a way that corresponds directly to the addition algorithm you used in part 1*. This may be different from what you did in part 2. Draw rough pictures to indicate the process you used. Compare with part 2.

4. Use expanded forms to solve the addition problem 147 + 195. First add like terms; then rewrite (regroup) the resulting number so that it is the expanded form of a number. This rewriting is the regrouping process.

$$1(100) + 4(10) + 7(1)$$
$$+ 1(100) + 9(10) + 5(1)$$

← First add like terms, remaining in expanded form.

← Then regroup so that you have the expanded form of a decimal number. You might want to take several steps to do so.

5. Compare and contrast your work in parts 1–4.

Class Activity 30:
Understanding the Common Subtraction Algorithm

Bundled toothpicks (or other small objects) would be useful for this activity.

1. Subtract the following numbers, using the standard paper-and-pencil method. Notice that regrouping is required.

$$125$$
$$- 68$$

2. If available, use bundles of toothpicks (or other objects) to solve the subtraction problem 125 − 68. Draw rough pictures to indicate the process.

3. If available, use bundles of toothpicks (or other objects) to solve the subtraction problem 125 − 68 *in a way that corresponds directly to the subtraction algorithm you used in part 1*. This may be different from what you did in part 2. Draw rough pictures to indicate the process. Compare with part 2.

4. Solve the subtraction problem 125 − 68, but now use expanded forms. Start by rewriting the number 125 in expanded form. Rewrite the number in several steps, so that it will be easy to take away 68. This rewriting is the regrouping process.

$$125 = 1(100) + 2(10) + 5(1) =$$

Write your regrouped number here $\rightarrow$

Subtract 68: $\underline{- \, [6(10) + 8(1)]}$

5. Compare and contrast your work in parts 1–4.

Class Activity 3P: A Third-Grader's Method of Subtraction

When asked to compute $423 - 157$, Pat (a third-grader) wrote the following:

4−

30−

34−

300

266

"You can't take 7 from 3; it's 4 too many, so that's negative 4. You can't take 50 from 20; it's 30 too many, so that's negative 30; and with the other 4, it's negative 34. 400 minus 100 is 300, and then you take the 34 away from the 300, so it's 266." [1]

1. Discuss Pat's idea for calculating $423 - 157$. Is her method legitimate? Analyze Pat's method in terms of expanded forms.

2. Could you use Pat's idea to calculate $317 - 289$? If so, write what you think Pat might write, and also use expanded forms.

Class Activity 3Q: Subtracting Across Zeros

1. David solves the subtraction problem $203 - 7$ as follows:

$$\begin{array}{r} {\scriptstyle 1 \;\; 13} \\ 20\rlap{/}3 \\ -\quad 7 \\ \hline 106 \end{array}$$

What mistake is David making? Explain why David's method is incorrect.

---

[1]This is taken from [1, p. 263].

2. Some subtraction problems require regrouping "across a 0," as does the previous problem as well as this problem

$$\begin{array}{r} 203 \\ -\ 86 \\ \hline \end{array}$$

Some people like to replace an intermediate 0 with a 9 when regrouping:

$$\begin{array}{r} 203 \\ -\ 86 \\ \hline \end{array} \rightarrow \quad \begin{array}{r} \overset{1\ 9\ 13}{2\cancel{0}\cancel{3}} \\ -\ 86 \\ \hline 117 \end{array}$$

Others prefer to regroup in two steps, first changing an intermediate 0 to a 10 and then changing the 10 to a 9:

$$\begin{array}{r} 203 \\ -\ 86 \\ \hline \end{array} \rightarrow \quad \begin{array}{r} \overset{1\ 10}{2\cancel{0}3} \\ -\ 86 \\ \hline \end{array} \rightarrow \quad \begin{array}{r} \overset{9}{\overset{1\ \cancel{10}\ 13}{2\cancel{0}\cancel{3}}} \\ -\ 86 \\ \hline 117 \end{array}$$

a. Explain why the first regrouping method described is just a shortcut of the second method.

b. Using bundled toothpicks, or rough drawings of bundled toothpicks, explain why both of the regrouping methods described make sense.

3. DeShun solves the subtraction problem $1002 - 248$ by crossing out 100 and replacing it with 99, as shown. Is this legitimate? To help your thinking, consider the following: The 100 is 100 of what?

$$\begin{array}{r} \overset{99\ \ 12}{\cancel{1002}} \\ -\ 248 \\ \hline 754 \end{array}$$

4. Can DeShun's method from the previous part be used in other situations? For example, could you use DeShun's method to subtract $20047 - 321$? Explain.

Class Activity 3R: Regrouping with Dozens and Dozens of Dozens

When we regroup in the decimal system we use the base-ten structure of place value: The value of each place is ten times the value of the next place to the right. We can also use the regrouping idea in other situations—for example, when objects are bundled in groups of a dozen instead of in groups of ten. The following problem asks you to regroup with dozens and dozens of dozens:

A store owner buys small, novelty party favors in bags of 1 dozen and boxes of 1-dozen bags (for a total of 144 favors in a box). The store owner has 5 boxes, 4 bags, and 3 individual party favors at the start of the month. At the end of the month, the store owner has 2 boxes, 9 bags, and 7 individual party favors left. How many favors did the store owner sell? Give the answer in terms of boxes, bags, and individual favors.

Solve this problem by working with a sort of *expanded form* for these party favors—in other words, working with the following representation:

$$5(\text{boxes}) + 4(\text{bags}) + 3(\text{individual})$$
$$2(\text{boxes}) + 9(\text{bags}) + 7(\text{individual})$$

Solve this problem by regrouping among the boxes, bags, and individual party favors.

Class Activity 3S: Regrouping with Seconds, Minutes, and Hours

When we regroup in the decimal system we use the base-ten structure of place value: The value of each place is ten times the value of the next place to the right. We can also use the regrouping idea in other situations—for example, with time. Just as 1 hundred is 10 tens and 1 ten is 10 ones, 1 hour is 60 minutes and 1 minute is 60 seconds. The following problem asks you to regroup among hours, minutes, and seconds:

Ruth runs around a lake two times. The first time takes 1 hour, 43 minutes, and 38 seconds. The second time takes 1 hour, 48 minutes, and 29 seconds. What is Ruth's total time for the two laps? Give the answer in hours, minutes, and seconds.

Solve this problem by working with a sort of *expanded form* for time—in other words, by working with

$$1(\text{hour}) + 43(\text{minutes}) + 38(\text{seconds})$$
$$1(\text{hour}) + 48(\text{minutes}) + 29(\text{seconds})$$

Solve this problem by regrouping among hours, minutes, and seconds.

3.4 Adding and Subtracting Fractions

Class Activity 3T: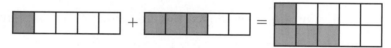

Why Do We Add and Subtract Fractions the Way We Do?

For part 2 of this activity, each person will need at least 5 identical strips of paper (or card stock).

1. When two fractions have the same denominator, we add or subtract them by keeping the same denominator and adding or subtracting the numerators. For example,

$$\frac{1}{5} + \frac{3}{5} = \frac{1+3}{5} = \frac{4}{5}$$

Patti says: "We should add the tops *and* the bottoms." She shows you this picture to explain why:

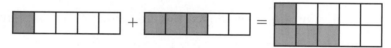

So according to Patti:

$$\frac{1}{5} + \frac{3}{5} = \frac{1+3}{5+5} = \frac{4}{10}$$

a. Why is Patti's method *not* a valid way to add fractions, and why doesn't Patti's picture prove that fractions can be added in her way? Explain what is wrong with Patti's reasoning.

b. Explain why the proper way to add $\frac{1}{5} + \frac{3}{5}$ makes sense. Are any aspects of the supports below helpful for your explanation?

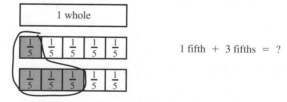

1 fifth + 3 fifths = ?

2. You need 5 identical strips of paper for this part.

a. Label one of the strips "1 whole," indicating that it is 1 unit long, and fold and label the other strips as indicated:

    b. Use the strips that are labeled with halves and thirds to show the following lengths:

$$\frac{1}{2} + \frac{1}{3}, \qquad \frac{2}{3} - \frac{1}{2}, \qquad \frac{2}{3} + \frac{1}{2}$$

(Fold and place your strips in a suitable way to show these lengths.) Make drawings to record your work.

    c. Now use the strips that are labeled with sixths to describe the lengths you showed in part (b). Relate the way you describe these lengths to the numerical procedure for adding and subtracting the fractions in part (b).

    d. Discuss: Why do we need to find common denominators to add or subtract fractions?

Class Activity 3U: How Do We Find a Suitable Common Denominator for Adding and Subtracting Fractions?

To add and subtract fractions, we need to give the fractions a common denominator first.

    1. For each of the next examples, decide what common denominator would be good to use.

$$\frac{2}{5} + \frac{7}{15}, \qquad \frac{1}{12} + \frac{3}{4}, \qquad \frac{1}{2} - \frac{1}{14}, \qquad \frac{9}{10} - \frac{1}{5}$$

What do all these examples have in common?

    2. For each of the next examples, decide what common denominator would be good to use.

$$\frac{1}{4} + \frac{2}{5}, \qquad \frac{2}{7} + \frac{1}{6}, \qquad \frac{5}{9} - \frac{1}{10}$$

What do all these examples have in common?

3. When we add fractions, *must* we use the least common denominator? Why or why not? Are there any advantages or disadvantages to using the least common denominator when adding fractions? Illustrate your answers with the example

$$\frac{3}{4} + \frac{1}{6}$$

and with other examples.

Class Activity 3V:
Mixed Numbers and Improper Fractions

1. Draw a picture to show how to convert $2\frac{3}{5}$ to an improper fraction. Relate your picture to the following numerical procedure for converting $2\frac{3}{5}$ to an improper fraction:

$$2\frac{3}{5} = \frac{2 \cdot 5 + 3}{5} = \frac{13}{5}$$

2. Sue showed Ramin the next diagram to explain why $1\frac{3}{4} = \frac{7}{4}$, but Ramin says that is shows $\frac{7}{8}$, not $\frac{7}{4}$. What must Sue and Ramin clarify?

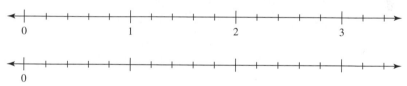

3. Label the first number line shown with fractions and mixed numbers. Label the second number line with proper and improper fractions. Then use the number lines to help you explain why the procedure for converting mixed numbers to improper fractions is valid.

Class Activity 3W: Adding and Subtracting Mixed Numbers

1. Each of the problems that follows shows some student work. Discuss the work: What is correct and what is not correct? In each case, either complete the work or modify it to make it correct. *Use the student's work; do not start from scratch.*
   a. Subtract: $3\frac{1}{4} - 1\frac{3}{4}$.

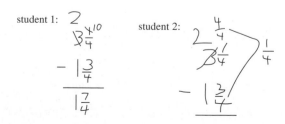

b. There are $2\frac{1}{3}$ cups of milk in a bowl. How much milk must be added to the bowl so that there will be 3 cups of milk in the bowl?

$$2 \quad 2\frac{1}{3} \quad 2\frac{2}{3} \quad 2\frac{3}{3} \overset{3}{}$$

2 more

c. There were 5 pounds of apples in a bag. After some of the apples were removed from the bag, there were $3\frac{1}{4}$ pounds of apples left. How many pounds of apples were removed?

$$5 \qquad \frac{4}{4} \quad \frac{4}{4} \quad \frac{4}{4} \quad \frac{4}{4} \quad \frac{4}{4}$$

$$\frac{1}{4} \quad \frac{3}{4}$$

d. Add: $2\frac{2}{3} + 1\frac{2}{3}$.

$2\frac{2}{3} + 1\frac{2}{3} = 3\frac{4}{6}$ because the fraction part is 4 out of 6.

2. Find at least two different ways to calculate

$$7\frac{1}{3} - 4\frac{1}{2}$$

and to give the answer as a mixed number. In each case, explain why your method makes sense.

Class Activity 3X: Addition with Whole Numbers, Decimals, Fractions, and Mixed Numbers: What Are Common Ideas?

Think about how we add (and subtract) whole numbers, decimals, fractions, and mixed numbers, and think about the ideas and reasoning that are involved. What is common in the way we add (and subtract) across all these different kinds of numbers?

Class Activity 3Y:

Are These Story Problems for $\frac{1}{2} + \frac{1}{3}$?

For each of the following story problems, determine whether the problem can be solved by adding $\frac{1}{2} + \frac{1}{3}$. If not, explain why not, and explain how the problem should be solved if there is enough information to do so. If there is not enough information to solve the problem, explain why not.

1. Tom pours $\frac{1}{2}$ cup of water into an empty bowl. Then Tom pours $\frac{1}{3}$ cup of water into the bowl. How many cups of water are in the bowl now?

2. Tom pours $\frac{1}{2}$ cup of water into an empty bowl. Then Tom pours in another $\frac{1}{3}$. How many cups of water are in the bowl now?

3. Starting at her apartment, Sally runs $\frac{1}{2}$ mile down the road. Then Sally turns around and runs $\frac{1}{3}$ mile back toward her apartment. How far has Sally run since leaving her apartment?

4. Starting at her apartment, Sally runs $\frac{1}{2}$ mile down the road. Then Sally turns around and runs $\frac{1}{3}$ mile back toward her apartment. How far down the road is Sally from her apartment?

5. $\frac{1}{2}$ of the land in Heeltoe County is covered with forest. $\frac{1}{3}$ of the and in the adjacent Toejoint County is covered with forest. What fraction of the land in the two-county Heeltoe–Toejoint region is covered with forest?

6. $\frac{1}{2}$ of the land in Heeltoe County is covered with forest. $\frac{1}{3}$ of the land in the adjacent Toejoint County is covered with forest. Heeltoe and Toejoint County have the same land area. What fraction of the land in the two-county Heeltoe–Toejoint region is covered with forest?

7. $\frac{1}{2}$ of the children at Martin Luther King Elementary School say they like to have pizza for lunch. $\frac{1}{3}$ of the children at Martin Luther King Elementary School say they like to have a hamburger for lunch. What fraction of the children at Martin Luther King Elementary School would like to have either pizza or a hamburger for lunch?

8. $\frac{1}{2}$ of the children at Timothy Elementary School like to have pizza for lunch, the other half does not like to have pizza for lunch. Of the children who do not like to have pizza for lunch, $\frac{1}{3}$ like to have a hamburger for lunch. What fraction of the children at Timothy Elementary School like to have either pizza or a hamburger for lunch?

Class Activity 3Z:
Are These Story Problems for $\frac{1}{2} - \frac{1}{3}$?

For each of the following story problems, determine whether the problem can be solved by subtracting $\frac{1}{2} - \frac{1}{3}$. If not, explain why not, and explain how the problem should be solved if there is enough information to do so. If there is not enough information to solve the problem, explain why not.

1. Zelha pours $\frac{1}{2}$ cup of water into an empty bowl. Then Zelha pours out $\frac{1}{3}$. How much water is in the bowl now?

2. Zelha pours $\frac{1}{2}$ cup of water into an empty bowl. Then Zelha pours out $\frac{1}{3}$ cup of water. How much water is in the bowl now?

3. Zelha pours $\frac{1}{2}$ cup of water into an empty bowl. Then Zelha pours out $\frac{1}{3}$ of the water that is in the bowl. How much water is in the bowl now?

4. Yesterday James ate $\frac{1}{2}$ of a pizza. Today James ate $\frac{1}{3}$ of a pizza of the same size. How much more pizza did James eat yesterday than today?

5. Yesterday James ate $\frac{1}{2}$ of a pizza. Today James ate $\frac{1}{3}$ of the whole pizza. Nobody else ate any of that pizza. How much pizza is left?

6. Yesterday James ate $\frac{1}{2}$ of a pizza. Today James ate $\frac{1}{3}$ of the pizza that was left over from yesterday. Nobody else ate any of that pizza. How much pizza is left?

Class Activity 3AA: What Fraction Is Shaded?

For each square shown, determine the fraction of the square that is shaded. Explain your reasoning. You may assume that all lengths that appear to be equal really are equal. Do not use any area formulas.

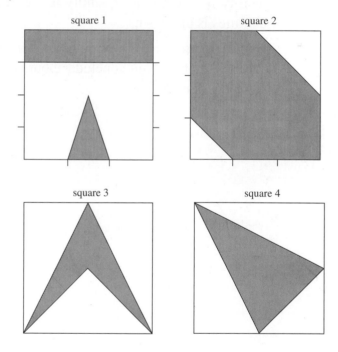

square 1   square 2

square 3   square 4

3.5 Adding and Subtracting Negative Numbers

Class Activity 3BB: Story Problems and Rules for Adding and Subtracting with Negative Numbers

In this activity you will write addition and subtraction story problems involving negative numbers. You will use these story problems to see why some of the rules for adding and subtracting with negative numbers make sense.

In writing your story problems, consider that negative numbers are nicely interpreted as amounts owed, temperatures below zero, locations below ground (such as in a building that has basement stories), or locations below sea level.

1. **a.** Write and solve an add to story problem for $(-5) + 5 = ?$.

   b. Thinking more generally about your story problem in part (a) and about its solution, what can you conclude about $(-N) + N$? Write an equation that shows your conclusion.

2. **a.** Write and solve a take away story problem for $(-2) - 5 = ?$.

   b. Write and solve a compare story problem for $(-2) - 5 = ?$ in which one quantity is -2 and the other quantity is 5 less and is unknown.

   c. Thinking more generally about your story problems in parts (a) and (b) and about their solutions, what can you conclude about how $(-A) - B$ and $A + B$ are related? Write an equation to show this relationship.

3. **a.** Write and solve a compare story problem for $2 - (-5) = ?$ in which one quantity is 2, the other quantity is -5, and the difference between the two quantities is unknown.

   b. Thinking more generally about your story problem in part (a) and about its solution, what can you conclude about $A - (-B)$? Write an equation that shows your conclusion.

Multiplication

4.1 Interpretations of Multiplication

Class Activity 4A: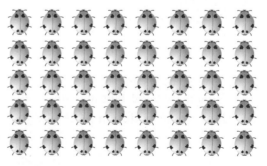
Showing Multiplicative Structure

Recall that according to our definition, $A \times B$ means the total in A groups of B.

$$A \times B$$
$$\uparrow \quad \uparrow$$

\# groups   \# in each group

1. Using the meaning of multiplication, explain why you can determine the number of ladybugs in the following picture by multiplying.

2. Fran has 3 pairs of pants, pants 1, 2, and 3, that coordinate perfectly with 4 different shirts, shirts A, B, C, and D. How many different outfits consisting of a pair of pants and a shirt can Fran make from these clothes?

   Apply the meaning of multiplication to explain why you can solve this problem with multiplication.

3. Eva's puppy weighs 9 pounds. Micah's puppy weighs 4 times as much as Eva's puppy. How much does Micah's puppy weigh?

   Draw a strip diagram for this problem and use it to help explain how to solve the problem.

4. Reword the previous problem about Eva's puppy so that it is still the same problem but you use a fraction in the statement of the problem.

Class Activity 4B: Problems about Pairs

1. A bag contains 6 tiles, labeled 1, 2, 3, 4, 5, 6. Reach into the bag, pick out a tile, and put it down. Then (without replacing the tile you picked out), reach into the bag again, pick out another tile, and put it down to the right of your first tile. The two tiles side by side make a 2-digit number. How many different 2-digit numbers can you possibly get this way?

   Explain how to solve this tile-pair problem. If multiplication is involved in your explanation, explain how the meaning of multiplication applies.

2. A bag contains a red, a blue, a yellow, a green, an orange, and a purple cube. Reach into the bag and pick out a pair of cubes (and then put the cubes back). How many different pairs of cubes can you possibly get this way?

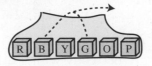

   Explain how to solve this cube-pair problem. If multiplication is involved in your explanation, explain how the meaning of multiplication applies.

3. How is the cube-pair problem different from the tile-pair problem?

4. How are the cube-pair and tile-pair problems different from this bear-pair problem?

    You have 6 bears. If you put these bears in pairs, how many pairs of bears will there be?

Class Activity 4C: Writing Multiplication Story Problems

Recall that according to our definition, $A \times B$ means the total in A groups of B.

$$A \times B$$
$$\uparrow \quad \uparrow$$
$$\text{\# groups} \quad \text{\# in each group}$$

1. Write a simple story problem that can be solved by multiplying 4×8. Explain why the problem can be solved by multiplying 4×8 (draw a picture to aid your explanation, if possible).

2. Write an *array* story problem that can be solved by multiplying 3×7. Explain why the problem can be solved by multiplying 3×7. How else can the story problem be solved? Explain.

3. Write an *ordered pair* story problem that can be solved by multiplying 8×5. Explain why the problem can be solved by multiplying 8×5. How else can the story problem be solved? Explain.

4. Write a *multiplicative comparison* story problem that can be solved by multiplying 5 × 9. Draw a strip diagram for the problem and explain why the problem can be solved by multiplying 5 × 9.

5. Reword your problem for part 4 so that it is the same problem but you use a fraction in the statement of the problem.

4.2 Why Multiplying Numbers by 10 Is Easy in the Decimal System

Class Activity 4D:
Multiplying by 10

1. Is the following statement correct in all circumstances?
   To multiply a number by 10, put a 0 at the end of the number.

2. The following statement is correct, but is it appropriate to use in all circumstances?
   To multiply a number by 10, move the decimal point one place to the right.

3. A different way to describe how to multiply by 10 is as follows:
   To multiply a number by 10, move all the digits one place to the left.

Explain why this statement about multiplying by 10 is true. To do so, use the picture below of 10 groups of 23, which represents 10 × 23. What happens to each of the 2 tens and what happens to each of the 3 ones when we multiply 23 by 10?

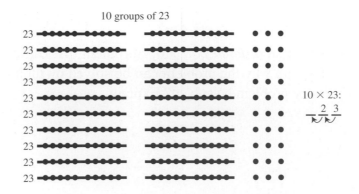

Class Activity 4E:
Multiplying by Powers of 10 Explains the Cycling of Decimal Representations of Fractions

When you use a calculator or long division, you will find that

$$\frac{1}{7} = 0.142857142857142857\ldots$$

Notice the repeating pattern—it turns out that it continues forever.

1. Look carefully at the sequence of digits in the decimal representations of the fractions listed. For $\frac{1}{7}$, this sequence is

$$1, 4, 2, 8, 5, 7, 1, 4, 2, 8, 5, 7, \ldots$$

How does the sequence of digits in these other decimal representations compare to this sequence?

$$\frac{1}{7} = 0.142857142857\ldots$$
$$\frac{2}{7} = 0.285714285714\ldots$$
$$\frac{3}{7} = 0.428571428571\ldots$$
$$\frac{4}{7} = 0.571428571428\ldots$$
$$\frac{5}{7} = 0.714285714285\ldots$$
$$\frac{6}{7} = 0.857142857142\ldots$$

2. By way of comparison, look at the decimal representations for various fractions with denominator 37. How is this similar to and how is this different from the situation in part 1?

$$\frac{1}{37} = 0.027027027027\ldots$$
$$\frac{2}{37} = 0.054054054054\ldots$$
$$\frac{3}{37} = 0.081081081081\ldots$$
$$\frac{4}{37} = 0.108108108108\ldots$$
$$\frac{5}{37} = 0.135135135135\ldots$$
$$\frac{10}{37} = 0.270270270270\ldots$$
$$\frac{26}{37} = 0.702702702702\ldots$$

The next several parts will help explain why the relationships you discovered in part 1 exist.

3. Calculate the following without the use of a calculator:

$$10 \times 0.142857142857142857\ldots =$$

$$100 \times 0.142857142857142857\ldots =$$

$$1,000 \times 0.142857142857142857\ldots =$$

$$10,000 \times 0.142857142857142857\ldots =$$

$$100,000 \times 0.142857142857142857\ldots =$$

$$1,000,000 \times 0.142857142857142857\ldots =$$

4. Write the following numbers as mixed numbers—in other words, with a whole number and a fractional part:

$$10 \times \frac{1}{7} = \frac{10}{7} = 1\frac{3}{7}$$

$$100 \times \frac{1}{7} = \frac{100}{7} =$$

$$1,000 \times \frac{1}{7} = \frac{1000}{7} =$$

$$10,000 \times \frac{1}{7} = \frac{10,000}{7} =$$

$$100,000 \times \frac{1}{7} = \frac{100,000}{7} =$$

$$1,000,000 \times \frac{1}{7} = \frac{1,000,000}{7} =$$

5. What is the relationship between the lists of numbers in parts 3 and 4? How are the fractional parts in part 4 related to your answers in part 3? Use this to explain the relationship you discovered in part 1.

4.3 The Commutative and Associative Properties of Multiplication, Areas of Rectangles, and Volumes of Boxes

Class Activity 4F:
Explaining and Illustrating the Commutative Property of Multiplication

1. Write one story problem for 5×3 and another for 3×5. Before determining the answers to the problems, discuss whether it would necessarily be obvious to a child that the answers are the same.

2. Use the next array to help you explain why 3×5 and 5×3 must be equal. In other words, explain why

$$3 \times 5 = 5 \times 3$$

☆ ☆ ☆ ☆ ☆
☆ ☆ ☆ ☆ ☆
☆ ☆ ☆ ☆ ☆

3. Why does the commutative property hold for numbers other than 3 and 5? In other words, why is it true that

$$A \times B = B \times A$$

no matter what counting numbers A and B are? To answer this question you may need to modify your explanation for why 3×5 is equal to 5×3 so that it is a general conceptual explanation, that is, one that *doesn't refer to the number 15 but refers only to 3 and 5 and to the underlying array.*

4. A third-grade math book explained the commutative property of multiplication by using a number line to show that

$$5 + 5 + 5$$

is equal to

$$3 + 3 + 3 + 3 + 3$$

Why is this not a good explanation? Why is it better to use an array?

5. A marching band is arranged in 20 rows of 4. Everybody in the band turns 90 degrees to their left. Now how is the band arranged? How can you use the marching band to illustrate the commutative property of multiplication?

6. There are 21 bags with 2 marbles in each bag. Ben calculates the number of marbles there are in all by counting by 2s 21 times:

$$2, 4, 6, 8, 10, \ldots, 40, 42$$

Kaia calculates $21 + 21 = 42$ instead.

   Discuss the two calculation methods. Are both legitimate? Explain.

Class Activity 4G: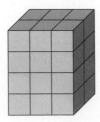
Multiplication, Areas of Rectangles, and the Commutative Property

1. The large rectangle shown here is 9 centimeters wide and 5 centimeters tall. Use the meaning of multiplication to explain why you can find the area of the rectangle by multiplying.

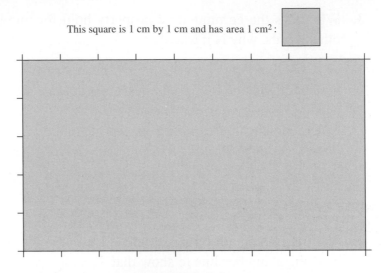

This square is 1 cm by 1 cm and has area 1 cm² :

2. Using the rectangle in part 1, explain why

$$5 \times 9 = 9 \times 5$$

3. Explain why

$$A \times B = B \times A$$

    is true for all counting numbers A and B.

Class Activity 4H:
Ways to Describe the Volume of a Box with Multiplication

You will need a set of blocks for parts 1 and 2 of this activity.

1. If you have cubic-inch blocks available, build a box that is 3 inches wide, 2 inches long, and 4 inches tall. It should look like this:

2. Subdivide your box into natural groups of blocks, and describe how you subdivided the box. How many groups were there and how many blocks were in each group? Using multiplication, write the corresponding expressions for the total number of blocks in the box. Now repeat, this time subdividing your box into natural groups in a different way.

3. The next figures show different ways of subdividing a box into groups. If you have built a box from blocks, subdivide your box in the ways shown in the figures. In each case, describe the number of groups and the number of blocks in each group. Then write an expression for the total number of blocks. Your expression should use multiplication, parentheses, and the numbers 2, 3, and 4.

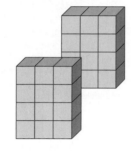

_____ groups of _____ blocks

On the following line, write an expression using multiplication, parentheses, and the numbers 2, 3, and 4 for the total number of blocks:

_____

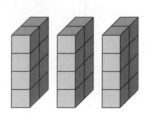

_____ groups of _____ blocks

On the following line, write an expression using multiplication, parentheses, and the numbers 2, 3, and 4 for the total number of blocks:

_____

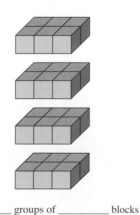

_____ groups of _____ blocks

On the following line, write an expression using multiplication, parentheses, and the numbers 2, 3, and 4 for the total number of blocks:

_____

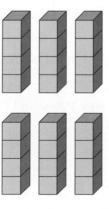

_____ groups of _____ blocks

On the following line, write an expression using multiplication, parentheses, and the numbers 2, 3, and 4 for the total number of blocks:

_____

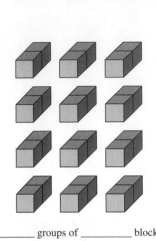

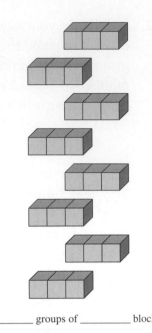

_____ groups of _____ blocks

On the following line, write an expression
using multiplication, parentheses, and the
numbers 2, 3, and 4 for the total number
of blocks:

_____

_____ groups of _____ blocks

On the following line, write an expression
using multiplication, parentheses, and the
numbers 2, 3, and 4 for the total number
of blocks:

_____

Class Activity 4I:
Explaining the Associative Property

1. Use some of the pictures and the expressions you wrote for part 3 of
   Class Activity 4H to help you explain why

   $$(4 \times 2) \times 3 = 4 \times (2 \times 3)$$

2. By describing the groups, explain how to see the following:

   The next design shows 6 groups of dots with 4×2 dots in each group;
   this design also shows 6×4 groups of dots with 2 dots in each group.

   Then write an equation to show that you must get the same number of dots, either
   way you count them.

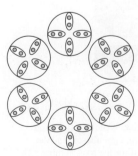

3. Use the next design to help you explain why

$$(5 \times 3) \times 4 = 5 \times (3 \times 4)$$

Your explanation should be general, in the sense that it explains why the equation is true when you replace the numbers 5, 3, and 4 with other counting numbers, and the design is changed accordingly.

Class Activity 4J:
Using the Associative and Commutative Properties of Multiplication

1. Which property of arithmetic is used in the following calculations? Where is the property used?

$$\begin{aligned}
8 \times 70 &= 8 \times (7 \times 10) \\
&= (8 \times 7) \times 10 \\
&= 56 \times 10 \\
&= 560
\end{aligned}$$

2. To multiply 4×60 mentally, we can multiply 4×6 first, and then put a 0 at the end to get the answer, 240. Write equations to show that this mental technique uses the associative property of multiplication. Use the next picture to explain why the mental technique makes sense.

3. How is the associative property of multiplication involved when viewing 20 groups of 10 as 2 groups of 100? Write equations to help explain.

4. Which properties of arithmetic are used in the following calculations? Where are the properties used?

$$\begin{aligned}
60 \times 4000 &= 6 \times 10 \times 4 \times 1000 \\
&= 6 \times 4 \times 10 \times 1000 \\
&= 24 \times 10 \times 1000 \\
&= 240 \times 1000 \\
&= 240,000
\end{aligned}$$

5. To multiply 30 × 40 mentally, we can multiply 3 × 4 first, and then put two zeros at the end to get the answer, 1200. Write equations to show that this mental technique uses the associative and commutative properties of multiplication. Use the next picture to explain why the mental technique makes sense.

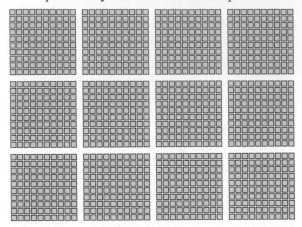

6. Marcie calculated 60 × 700 mentally as follows:

    6 times 7 is 42,   10 times 100 is 1000,   42 times 1000 is 42,000.

Write a sequence of equations that shows why Marcie's method of calculation is valid. Which properties of arithmetic are involved? Write your equations in the following form:

$$
\begin{aligned}
60 \times 700 &= \text{some expression}\\
&= \text{some expression}\\
&= \vdots\\
&= 42{,}000
\end{aligned}
$$

Class Activity 4K: Different Ways to Calculate the Total Number of Objects

1. Use only the numbers 3, 4, and 5, the multiplication symbol × (or ·), and parentheses to write at least two different expressions for the total number of hearts in the next figure. In each case, evaluate your expression to calculate the total number of hearts.

2. Write at least two different expressions for the total number of stars shown next. In each case, evaluate your expression in order to calculate the total number of stars.

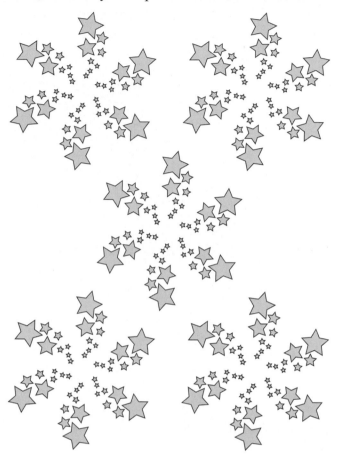

Class Activity 4L: Using Multiplication to Estimate How Many

1. Use multiplication to estimate how many curlicues there are in the figure.

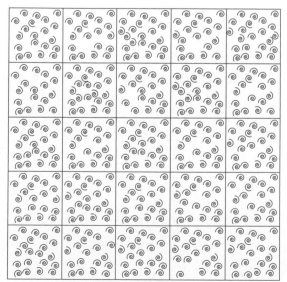

2. Use multiplication to estimate how many dots are shown. Describe your strategy.

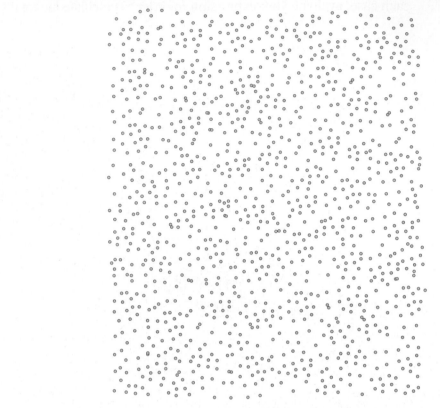

3. Describe a *realistic* strategy for determining approximately how many hairs are on a person's head. If possible, carry out your strategy.

Class Activity 4M: How Many Gumdrops?

You will need a box filled with small objects such as snap cubes or counting bears as well as measuring cups, measuring spoons, or scoops for part 2 of this activity.

1. The container shown has a square base, so that all four vertical sides of the container are identical; the picture shows one of those four sides. Use multiplication to determine approximately how many gumdrops are in the container. Explain your method.

2. Describe several different realistic methods for determining approximately how many snap cubes (or counting bears or other small objects) are in a box, *without* counting all the items one by one. If possible, carry out your methods.

4.4 The Distributive Property

Class Activity 4N: Order of Operations

You will need a calculator for part 1(b) of this activity.

1. **a.** Evaluate the expression $4 \times 5 - 18 \div 3 + 12 \times 10$ without a calculator.

   b. Using a calculator, enter the numbers and operations in the expression $4 \times 5 - 18 \div 3 + 12 \times 10$ in the order in which they appear, pressing the = sign or "enter" button each time after you enter a number. Do you get the correct answer this way? If not, why not?

2. For each of the following expressions, write a story problem for that expression and explain briefly why your story problem is appropriate for the expression.

a. $3 + 4 \times 6$

b. $3 + 4 \quad \times 6$ (Does it matter if there is a big space between the $\times$ and the 4?)

c. $(3 + 4) \times 6$

d. $6 \times 4 + 3 \times 5$

Class Activity 4O:
Explaining the Distributive Property

1. There are 6 goodie bags. Each goodie bag contains 3 eraser tops and 4 stickers.

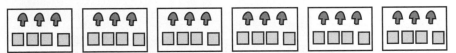

a. Explain why the expression

$$6 \times 3 + 6 \times 4$$

describes the total number of items in the goodie bags. Your explanation should *not* refer explicitly to the number 42.

b. Explain why the expression

$$6 \times (3 + 4)$$

describes the total number of items in the goodie bags. Your explanation should *not* refer explicitly to the number 42.

c. Use parts (a) and (b) to explain why

$$6 \times (3 + 4) = 6 \times 3 + 6 \times 4$$

Your explanation should *not* refer explicitly to the number 42.

d. State the distributive property. Now discuss how to view your explanation in part (c) as explaining why the distributive property makes sense for all counting numbers.

Note: parts (a), (b), and (c) asked you not to refer explicitly to the number 42 so that you could produce a general explanation that is valid even when you replace the numbers 6, 4, and 3 with other counting numbers.

2. Use the different shading shown in the rectangle, and use the meaning of multiplication, to explain why

$$3 \times (2 + 4) = 3 \times 2 + 3 \times 4$$

Your explanation should be general in the sense that you could use it to explain why

$$A \times (B + C) = A \times B + A \times C$$

for *all* counting numbers *A, B,* and *C.*

3. On the graph paper shown, draw a rectangle and shade it to illustrate the equation

$$8 \times (10 + 5) = 8 \times 10 + 8 \times 5$$

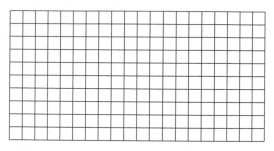

Class Activity 4P:

Using the Distributive Property

1. Use the multiplication facts

$$15 \times 15 = 225$$
$$2 \times 15 = 30$$

to help you mentally calculate

$$17 \times 15$$

Explain how your calculation method is related to the following array, which consists of 17 rows of dots with 15 dots in each row:

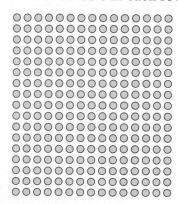

2. Write equations showing how your mental strategy for calculating 17×15 in part 1 involves the distributive property.

3. Write an equation that uses subtraction and the distributive property and that goes along with the following array:

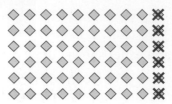

4. Mentally calculate 20 × 15, and use your answer to mentally calculate 19 × 15. Write an equation that uses subtraction and the distributive property and that goes along with your strategy. Without drawing all the detail, draw a rough picture of an array that illustrates this calculation strategy.

Class Activity 4Q: Why Isn't 23 × 23 Equal to 20 × 20 + 3 × 3?

Kylie has an idea for how to calculate 23 × 23. She says,

> Twenty times 20 is 400, and 3 times 3 is 9; so 23 × 23 should be 400 plus 9, which is 409.

Is Kylie's method valid? If not, how could you modify her work to make it correct? Don't just start over in a different way; work with Kylie's idea. Use the large square below, which consists of 23 rows with 23 small squares in each row, to help you explain your answer.

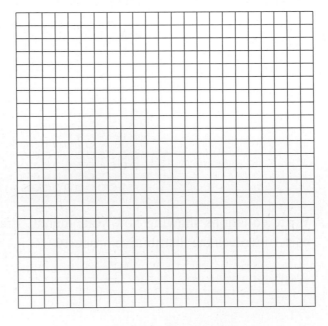

Class Activity 4R: The Distributive Property and FOIL

If you have studied algebra, then you probably learned the FOIL method for multiplying expressions of the form

$$(A + B) \cdot (C + D)$$

FOIL stands for *First, Outer, Inner, Last,* and reminds us that

$$(A + B) \cdot (C + D) = A \cdot C + A \cdot D + B \cdot C + B \cdot D$$

Where $A \cdot C$ is *First,* $A \cdot D$ is *Outer,* $B \cdot C$, is *Inner*, and $B \cdot D$ is *Last.*

This class activity will help you explain in several different ways why the FOIL equation is valid.

1. Use the shading shown in the next rectangle and use the meaning of multiplication to explain why

$$(2 + 3) \cdot (7 + 4) = 2 \cdot 7 + 2 \cdot 4 + 3 \cdot 7 + 3 \cdot 4$$

Your explanation should be general in the sense that you could use it to explain why

$$(A + B) \cdot (C + D) = A \cdot C + A \cdot D + B \cdot C + B \cdot D$$

is true for all counting numbers A, B, C, and D

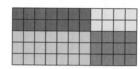

2. Relate the preceding subdivided rectangle to the following sequence of equations:

$$(2 + 3) \cdot (7 + 4) = 2 \cdot (7 + 4) + 3 \cdot (7 + 4)$$
$$= 2 \cdot 7 + 2 \cdot 4 + 3 \cdot 7 + 3 \cdot 4$$

Which properties of arithmetic do these equations use? Where are the properties used?

3. On the graph paper shown, draw and shade a rectangle to show why the following equation is true:

$$(10 + 3) \cdot (20 + 4) = 10 \cdot 20 + 10 \cdot 4 + 3 \cdot 20 + 3 \cdot 4$$

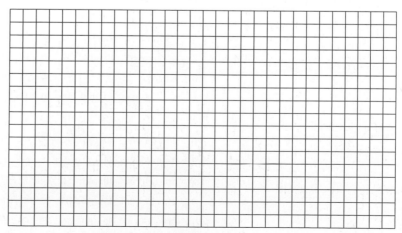

4. Use the distributive property several times to write a sequence of equations which proves that

$$(10 + 3) \cdot (20 + 4) = 10 \cdot 20 + 10 \cdot 4 + 3 \cdot 20 + 3 \cdot 4$$

Your work should be general in the sense that it would remain valid if other numbers were to replace 10, 3, 20, and 4.

5. Relate each step in your sequence of equations in part 4 to the subdivided rectangle you created in part 3.

6. Find a different expression that is equal to $(A + B) \cdot (C + D + E)$, and explain why the two expressions are equal.

Class Activity 4S: Squares and Products Near Squares

If available, a set of square tiles would be helpful for part 2.

The word *square* can refer to a geometric shape or to a related amount of area, such as a "square inch." But there are also square *numbers*. The **square number** or **perfect squares** are the counting numbers that can be written as a counting number times itself; for example,

$$1 \times 1, \quad 2 \times 2, \quad 3 \times 3, \quad \dots, \quad 9 \times 9, \quad \dots$$

are squares. In the multiplication table, the squares are usually easy to remember; the squares lie on a diagonal, as in the following multiplication table:

×	1	2	3	4	5	6	7	8	9	10
1	1	2	3	4	5	6	7	8	9	10
2	2	4	6	8	10	12	14	16	18	20
3	3	6	9	12	15	18	21	24	27	30
4	4	8	12	16	20	24	28	32	36	40
5	5	10	15	20	25	30	35	40	45	50
6	6	12	18	24	30	36	42	48	54	60
7	7	14	21	28	35	42	49	56	63	70
8	8	16	24	32	40	48	56	64	72	80
9	9	18	27	36	45	54	63	72	81	90
10	10	20	30	40	50	60	70	80	90	100

1. Compare each square in the multiplication table with the entry that is diagonally above and to the right of it (or diagonally below and to the left). For example, compare 49 (which is 7 × 7) with 48 (which is 6 × 8). What pattern do you notice?

2. Use arrays to help you explain why the pattern you described in part 1 exists. If available, use square tiles to make your arrays; rearrange the tiles to relate multiplication facts. If tiles are not available, draw the arrays instead.

3. Now apply the distributive property or FOIL to the expression
$$(A - 1) \cdot (A + 1)$$
    to explain why the pattern you discovered in part 1 exists.

4. Why are the squares 1 × 1, 2 × 2, 3 × 3, ... called squares?

5. Annie is working on the multiplication problem 19 × 21. Annie says that 19 × 21 should equal 20 × 20 because 19 is one less than 20 and 21 is one more than 20.

    Annie has a wonderful idea, but is it correct? If not, use the dots shown to help you explain to Annie why not. There are 20 rows of dots with 21 dots in each row.

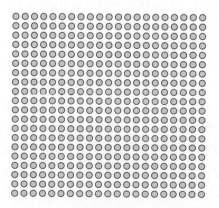

6. Mary is working on the multiplication problem 19 × 21. Mary says that 19 × 21 is 21 less than 20 × 21, and 20 × 21 is 20 more than 20 × 20, which she knows is 400. Mary thinks this ought to help her calculate 19 × 21, but she can't quite figure it out.

   Discuss Mary's idea in detail. Can you make her explanation work?

4.5 Properties of Arithmetic, Mental Math, and Single-Digit Multiplication Facts

Class Activity 4T:
Using Properties of Arithmetic to Aid the Learning of Basic Multiplication Facts

In school, children must learn the single-digit multiplication facts from 1 × 1 = 1 to 9 × 9 = 81. These are 81 separate facts, but many of these facts are related by properties of arithmetic. By knowing how some facts are related to other facts, children can structure their understanding of the single-digit facts in order to learn them better.

2 × 2 = 4	3 × 2	4 × 2	5 × 2	6 × 2	7 × 2	8 × 2	9 × 2
2 × 3 = 6	3 × 3 = 9	4 × 3	5 × 3	6 × 3	7 × 3	8 × 3	9 × 3
2 × 4 = 8	3 × 4 = 12	4 × 4 = 16	5 × 4	6 × 4	7 × 4	8 × 4	9 × 4
2 × 5 = 10	3 × 5 = 15	4 × 5 = 20	5 × 5 = 25	6 × 5	7 × 5	8 × 5	9 × 5
2 × 6 = 12	3 × 6 = 18	4 × 6 = 24	5 × 6 = 30	6 × 6 = 36	7 × 6	8 × 6	9 × 6
2 × 7 = 14	3 × 7 = 21	4 × 7 = 28	5 × 7 = 35	6 × 7 = 42	7 × 7 = 49	8 × 7	9 × 7
2 × 8 = 16	3 × 8 = 24	4 × 8 = 32	5 × 8 = 40	6 × 8 = 48	7 × 8 = 56	8 × 8 = 64	9 × 8
2 × 9 = 18	3 × 9 = 27	4 × 9 = 36	5 × 9 = 45	6 × 9 = 54	7 × 9 = 63	8 × 9 = 72	9 × 9 = 81

1. Examine the darkly shaded, lightly shaded, and unshaded regions in the preceding multiplication table. Explain how to obtain the unshaded facts quickly and easily from the shaded facts. In doing so, what property of arithmetic do you use? How does knowing this property of arithmetic lighten the load for children of learning the single-digit multiplication facts?

2. Multiplication facts involving the numbers 6, 7, and 8 are often hard to learn. For each fact in the lightly shaded regions in the table, describe a way to obtain the fact from facts in the darkly shaded region as follows:

   a. Draw an array for the fact, and show how to subdivide the array in order to relate the fact to one or more other facts. Try to find several different ways to subdivide the array this way.

b. Write equations that correspond to your subdivided array from part (a) and that show how the multiplication fact is related to darkly shaded facts. Specify the properties of arithmetic that your equations used.

　　　For example, you could draw either of the two subdivided arrays shown here for the fact 3×7 and write the corresponding equations shown underneath them. Both equations use the distributive property.

$$3 \times 7 = 2 \times 7 + 1 \times 7$$
$$= 14 + 7 = 21$$

$$3 \times 7 = 3 \times 3 + 3 \times 4$$
$$= 9 + 12 = 21$$

3. The *5 × table* is easy to learn because it is "half of the *10 × table*."

$5 \times 1 = 5$	$10 \times 1 = 10$
$5 \times 2 = 10$	$10 \times 2 = 20$
$5 \times 3 = 15$	$10 \times 3 = 30$
$5 \times 4 = 20$	$10 \times 4 = 40$
$5 \times 5 = 25$	$10 \times 5 = 50$
$5 \times 6 = 30$	$10 \times 6 = 60$
$5 \times 7 = 35$	$10 \times 7 = 70$
$5 \times 8 = 40$	$10 \times 8 = 80$
$5 \times 9 = 45$	$10 \times 9 = 90$

Write an equation showing the relationship between 10×7 and 5×7 that fits with the statement about the *5 × table* being half of the *10 × table*. Which property of arithmetic do you use?

4. The *9 × table* is easy to learn because you can just subtract a number that is to be multiplied by 9 from that number with a 0 placed behind it, as shown next. Explain why this way of multiplying by 9 is valid.

$$9 \times 1 = 10 - 1 = 9$$
$$9 \times 2 = 20 - 2 = 18$$
$$9 \times 3 = 30 - 3 = 27$$
$$9 \times 4 = 40 - 4 = 36$$
$$9 \times 5 = 50 - 5 = 45$$
$$9 \times 6 = 60 - 6 = 54$$
$$9 \times 7 = 70 - 7 = 63$$
$$9 \times 8 = 80 - 8 = 72$$
$$9 \times 9 = 90 - 9 = 81$$

5. What is another pattern (other than the one described in part 4) in the *9 × table*?

Class Activity 4U: Solving Arithmetic Problems Mentally

For each of the following arithmetic problems, describe a way to make the problem easy to solve mentally:

1. 4×99

2. 16×25 (Try to find several ways to solve this problem mentally.)

3. $45\% \times 680$

4. 12×125 (Try to find several ways to solve this problem mentally.)

5. $125\% \times 120$

Class Activity 4V: Which Properties of Arithmetic Do These Calculations Use?

The sequences of equations that follow correspond to efficient mental strategies for solving the arithmetic problems of the previous class activity. In each case, describe the strategy in words. That is, describe what a person who is solving the problem mentally in a way that corresponds to the given equations might say to himself or herself. Also, determine which properties of arithmetic were used, and where they were used. Be specific.

1. $\begin{aligned} 4 \times 99 &= 4 \times (100 - 1) \\ &= 4 \times 100 - 4 \times 1 \\ &= 400 - 4 \\ &= 396 \end{aligned}$

2. $16 \times 25 = (4 \times 4) \times 25$
$= 4 \times (4 \times 25)$
$= 4 \times 100$
$= 400$

3. $16 \times 25 = 4 \times 4 \times 5 \times 5$
$= 4 \times 5 \times 4 \times 5$
$= 20 \times 20$
$= 400$

4. $45\% \times 680 = (50\% - 5\%) \times 680$
$= 50\% \times 680 - 5\% \times 680$
$= \dfrac{1}{2} \times 680 - \dfrac{1}{2} \times 10\% \times 680$
$= 340 - \dfrac{1}{2} \times 68$
$= 340 - 34$
$= 306$

5. $12 \times 125 = 10 \times 125 + 2 \times 125$
$= 1250 + 2 \times 100 + 2 \times 25$
$= 1250 + 200 + 50$
$= 1500$

6. $12 \times 125 = (3 \times 4) \times 125$
$= 3 \times (4 \times 125)$
$= 3 \times (4 \times 100 + 4 \times 25)$
$= 3 \times (400 + 100)$
$= 3 \times 500$
$= 1500$

7. $125\% \times 120 = (100\% + 25\%) \times 120$
$$= 100\% \times 120 + 25\% \times 120$$
$$= 120 + \frac{1}{4} \times 120$$
$$= 120 + 30$$
$$= 150$$

Class Activity 4W: Writing Equations That Correspond to a Method of Calculation

Each arithmetic problem in this activity has a description of the problem solution. In each case, write a sequence of equations that corresponds to the given description. Which properties of arithmetic were used and where? Write your equations in the following form:

$$\text{original} = \text{some expression}$$
$$= \vdots$$
$$= \text{some expression}$$

1. $6 \times 800 = ?$

    6 times 8 is 48; then 48 times 100 is 4800.

2. $51 \times 4 = ?$

    50 times 4 is 200, plus another 4 is 204.

3. $35 \times 2 = ?$

    35 twos is two 35s, which is 70.

4. What is 55% of 120?

    Half of 120 is 60. 10% of 120 is 12, so 5% of 120 is half of that 10%, which is 6. So the answer is 60 plus 6, which is 66.

5. What is 35% of 80?

    25% is $\frac{1}{4}$, so 25% of 80 is one-fourth of 80, which is 20. 10% of 80 is 8. So 35% of 80 is 20 plus 8, which is 28.

6. What is 90% of 350?

    10% of 350 is 35. Taking 35 away from 350 leaves 315. So the answer is 315.

7. What is $\frac{7}{8}$ of 2400?

    One-eighth of 2400 is 300. Taking 300 away from 2400 leaves 2100. The answer is 2100.

Class Activity 4X:
Showing the Algebra in Mental Math

For each arithmetic problem in this activity, find ways to use properties of arithmetic to make the problem easy to do mentally. Describe your method in words, and write equations that correspond to your method. Write your equations in the following form:

$$\text{original} = \text{some expression}$$
$$= \vdots$$
$$= \text{some expression}$$

1. 6×12 (Try to find several different ways to solve this problem mentally.)

2. 24×25 (Try to find several different ways to solve this problem mentally.)

3. $5\% \times 48$

4. 15% × $44

5. 26% × 840

6. 9 × 99 (Try to find several different ways to solve this problem mentally.)

7. $\frac{7}{8}$ × 128

4.6 Why the Common Algorithm for Multiplying Whole Numbers Works

Class Activity 4Y: The Standard versus the Partial-Products Multiplication Algorithm

1. Use the standard multiplication algorithm and then the partial-products algorithm to solve the following multiplication problems:

$$
\begin{array}{r}
495 \\
\times\ \ 7 \\
\hline
\end{array}
\qquad
\begin{array}{r}
495 \\
\times\ \ 7 \\
\hline
\end{array}
$$

$$
\begin{array}{r}
84 \\
\times\ 69 \\
\hline
\end{array}
\qquad
\begin{array}{r}
84 \\
\times\ 69 \\
\hline
\end{array}
$$

2. Compare the two algorithms. How are they the same, and how are they different? Why do both produce the same answer? Compare how "carrying" is handled in the two algorithms. Compare how place value is handled in the two algorithms.

Class Activity 4Z:

Why the Multiplication Algorithms Give Correct Answers, Part 1

Graph paper would be helpful for part 5 of this activity.

This class activity will help you explain why the partial-products algorithm, and therefore also the standard algorithm, gives correct answers to multiplication problems. Approach this activity and the next from a smart child's perspective. Pretend you don't know any multiplication algorithms yet, but you *do* know what multiplication means and you want to understand how to multiply and *why* it works.

Consider the multiplication problem 6×38.

1. Use the partial-products multiplication algorithm to calculate 6×38.

2. The array shown next consists of 6 rows of dots with 38 dots in each row. Subdivide the array into pieces that correspond to the steps in the partial-products algorithm. Use this to explain why the partial-products algorithm calculates the correct answer to 6×38. Begin your explanation by using the meaning of multiplication to relate the array to the multiplication problem 6×38.

3. Now solve the multiplication problem 6×38 by working with expanded forms and using the distributive property.

$$6 \times 38 = 6 \times (30 + 8)$$
$$=$$

Relate the equations you just wrote to the steps in the partial-products algorithm. Use this relationship to explain why the partial-products algorithm calculates the correct answer to 6×38.

4. Compare the two explanations you gave in parts 2 and 3 to show why the partial-products algorithm calculates the correct answer to 6×38.

5. **a.** Use the partial-products algorithm to calculate 9×26.

   b. Draw an array for 9×26 (if it's available, use graph paper; otherwise, indicate the array by drawing a rectangle). Subdivide the array in a natural way so that the parts of the array correspond to the steps in the partial-products algorithm.

   c. Solve 9×26 by writing equations that use expanded forms and the distributive property. Relate your equations to the steps in the partial-products algorithm.

Class Activity 4AA:
Why the Multiplication Algorithms Give Correct Answers, Part 2

Graph paper would be helpful for part 7 of this activity.

This class activity will help you explain why the partial-products multiplication algorithm, and therefore also the standard algorithm, gives correct answers to multiplication problems. It will also help you relate the standard and partial-products algorithms.

Consider the multiplication problem 23×45.

1. Use the partial-products and standard algorithms to calculate

$$
\begin{array}{r}
45 \\
\times\ 23 \\
\hline
\end{array}
\qquad
\begin{array}{r}
45 \\
\times\ 23 \\
\hline
\end{array}
$$

2. The next array consists of 23 rows of squares with 45 squares in each row. Relate this array, and the way it has been subdivided, to the steps in the partial-products algorithm. Use this relationship to explain why the partial-products algorithm calculates the correct answer to 23 × 45. Begin your explanation by using the meaning of multiplication to relate the array to the multiplication problem 23 × 45.

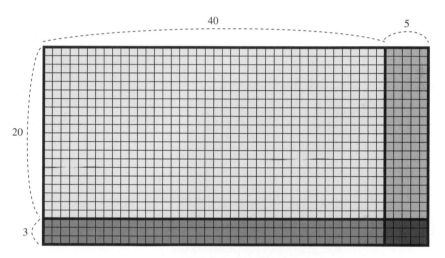

3. Now describe the pieces of the previous array that correspond to the steps in the *standard algorithm*. Relate these pieces to the pieces for the partial-products algorithm that you discussed in part 2.

4. Solve the multiplication problem 23 × 45 by working with expanded forms and using the distributive property several times.

$$23 \times 45 = (20 + 3) \times (40 + 5)$$
$$=$$

Relate the equations you just wrote to the steps in the partial-products algorithm. Use this relationship to explain why the partial-products algorithm calculates the correct answer to 23 × 45.

5. Compare the two explanations you gave in parts 2 and 4 to show why the partial-products algorithm calculates the correct answer to 23 × 45.

6. Write equations that use the distributive property and that correspond to the steps in the standard algorithm for 23 × 45. (Put one of the numbers in expanded form.) Relate to part 3.

7. **a.** Use the partial-products and standard algorithms to calculate 17 × 28.

    b. Draw an array for 17 × 28. (Draw your array by drawing a rectangle on graph paper; if you don't have graph paper, draw a rectangle to represent the array rather than drawing 17 rows of 28 items.) Subdivide the array in a natural way so that the parts of the array correspond to the steps in the partial-products algorithm.

    c. Now subdivide your array from part (b) in a natural way so that the parts of the array correspond to the steps in the standard algorithm. Relate these parts to the parts in part (b).

    d. Solve 17 × 28 by writing equations that use expanded forms and the distributive property. Relate your equations to the steps in the partial-products algorithm.

    e. Write equations that use the distributive property and that correspond to the steps in the standard algorithm for 17 × 28. Relate to part (c).

Class Activity 4BB: The Standard Multiplication Algorithm Right Side Up and Upside Down

1. Use the standard algorithm to calculate

$$\begin{array}{r} 347 \\ \times\ 26 \\ \hline \end{array}$$

2. Draw a rectangle to represent an array for 26×347. (The rectangle need not be to scale.) Subdivide the rectangle in a natural way so that the parts of the rectangle correspond to the steps of the standard algorithm in part 1.

3. Now use the standard algorithm to calculate

$$\begin{array}{r} 26 \\ \times\ 347 \\ \hline \end{array}$$

      Are the steps the same as in part 1? Is the answer the same as in part 1?

4. Can you show the steps of the standard algorithm in part 3 on the rectangle in part 2? If so, how?

5. Why must the answers in 1 and 3 be the same even though the steps are different? How is this question related to the rectangle in part 2? Which property of arithmetic is relevant here?

Multiplication of Fractions, Decimals, and Negative Numbers

5.1 Multiplying Fractions

Class Activity 5A:
The Meaning of Multiplication for Fractions

In Chapter 4 we said that if A and B are nonnegative numbers, then $A \cdot B$ is the "amount in A groups of B." This shorthand definition applies to fractions, but we'll need to "massage" the wording and think carefully about its meaning to make sense of what fraction multiplication means. So let's start by thinking about the meaning of whole number multiplication and rephrasing it slightly:

$$3 \cdot 4 = \text{amount of stuff in 3 groups}$$

$$\uparrow \quad \uparrow$$

# of groups   amount of stuff in one whole group

For each of the following fraction multiplication problems, annotate the problem so that it looks like the annotated equation above. Then use your annotation to discuss the meaning of the fraction multiplication problem and to help you make sense of it. As part of your discussion, write a simple story problem and draw a simple picture.

1. $2 \cdot \dfrac{1}{3}$ **2.** $\dfrac{1}{2} \cdot \dfrac{1}{3}$ **3.** $\dfrac{1}{3} \cdot 2$ **4.** $3 \cdot \dfrac{4}{5}$

Class Activity 5B: Misconceptions with Fraction Multiplication

1. Maisy draws a picture like the one shown to depict $3 \cdot \frac{4}{5}$. Maisy concludes from her picture that

$$3 \cdot \frac{4}{5} = \frac{12}{15}$$

because 12 pieces out of 15 are shaded. Is Maisy right? If not, where is her reasoning flawed?

2. Joey, a fourth-grader, wanted to figure out how many calories were in a piece of candy. According to the label on the bag, there were 50 calories in 3 pieces. Joey knew he had to find $\frac{1}{3}$ of 50, and he gave the answer $16\frac{2}{6}$. Joey explained his answer this way:

    3 sixteens is 48 and $\frac{1}{3}$ of the other 2 calories is $\frac{2}{6}$.

    Joey drew the following picture to explain the $\frac{2}{6}$. What was Joey confused about?

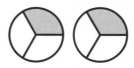

Class Activity 5C:
Explaining Why the Procedure for Multiplying Fractions Gives Correct Answers

This class activity will help you explain how the procedure for multiplying fractions comes from the meaning of fractions and the meaning of multiplication.

1. Use the meaning of fractions, the meaning of multiplication, and the next diagram to help you explain why

$$\frac{2}{3} \cdot \frac{5}{8} = \frac{2 \cdot 5}{3 \cdot 8}$$

In particular, explain why it makes sense to multiply the numerators and why it makes sense to multiply the denominators.

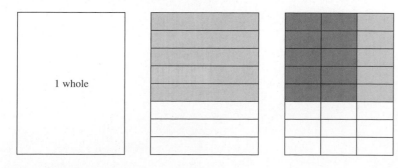

1 whole

2. Use the meaning of fractions, the meaning of multiplication, and the rectangles in the next figure to help you explain why

$$\frac{2}{5} \cdot \frac{3}{7} = \frac{2 \cdot 3}{5 \cdot 7}$$

In particular, explain why it makes sense to multiply the numerators and why it makes sense to multiply the denominators.

Class Activity 5D:
When Do We Multiply Fractions?

As a teacher, you will probably write story problems for your students. This activity will help you see how slight changes in the wording of a problem can produce big changes in the meaning of the problem and the operation that is used to solve the problem.

1. *A mulch pile problem:* Originally, there was $\frac{3}{4}$ of a cubic yard of mulch in a mulch pile. Then $\frac{1}{3}$ of the mulch in the mulch pile was removed. Now how much mulch is left in the mulch pile?

   a. Is the mulch pile problem a story problem for $\frac{1}{3} \cdot \frac{3}{4}$, is it a story problem for $\frac{3}{4} - \frac{1}{3}$, or is it not a story problem for either of these? Explain.

   b. Write a new mulch pile story problem for $\frac{1}{3} \cdot \frac{3}{4}$ and write a new mulch pile story problem for $\frac{3}{4} - \frac{1}{3}$. Make clear which is which.

2. Which of the following problems are story problems for $\frac{2}{3} \cdot \frac{1}{4}$, and which are not? Why?

   a. Joe is making $\frac{2}{3}$ of a recipe. The full recipe calls for $\frac{1}{4}$ cup of water. How much water should Joe use?

   b. $\frac{1}{4}$ of the students in Mrs. Watson's class are doing a dinosaur project. $\frac{2}{3}$ of the children doing the dinosaur project have completed it. How many children have completed a dinosaur project?

   c. $\frac{1}{4}$ of the students in Mrs. Watson's class are doing a dinosaur project. $\frac{2}{3}$ of the children doing the dinosaur project have completed it. What fraction of the students in Mrs. Watson's class have completed a dinosaur project?

   d. There is $\frac{1}{4}$ of a cake left. $\frac{2}{3}$ of Mrs. Watson's class would like to have some cake. What fraction of the cake does each student who wants cake get?

   e. Carla is making snack bags that each contain $\frac{1}{4}$ package of jelly worms. $\frac{2}{3}$ of Carla's grab bags have been bought. What fraction of Carla's jelly worms have been bought?

Class Activity 5E: Multiplying Mixed Numbers

1. Write a story problem for $2\frac{1}{2} \times 1\frac{1}{2}$.

2. Use pictures and the meaning of multiplication to solve your problem from part 1.

3. Use the distributive property (or FOIL) to calculate $2\frac{1}{2} \times 1\frac{1}{2}$ by rewriting this product as $(2 + \frac{1}{2}) \times (1 + \frac{1}{2})$.

4. Identify the four terms produced by the distributive property or FOIL (in part 3) in your picture in part 2.

5. Now write the mixed numbers $2\frac{1}{2}$ and $1\frac{1}{2}$ as improper fractions, and use the procedure for multiplying fractions to calculate $2\frac{1}{2} \times 1\frac{1}{2}$. How can you see the product of the numerators in your picture in part 2? How can you see the product of the denominators in your picture?

Class Activity 5F: What Fraction Is Shaded?

1. For each of the next figures, write an expression that uses both multiplication and addition (or subtraction) to describe the total fraction of the figure that is shaded. (For example, $\frac{5}{7} \cdot \frac{2}{9} + \frac{1}{3}$ is an expression that uses both multiplication and addition). Explain your reasoning. Then determine what fraction of the figure is shaded (in simplest form). In each figure, you may assume that lengths which appear to be equal really are equal.

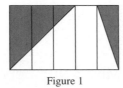

Figure 1

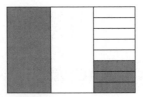

Figure 2

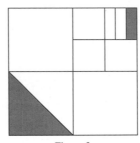

Figure 3

2. Draw a figure in which you shade $\frac{1}{3} \cdot \frac{2}{7} + \frac{1}{2} \cdot \frac{3}{7}$ of the figure.

5.2 Multiplying Decimals

Class Activity 5G: Multiplying Decimals

1. Write a story problem for 2.7×1.35.

2. Ben wants to multiply 3.46×1.8. He first multiplies the numbers by ignoring the decimal points:

$$\begin{array}{r} 3.46 \\ \times\ 1.8 \\ \hline 6228 \end{array}$$

Ben knows that he just needs to figure out where to put the decimal point in his answer, but he can't remember the rule about where to put the decimal point. Explain how Ben could reason about the sizes of the numbers to determine where to put the decimal point in his answer.

3. Lameisha used a calculator and found that

$$1.5 \times 1.2 = 1.8$$

Lameisha wants to know why the rule about adding the number of places behind the decimal point doesn't work in this case. Why aren't there 2 digits to the right of the decimal point in the answer? Is Lameisha right that the rule about adding the number of places behind the decimal points doesn't work in this case? Explain.

Class Activity 5H:
Explaining Why We Place the Decimal Point
Where We Do When We Multiply Decimals

1. As indicated in the next diagram, to get from 1.36 to 136, we multiply by 10×10. To get from 2.7 to 27, we multiply by 10. In other words,

$$136 = 10 \times 10 \times 1.36 \qquad \text{and} \qquad 27 = 10 \times 2.7$$

$$
\begin{array}{r}
136 \\
\times \; 27 \\
\hline
952 \\
2720 \\
\hline
3672
\end{array}
$$

Therefore,

$$
\begin{array}{r}
1.36 \\
\times \; 2.7 \\
\hline
952 \\
2720 \\
\end{array}
\qquad
\begin{array}{r}
136 \\
\times \; 27 \\
\hline
952 \\
2720 \\
\hline
3672
\end{array}
$$

Therefore, what should we do to

$$136 \times 27 = 3672$$

to get back to

$$1.36 \times 2.7?$$

Use your answer to explain the placement of the decimal point in 1.36×2.7.

2. Use the next diagram to help you explain where to put the decimal point in 2.476×1.83.

$$
\begin{array}{c}
2.476 \\
\times \ 1.83
\end{array}
\longrightarrow
\begin{array}{c}
2476 \\
\times \ 183
\end{array}
$$

Therefore,

$$
\begin{array}{c}
2.476 \\
\times \ 1.83
\end{array}
\longleftarrow
\begin{array}{c}
2476 \\
\times \ 183
\end{array}
$$

3. Working with products of tens and using the idea of parts 1 and 2, explain why the following makes sense: If you multiply a number that has 3 digits to the right of its decimal point by a number that has 4 digits to the right of its decimal point, you should place the decimal point $3 + 4 = 7$ places from the end of the product calculated without the decimal points.

Class Activity 5I: Decimal Multiplication and Areas of Rectangles

In Section 4.3, we decomposed rectangles into groups of squares to explain why we can multiply to find areas of rectangles. Our focus in that section was on rectangles whose side lengths are whole numbers. In this activity, you will see that the area formula for rectangles is compatible with the meaning of multiplication, even for rectangles whose side lengths are decimals. You will also take apart and recombine a rectangle to determine its area.

Recall that the area of a region, in square units, is the number of 1-unit-by-1-unit squares it takes to cover the region without gaps or overlaps.

1. Explain how to see the 2.3-unit-by-1.8-unit rectangle in Figure 5I.1 as consisting of 2.3 groups of 1.8 squares.

Therefore, to say that this rectangle has an area of 2.3 × 1.8 square units is compatible with the meaning of multiplication as we have described it.

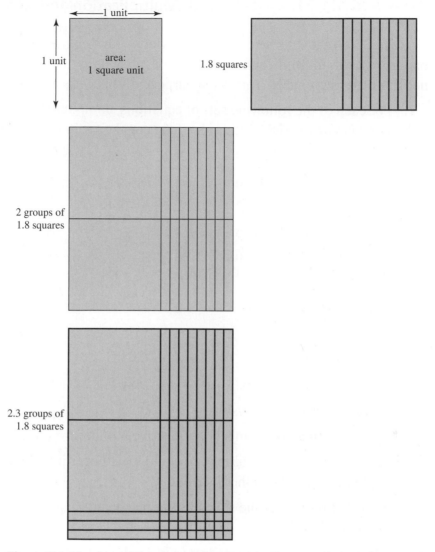

Figure 5I.1 Viewing a 2.3-unit-by-1.8-unit rectangle as consisting of 2.3 groups with 1.8 squares in each group

2. Draw pictures showing how to rearrange portions of the 2.3-unit-by-1.8-unit rectangle in Figure 5I.1 so that you can determine the area of this rectangle. Calculate 2.3 × 1.8, and verify that it produces the correct area.

3. Discuss the following questions: How is the 2.3-unit-by-1.8-unit rectangle in Figure 5I.1 related to an array for 23 × 18? How is 2.3 × 1.8 related to 23 × 18?

5.3 Multiplying Negative Numbers

Class Activity 5J: Patterns with Multiplication and Negative Numbers

How can we make sense of multiplication with negative numbers? By extending patterns in the multiplication tables, we can see why the rules for multiplying with negatives are reasonable. This is the purpose of this class activity.

1. For each of the following sets of equations, complete the set so that the pattern of numbers on the right-hand side of the equal sign continues. Describe the patterns.

$$6 \times 4 = 24 \qquad 4 \times 7 = 28 \qquad -8 \times 4 = -32$$
$$6 \times 3 = 18 \qquad 3 \times 7 = 21 \qquad -8 \times 3 = -24$$
$$6 \times 2 = 12 \qquad 2 \times 7 = 14 \qquad -8 \times 2 = -16$$
$$6 \times 1 = 6 \qquad 1 \times 7 = 7 \qquad -8 \times 1 = -8$$
$$6 \times 0 = 0 \qquad 0 \times 7 = 0 \qquad -8 \times 0 = 0$$
$$6 \times -1 = \qquad -1 \times 7 = \qquad -8 \times -1 =$$
$$6 \times -2 = \qquad -2 \times 7 = \qquad -8 \times -2 =$$
$$6 \times -3 = \qquad -3 \times 7 = \qquad -8 \times -3 =$$
$$6 \times -4 = \qquad -4 \times 7 = \qquad -8 \times -4 =$$
$$6 \times -5 = \qquad -5 \times 7 = \qquad -8 \times -5 =$$

2. Assume a student knows that

$$(\text{positive number}) \times (\text{positive number}) = (\text{positive number})$$

   a. What rule about multiplying could the student infer by considering the first list in part 1 and other lists like it?

   b. What rule could the student infer by considering the second list in part 1 and other lists like it?

   c. What rule could the student infer by considering the third list in part 1 and other lists like it?

Class Activity 5K: Explaining Multiplication with Negative Numbers (and 0)

1. Write a story problem for 3×-5. Solve the story problem, thereby explaining why 3×-5 is negative. Interpret negative numbers as amounts owed.

2. Explain why the following make sense:

$$0 \times (\text{any number}) = 0$$
$$(\text{any number}) \times 0 = 0$$

3. Assume that you don't yet know what $(-3) \times 5$ is, but you do know that $3 \times 5 = 15$. Use the distributive property to show that the expression

$$(-3) \times 5 + 3 \times 5$$

is equal to 0. Then use that result to determine what $(-3) \times 5$ must be equal to.

4. Assume that you don't yet know what $(-3) \times (-5)$ is, but you do know that $(-3) \times 5 = -15$ from part 3. Use the distributive property to show that the expression

$$(-3) \times (-5) + (-3) \times 5$$

is equal to 0. Then use that result to determine what $(-3) \times (-5)$ must be equal to.

Class Activity 5L: Using Checks and Bills to Interpret Multiplication with Negative Numbers

1. For each of the following transactions, compare the amount of money you will have before and after the transaction takes place:

   a. You get 3 checks, each for $5.

   b. You get 3 bills, each for $5. (Each bill tells you that you owe $5.)

   c. You give away 3 checks, each for $5.

   d. You give away 3 bills, each for $5.

2. Write a consistent set of multiplication problems that describe how the amount of money you have changes due to the transactions in part 1. Use negative numbers wherever it makes sense to do so.

Class Activity 5M: Does Multiplication Always Make Larger?

1. In ordinary language, the term *multiply* means *make larger*, as in Go forth and multiply.

   In mathematics, does multiplying always make a quantity larger? Give some examples to help you explain your answer.

2. For which numbers, N, is $N \times 3$ greater than 3? In other words, for which numbers, N, is $N \times 3 > 3$? Consider all kinds of numbers for N: fractions, decimals, positive, negative. Investigate this question by trying a number of examples and by thinking about the meaning and rules of multiplication.

3. For which numbers, N, is $N \times -3$ greater than -3? In other words, for which numbers, N, is $N \times -3 > -3$? Consider all kinds of numbers for N: fractions, decimals, positive, negative. Investigate this question by trying a number of examples and by thinking about the meaning and rules of multiplication.

5.4 Powers and Scientific Notation

Class Activity 5N: Multiplying Powers of Ten

Remember that if A is a counting number, the expression

$$10^A$$

stands for A 10s multiplied together:

$$10^A = \underbrace{10 \times 10 \times \cdots \times 10}_{A \text{ times}}$$

1. Use the meaning of powers of ten to show how to write each of the expressions (a), (b), and (c) as a single power of ten (i.e., in the form 10^A for some exponent A). For example, 10^2 means 10×10, and 10^3 means $10 \times 10 \times 10$; therefore,
$$10^2 \times 10^3 = (10 \times 10) \times (10 \times 10 \times 10)$$
$$= 10^5$$

   a. $10^3 \times 10^4$

   b. $10^2 \times 10^5$

   c. $10^3 \times 10^3$

2. In each of (a), (b), and (c) in part 1, relate the exponents in the product with the exponent in the answer. (For the example given at the beginning of part 1, relate 2 and 3 to 5). In each case, how are the three exponents related?

3. Explain why it is always true that $10^A \times 10^B = 10^{A+B}$ when A and B are counting numbers.

4. Assume now that we want the equation $10^A \times 10^B = 10^{A+B}$ to be true not just when A and B are counting numbers, but even when A or B is 0. With this assumption, explain why it makes sense that 10^0 should be equal to 1.

5. Assume now that we want the equation $10^A \times 10^B = 10^{A+B}$ to be true not just when A and B are whole numbers, but even when A or B is a negative integer. Also assume that $10^0 = 1$.

   a. Explain why it makes sense that 10^{-1} should be equal to $\frac{1}{10}$.

   b. Explain why it makes sense that 10^{-2} should be equal to $\frac{1}{100}$.

   c. More generally, explain why 10^{-N} should be equal to $\frac{1}{10^N}$.

Class Activity 5O: Scientific Notation versus Ordinary Decimal Notation

1. A $1.3 trillion tax cut was approved. Write 1.3 trillion in scientific notation and in ordinary decimal notation.

2. The population of the United States is approximately 310 million. Write 310 million in scientific notation and in ordinary decimal notation.

3. Use a calculator to multiply
$$123{,}456{,}789 \times 987{,}654{,}321$$

   a. Does your calculator's display show all the digits in the product $123{,}456{,}789 \times 987{,}654{,}321$? If not, why not? What does your calculator's display mean?

b. Based on your calculator's display, what can you determine about the ordinary decimal representation of the product $123,456,789 \times 987,654,321$?

c. Can you use the calculator's display to determine how many digits the decimal representation of the product $123,456,789 \times 987,654,321$ has? Explain.

d. Explain how you can "break up" the numbers $123,456,789$ and $987,654,321$ and use the distributive property or FOIL in conjunction with a calculator to determine all the digits in the product $123,456,789 \times 987,654,321$. Do not just multiply longhand.

Class Activity 5P: ↻
How Many Digits Are in a Product of Counting Numbers?

When you multiply two counting numbers, how many digits does the product have? This class activity will help you discover the answer to this question.

1. a. Multiply many 2-digit counting numbers with 3-digit counting numbers. How many digits do the products have?

b. Multiply many 3-digit counting numbers with 4-digit counting numbers. How many digits do the products have?

c. Multiply many 2-digit counting numbers with 4-digit counting numbers. How many digits do the products have?

    d. In your examples, how are the number of digits in the two factors related to the number of digits in the product? (Your answer should involve "either . . . or . . .")

    2. Based on your results in part 1, predict what will happen in other situations. If you multiply a 9-digit counting number with an 11-digit counting number, how many digits will the product have? In general, if you multiply an n-digit counting number with an m-digit counting number, how many digits will the product have? Give "either . . . or . . ." answers.

Class Activity 5Q:
Explaining the Pattern in the Number of Digits in Products

This class activity continues the previous activity. In this activity, you will explain why the pattern you found in the previous class activity must hold. The key is to relate the number of digits in a counting number to the exponent on the 10 when the number is written in scientific notation.

    1. Based on what you discovered in the previous class activity, predict how many digits the product $123{,}456{,}789 \times 23{,}456{,}789$ has.

    2. Now use a calculator to compute $123{,}456{,}789 \times 23{,}456{,}789$. Use the calculator's display to determine how many digits the product $123{,}456{,}789 \times 23{,}456{,}789$ has.

    3. In general, what is the relationship between the number of digits of a counting number and the exponent on the 10 when that number is written in scientific notation? Explain.

4. Write the numbers 123,456,789 and 23,456,789 and the product 123,456,789 × 23,456,789 in scientific notation. Look carefully at the exponents on the 10s. What relationship do you notice among these three exponents?

5. Take another pair of whole numbers and write them and their product in scientific notation. What is the relationship among the exponents on the 10s? Do this many times, with many pairs of numbers. Do you always get the same relationship as in the last problem, or not?

6. What happens when we multiply numbers that are in scientific notation? Fill in the correct exponents for the 10s on the right in the following equations:

$$(1.2 \times 10^3) \times (3.7 \times 10^5) = \quad (1.2 \times 3.7) \times 10^3 \times 10^5 = \quad (1.2 \times 3.7) \times 10\underline{\quad}$$

$$(7.63 \times 10^4) \times (8.14 \times 10^6) = (7.63 \times 8.14) \times 10^4 \times 10^6 = (7.63 \times 8.14) \times 10\underline{\quad}$$

$$(4.5 \times 10^7) \times (5.2 \times 10^8) = \quad (4.5 \times 5.2) \times 10^7 \times 10^8 = \quad (4.5 \times 5.2) \times 10\underline{\quad}$$

7. Now put the numbers from the previous problem in scientific notation. In some cases, the exponent on the 10 changes. Why?

$$(1.2 \times 3.7) \times 10\underline{\quad\quad} =$$
$$(7.63 \times 8.14) \times 10\underline{\quad\quad} =$$
$$(4.5 \times 5.2) \times 10\underline{\quad\quad} =$$

8. Suppose you have a 7-digit counting number and an 8-digit counting number. What will they look like in scientific notation? Use this to explain why the product of a 7-digit counting number with an 8-digit counting number will have 14 or 15 digits.

Division

6.1 Interpretations of Division

Class Activity 6A:
What Does Division Mean?

1. Write a simple story problem and draw a simple picture that you could use to help children understand what $10 \div 2$ means.

2. Just as every subtraction problem can be reformulated as an addition problem, a division problem

$$A \div B = ?$$

can be reformulated as a multiplication problem, either as

$$B \times ? = A \quad \text{or as} \quad ? \times B = A$$

Reformulate the division problem $10 \div 2 = ?$ as

$$2 \times ? = 10 \quad \text{or as} \quad ? \times 2 = 10$$

whichever fits with your story problem in part 1 and with the way we have described multiplication.

3. Now write another simple division story problem for $10 \div 2$, one that fits with the *other* multiplication equation identified in part 2. Draw a simple picture that fits with your new story problem.

Class Activity 6B: 🎲
Division Story Problems

1. For each of the following problems, write the corresponding numerical division problem, write the corresponding multiplication equation, and decide which interpretation of division is involved (the "how many groups?" or the "how many in each group?" interpretation). Solve the problems.

   For example:

   > Gloria has 35 candies to distribute equally among 5 children. How many candies will each child get?

   - Corresponding equations:
   $$35 \div 5 = ? \qquad 5 \times ? = 35$$
   - "How many in each group"—because each child is a "group"
   - Solution: Each child gets 7 candies because $35 \div 5 = 7$.

   a. Bill has a muffin recipe that calls for 2 cups of flour. How many batches of muffins can Bill make if he has 8 cups of flour available? (Assume that Bill has all the other ingredients too.)

   b. If 6 limes cost $3, then how much should one lime cost (assuming that all limes are priced equally)?

   c. If 6 limes cost $3, then how many limes can you buy for $1?

   d. One foot is 12 inches. If a piece of rope is 96 inches long, then how long is it in feet?

   e. Francine has 32 yards of rope that she wants to cut into 8 equal pieces. How long will each piece be?

f. A gallon of water weighs 8 pounds. How many gallons is 400 pounds of water?

g. If you drive 220 miles at a constant speed and it takes you 4 hours, then how fast did you go?

2. For each of the story problems in part 1, label the numerical division problem and its solution with the corresponding units (such as inches, dollars, cups, candies, etc.). For the example, write

$$33 \quad \div \quad 5 \quad = \quad 7$$

candies   children   candies

What do the "how many groups?" problems have in common? What do the "how many in each group?" have in common?

Class Activity 6C:
Why Can't We Divide by Zero?

1. A division problem

$$A \div B = ?$$

can always be rewritten as a multiplication problem, namely, as

$$? \times B = A$$

or as

$$B \times ? = A$$

Use the fact that every division problem can be rewritten as a multiplication problem to explain why $2 \div 0$ is not defined.

2. Write story problems for the two interpretations of $2 \div 0$. Use your problems to explain why $2 \div 0$ is not defined. Link your story problems to your multiplication equations from part 1.

3. Write story problems for the two interpretations of $0 \div 2$. Use your problems to explain why $0 \div 2$ *is* defined. Explain the difference between $2 \div 0$ and $0 \div 2$.

4. Explain why $0 \div 0$ is undefined by viewing division in terms of multiplication. (We can also say that $0 \div 0$ is "indeterminate.") Can you give the same explanation as for why $2 \div 0$ is not defined? If not, how are the explanations different?

6.2 Division and Fractions and Division with Remainder

Class Activity 6D:
Relating Fractions and Division

1. There are 3 pizzas that will be divided equally among 4 people. How much pizza will each person get? Explain. What does your answer tell you about $3 \div 4$?

2. There are 3 pizzas that will be divided equally among 5 people. How much pizza will each person get? Explain. What does your answer tell you about $3 \div 5$?

3. There are 3 pizzas that will be divided equally among 7 people. How much pizza will each person get? Explain. What does your answer tell you about $3 \div 7$?

4. How are $A \div B$ and $\frac{A}{B}$ related? Explain.

Class Activity 6E: Division with Remainder Notation

1. Even though

$$25 \div 12 \text{ is 2, remainder 1}$$

and

$$21 \div 10 \text{ is } 2, \text{ remainder } 1$$

would it be correct to say that

$$25 \div 12 = 21 \div 10?$$

Explain.

Class Activity 6F: What to Do with the Remainder?

1. Consider these two story problems for $14 \div 3$:

   A cookie baking problem: A batch of cookies requires 3 cups of flour. How many batches of cookies can you make if you have 14 cups of flour (and all the other ingredients you need)?

   A brownie problem: You have 14 brownies which you will divide equally among 3 bags. How many brownies should you put in each bag?

   a. Discuss how to interpret $14 \div 3 = 4$, remainder 2, in the context of the cookie baking problem and in the context of the brownie problem. How are the interpretations different? How is this difference related to the type of division story problems the two problems represent?

   b. Discuss how to interpret $14 \div 3 = 4\frac{2}{3}$ in the context of the cookie baking problem and in the context of the brownie problem. In particular, discuss the meaning of the fraction $\frac{2}{3}$ in each case and discuss how the fraction $\frac{2}{3}$ is related to the "remainder 2" in each case.

2. Write a story problem for which you would calculate $14 \div 3$ in order to solve the problem, but which has the answer 5.

3. *A calendar problem:* What day of the week will it be 31 days from today?

   Explain how $31 \div 7$ is relevant to solving the calendar problem.

4. Consider these three problems about distance, speed, and time:

   i. How long will it take you to drive 180 miles if you drive at the constant speed of 55 mph?

   ii. How long will it take you to drive 195 miles if you drive at the constant speed of 60 mph?

   iii. How long will it take you to drive 105 miles if you drive at the constant speed of 30 mph?

   a. Write numerical division problems to solve problems (i), (ii), and (iii) and give the mixed number answers and whole-number-with-remainder answers to these numerical problems.

   b. Interpret the meaning of the mixed number answers and whole-number-with-remainder answers you gave in part (a) in terms of the original story problems.

   c. For problem (i) Josh says: "The 3, remainder 15, answer tells you that it will take 3 full hours, and the remainder 15 tells you it will take another 15 minutes." Explain why Josh's comment is not completely correct, but is approximately correct.

6.3 Why the Common Long Division Algorithm Works

Class Activity 6G: Can We Use Properties of Arithmetic to Divide?

In Chapter 4, we often used properties of arithmetic to solve multiplication problems. We will also use properties of arithmetic to solve division problems, but first think carefully about each of the following:

1. Is division commutative? Explain your answer.

2. Is division associative? Explain your answer.

3. Is the following statement true?

$$200 \div 45 = 200 \div 40 + 200 \div 5$$

Why, or why not? Explain your answer carefully; include a drawing if possible.

4. Is the following statement true?

$$365 \div 7 = 300 \div 7 + 60 \div 7 + 5 \div 7$$

Does it depend on how you express the answer (as a whole number with remainder, a mixed number, or a decimal)?

Class Activity 6H: Dividing Without Using a Calculator or Long Division

1. Antrice is working on the following problem: There are 260 pencils to be put in packages of 12. How many packages of pencils can be made, and how many pencils will be left over? Here are Antrice's ideas:

10 packages will use up 120 pencils. After another 10 packages, 240 pencils will be used up. After 1 more package, 252 pencils are used. Then there are only 8 pencils left, and that's not enough for another package. So the answer is 21 packages of pencils with 8 pencils left over.

Explain why the equations

$$10 \cdot 12 + 10 \cdot 12 + 1 \cdot 12 + 8 = 260 \tag{6.1}$$
$$(10 + 10 + 1) \cdot 12 + 8 = 260 \tag{6.2}$$
$$21 \cdot 12 + 8 = 260 \tag{6.3}$$

correspond to Antrice's work, and explain why the last equation shows that $260 \div 12 = 21$, remainder 8.

2. Ashley is working on the division problem 258 ÷ 6. She writes:

$$258 \div 6 = ?$$

10	→	60		240	←	40
20	→	120		+12	←	2
40	→	240		252	←	42
				+6		
				258	←	43

a. Explain what Ashley did and why her strategy makes sense. It may help you to work with a story problem for 258 ÷ 6.

b. Write equations like equations 6.1, 6.2, and 6.3 that correspond to Ashley's work and which demonstrate that 258 ÷ 6 = 43.

3. Maya is working on the division problem 245 ÷ 15. She writes the following:

$$
\begin{array}{r}
15 \\
\times\ 2 \\
\hline
30
\end{array}
\qquad 8 \times 30 = 240 \qquad 8 \times 2 = 16 \qquad \boxed{16\ R\ 5}
$$

a. Explain why Maya's strategy makes sense. It may help you to work with a story problem for 245 ÷ 15.

b. Write equations like Equations 6.1, 6.2, and 6.3 that correspond to Maya's work and which demonstrate that 245 ÷ 15 = 16, remainder 5. One side of each equation should be 245.

4. Zane is working on the division problem 245 ÷ 15. He writes

$$
\begin{array}{r}
15 \\
\times\ 2 \\
\hline
30 \\
\times\ 2 \\
\hline
60 \\
\times\ 4 \\
\hline
240
\end{array}
\qquad 2 \times 2 \times 4 = 16\,R\,5
$$

5 left

a. Explain why Zane's strategy makes sense. It may help you to work with a story problem for 245 ÷ 15.

b. Write equations like Equations 6.1, 6.2, and 6.3 that correspond to Zane's work and which demonstrate that 245 ÷ 15 = 16, remainder 5.

5. Assume that you don't have a calculator and have forgotten how to do longhand division. Explain how you can calculate 1000 ÷ 6.

Class Activity 6I:
Why the Scaffold Method of Long Division Works

1. Interpret each of the steps in the next scaffold in terms of the following story problem:

> You have 3475 marbles, and you want to put these marbles into bags with 8 marbles in each bag. How many bags of marbles can you make, and how many marbles will be left over?

$$
\begin{array}{r}
4 \\
30 \\
400 \\
\hline
8\overline{)3475} \\
-\ 3200 \\
\hline
275 \\
-\ 240 \\
\hline
35 \\
-\ 32 \\
\hline
3
\end{array}
$$

2. Explain how the equations

$$3475 - 400 \times 8 - 30 \times 8 - 4 \times 8 = 3$$
$$3475 - (400 + 30 + 4) \times 8 = 3$$
$$3475 - 434 \times 8 = 3$$

relate the scaffold to the story problem in part 1. Then explain why the last equation shows that $3475 \div 8 = 434$, remainder 3.

3. Use the scaffold method to calculate $8321 \div 6$. Interpret each step in your scaffold in terms of the following story problem:

You have 8321 pickles, and you want to put these pickles in packages with 6 pickles in each package. How many packages can you make, and how many pickles will be left over?

4. Write equations like those in part 2 for your scaffold in part 3. Explain how your equations relate to the scaffold and to the story problem of part 3.

Class Activity 6J: Using the Scaffold Method Flexibly

1. Cassie writes the following scaffold to calculate $7549 \div 12$:

$$
\begin{array}{r}
1 \\
8 \\
20 \\
100 \\
500 \\
\hline
12\overline{)7549} \\
-\ 6000 \\
\hline
1549 \\
-\ 1200 \\
\hline
349 \\
-\ 240 \\
\hline
109 \\
-\ 96 \\
\hline
13 \\
-\ 12 \\
\hline
1
\end{array}
$$

Then Cassie writes the following:

$$500 + 100 + 20 + 8 + 1 = 629, \text{ so } 7549 \div 12 = 629, \text{ remainder } 1.$$

a. Show how Cassie could have written a scaffold with fewer steps to solve $7549 \div 12$.

b. Even though Cassie used more steps than she had to, is her method legitimate? In other words, is her method based on sound reasoning? Explain.

2. Manuel calculates $427 \div 11$, using the following reasoning:

10 elevens is 110. After another 10 elevens and another 10 elevens, I'm up to 330. After another 5 elevens, I'm up to 385. One more eleven makes 396. Then one more eleven makes 407. One more eleven makes 418. Then there are 9 left. So the answer is 38, remainder 9.

Write a scaffold for $427 \div 11$ that is based on Manuel's reasoning. The arithmetic in the scaffold will not correspond exactly to Manuel's. Why not?

3. Use the scaffold method and the common long division method to calculate $3895 \div 14$. Discuss how the two methods are related.

Class Activity 6K:
Interpreting the Standard Division Algorithm
as Dividing Bundled Toothpicks

1. Use the standard long division algorithm to calculate $1372 \div 3$. Interpret each step in the algorithm in terms of dividing 1372 toothpicks equally among 3 groups, where the toothpicks are arranged in bundles of 1 thousand, 3 hundreds, 7 tens, and 2 individual toothpicks. Show the steps pictorially by drawing how bundles will be unbundled and divided step-by-step among the 3 groups shown. How is the "bringing down" step in long division related to unbundling toothpicks?

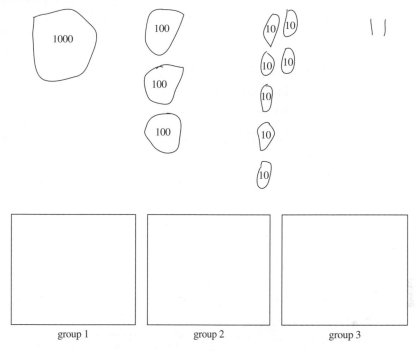

group 1   group 2   group 3

2. Use the standard long division algorithm to calculate $1413 \div 2$. Interpret each step in the algorithm in terms of dividing 1413 toothpicks equally between 2 groups, where the toothpicks are arranged in bundles of 1 thousand, 4 hundreds, 1 ten, and 3 individual toothpicks. Show the steps pictorially by drawing how bundles will be unbundled and divided step-by-step between the 2 groups shown. How is the "bringing down" step in long division related to unbundling toothpicks?

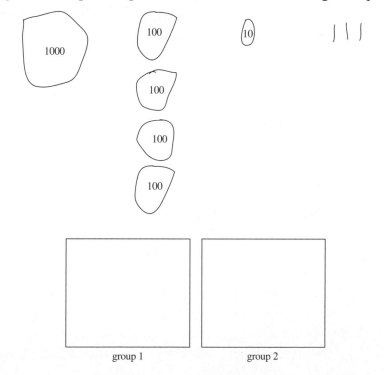

group 1   group 2

Class Activity 6L: Interpreting the Standard Division Algorithm in Terms of Area

1. If a rectangle has area 948 square units and one side is 4 units long, then the adjacent side length is found by dividing $4\overline{)948}$. Examine the "rectangle sections" method shown below. It works by thinking about the area and side length of the rectangle in chunks. Explain each step and relate it to the standard way of writing the standard division algorithm (shown right).

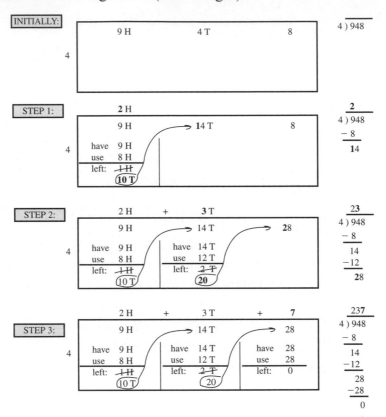

2. Now use "rectangle sections" to explain how to calculate $5\overline{)1543}$ with the standard algorithm.

Class Activity 6M: Student Errors in Using the Division Algorithm

1. Identify the errors that the (hypothetical) students have made in the calculations shown next. Why might they have made these errors?

$$
\begin{array}{r}
39 \\
12\overline{)3711} \\
-36 \\
\hline
111 \\
-108 \\
\hline
3
\end{array}
$$

$$
\begin{array}{r}
18 \\
4\overline{)729} \\
-4 \\
\hline
32 \\
-32 \\
\hline
0
\end{array}
\qquad
\begin{array}{r}
13 \\
7\overline{)940} \\
-7 \\
\hline
24 \\
-21 \\
\hline
3
\end{array}
$$

The student stops here.   The student stops here.

2. Use the scaffold method to calculate $3711 \div 12$, $729 \div 4$, and $940 \div 7$. Discuss why it is easier to avoid the errors of part 1 when using the scaffold method than when using standard long division.

Class Activity 6N:

Interpreting the Calculation of Decimal Answers to Whole Number Division Problems in Terms of Money

Use the standard long division algorithm to determine the decimal answer to $2674 \div 3$ to the hundredths place. Interpret each step in your calculation in terms of dividing $2674 equally among 3 people by imagining that you distribute the money in stages: First distribute hundreds, then tens, then ones, then dimes (tenths), then pennies (hundredths).

Class Activity 6O: Errors in Decimal Answers to Division Problems

1. Given that the answer to a whole number division problem is 4, remainder 1, can you tell what the decimal answer to the division problem is without any additional information? If not, what other information would you need to determine the decimal answer?

2. Ben has been making errors in his division problems. Here are some of Ben's answers:

$$251 \div 6 = 41.5$$
$$269 \div 7 = 38.3$$
$$951 \div 21 = 45.6$$

Use long division to calculate the correct answers to Ben's division problems. Based on your work, determine what Ben is likely to be confused about.

Class Activity 6P: Using Division to Calculate Decimal Representations of Fractions

1. Use long division to determine the decimal representation of $\frac{1}{8}$. Interpret each of your long-division steps in terms of dividing $1 equally among 8 people, using dollars, dimes, and pennies. (Note that you will not be able to divide evenly without being able to split a penny.)

2. Interpret each of your long-division steps in part 1 in terms of dividing the following square into 8 equal parts:

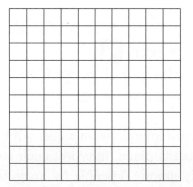

Class Activity 6Q: Rounding to Estimate Solutions to Division Problems

1. Suppose you want to estimate

$$615 \div 29$$

by rounding 29 up to 30. Both $600 \div 30$ and $630 \div 30$ are easy to calculate mentally. Use reasoning about division to determine which division problem, $600 \div 30$ or $630 \div 30$, should give you a better estimate to $615 \div 29$. Then check your answer by solving the division problems.

2. Suppose you want to estimate

$$615 \div 31$$

by rounding 31 down to 30. Both $600 \div 30$ and $630 \div 30$ are easy to calculate mentally. Use reasoning about division to determine which division problem, $600 \div 30$ or $630 \div 30$, should give you a better estimate to $615 \div 31$. Then check your answer by solving the division problems.

3. Suppose you want to estimate $527 \div 48$. What is a good way to round the numbers 527 and 48 so as to obtain an easy division problem that will give a good estimate to $527 \div 48$? Explain, drawing on what you learned from parts 1 and 2.

4. Suppose you want to estimate $527 \div 52$. What is a good way to round the numbers 527 and 52 so as to obtain an easy division problem that will give a good estimate to $527 \div 52$? Explain, drawing on what you learned from parts 1 and 2.

6.4 Fraction Division from the "How Many Groups?" Perspective

Class Activity 6R:
"How Many Groups?" Fraction Division Problems

1. **a.** Write a simple "how many groups?" story problem for $6 \div 2$.

b. Write a simple "how many groups?" story problem for $3 \div \frac{3}{4}$. (If it works, you may modify your story problem from part (a).)

c. Assume that you don't know the "invert and multiply" method for dividing fractions. Solve your story problem for $3 \div \frac{3}{4}$ in a simple and concrete way, for example, by drawing simple pictures, such as strip diagrams. Explain your solution.

2. Tonya and Chrissy are trying to understand $1 \div \frac{2}{3}$ by using the following story problem:

> One serving of rice is $\frac{2}{3}$ of a cup. I ate 1 cup of rice. How many servings of rice did I eat?

To solve the problem, Tonya and Chrissy draw a diagram divided into three equal pieces, and they shade two of those pieces.

Tonya says, "There is one $\frac{2}{3}$-cup serving of rice in 1 cup, and there is $\frac{1}{3}$ cup of rice left over, so the answer should be $1\frac{1}{3}$."

Chrissy says, "The part left over is $\frac{1}{3}$ cup of rice, but the answer is supposed to be $\frac{3}{2} = 1\frac{1}{2}$. Did we do something wrong?"

Help Tonya and Chrissy.

3. a. Write a simple "how many groups?" story problem for $8 \div 3$. Choose your story problem so that a mixed-number answer makes sense.

b. Write a simple "how many groups?" story problem for $1\frac{1}{2} \div \frac{1}{3}$. (If it works, you may modify your story problem from part (a).)

c. Assume that you don't know the "invert and multiply" method for dividing fractions. Solve your story problem for $1\frac{1}{2} \div \frac{1}{3}$ in a simple and concrete way, for example, by drawing simple pictures, such as strip diagrams. Explain your solution.

4. a. Write a simple "how many groups?" story problem for $\frac{1}{3} \div \frac{3}{4}$.

    b. Assume that you don't know the "invert and multiply" method for dividing fractions. Solve your story problem for $\frac{1}{3} \div \frac{3}{4}$. in a simple and concrete way, for example, by drawing simple pictures, such as strip diagrams. Explain your solution.

Class Activity 6S: Dividing Fractions by Dividing the Numerators and Dividing the Denominators

If you did the previous activity you may have noticed that to solve "how many groups?" fraction division story problems with the aid of a simple drawing, it was helpful to give the fractions a common denominator. Once the fractions had a common denominator, you really only had to divide the numerators. In this activity, you'll see that this method is part of a general method for dividing fractions, and that we can also explain why the "invert and multiply" procedure for fraction division is valid by giving fractions common denominators. To develop these methods, we'll need to view division problems as multiplication problems that have an unknown factor:

$$A \div B = ? \qquad \text{is equivalent to} \qquad ? \times B = A$$

1. Consider the two division problems

$$\frac{6}{5} \div \frac{2}{5} = ? \qquad \text{and} \qquad 6 \div 2 = ?$$

Explain in two ways why these division problems must have the same solution:

• by working with this strip diagram:

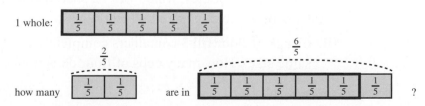

- by rewriting the division problems as multiplication problems with unknown factors

2. Explain why you can divide fractions by dividing the numerators and dividing the denominators like this:

$$\frac{6}{20} \div \frac{3}{4} = \frac{6 \div 3}{20 \div 4} = \frac{2}{5}$$

by rewriting

$$\frac{6}{20} \div \frac{3}{4} = \frac{?}{?} \qquad \text{as} \qquad \frac{?}{?} \times \frac{3}{4} = \frac{6}{20}$$

3. Give another example where you can divide fractions by dividing the numerators and dividing the denominators. Use the reasoning of part 2 to explain why this method works.

4. The next equations make use of the method of dividing the numerators and dividing the denominators to divide fractions. Explain the strategy behind these equations. What do these equations show? Will the same strategy work if other numbers replace 5, 7, 3, and 4?

$$\frac{5}{7} \div \frac{3}{4} = \frac{5 \times 3 \times 4}{7 \times 3 \times 4} \div \frac{3}{4} = \frac{5 \times 4}{7 \times 3} = \frac{5}{7} \times \frac{4}{3}$$

6.5 Fraction Division from the "How Many in One Group?" Perspective

Class Activity 6T:

"How Many in One Group?" Fraction Division Problems

1. **a.** Verify that the following problems are "how many in one group?" problems for $6 \div 3$:

   i. There are 6 cookies, which will be shared equally among 3 children. How many cookies will each child get?

   ii. 6 cups of flour fill 3 containers completely full (all of which are the same size). How many cups of flour does it take to fill one container?

iii. Walking at a steady pace, Anna walked 6 miles in 3 hours. How far did Anna walk each hour?

b. Write a "how many in one group?" story problem for $3 \div \frac{1}{4}$.

c. Assume that you don't know the "invert and multiply" method for dividing fractions. Solve your story problem for $3 \div \frac{1}{4}$ in a simple and concrete way, for example, by drawing pictures. Explain your solution.

d. Solve $3 \div \frac{1}{4}$ numerically by "inverting and multiplying"—in other words, by multiplying 3 by $\frac{4}{1}$. Explain how your solution in part (c) shows this process of multiplying 3 by $\frac{4}{1}$.

2. a. Write a "how many in one group?" story problem for $6 \div \frac{3}{4}$.

b. Assume that you don't know the "invert and multiply" method for dividing fractions. Solve your story problem for $6 \div \frac{3}{4}$ in a simple and concrete way, for example, by drawing pictures. Explain your solution.

c. Solve $6 \div \frac{3}{4}$ numerically by "inverting and multiplying"—in other words, by multiplying 6 by $\frac{4}{3}$. Explain how your solution in part (b) shows this process of multiplying 6 by $\frac{4}{3}$.

3. a. Write a "how many in one group?" story problem for $\frac{1}{2} \div \frac{2}{3}$.

    b. Assume that you don't know the "invert and multiply" method for dividing fractions. Solve your story problem for $\frac{1}{2} \div \frac{2}{3}$ in a simple and concrete way, for example, by drawing pictures. Explain your solution.

    c. Solve $\frac{1}{2} \div \frac{2}{3}$ numerically by "inverting and multiplying,"—in other words, by multiplying $\frac{1}{2}$ by $\frac{3}{2}$. Explain how your solution in part (b) shows this process of multiplying $\frac{1}{2}$ by $\frac{3}{2}$.

Class Activity 6U: Using Double Number Lines to Solve "How Many in One Group?" Division Problems

One helpful aid for solving "how many in one group?" division story problems is a double number line, such as the one that follows.

1. Will found that $\frac{1}{2}$ pound of nails was $\frac{3}{4}$ of the nails he needed for a project. How many pounds of nails does Will need for the project?

Use the next double number line to help you solve this problem. Explain your reasoning.

2. It takes Gloria $\frac{1}{3}$ of an hour to walk $\frac{3}{5}$ of a mile. At that rate, how far will Gloria walk in 1 hour? How long does it take for Gloria to walk 1 mile? Use double number lines to help you solve these problems. Explain your reasoning.

3. Six liters of juice filled a container $2\frac{1}{2}$ times. How many liters of juice does the container hold?

Use a double number line to solve this problem. Explain your reasoning.

Class Activity 6V: Are These Division Problems?

Which of the following are story problems for the division problem $\frac{3}{4} \div \frac{1}{2}$? For those that are, which interpretation of division is used? For those that are not, determine how to solve the problem if it can be solved.

1. Beth poured $\frac{3}{4}$ cup of cereal in a bowl. The cereal box says that one serving is $\frac{1}{2}$ cup. How many servings are in Beth's bowl?

2. Beth poured $\frac{3}{4}$ cup of cereal in a bowl. Then Beth took $\frac{1}{2}$ of that cereal and put it into another bowl. How many cups of cereal are in the second bowl?

3. A crew is building a road. So far, the road is $\frac{3}{4}$ mile long. This is $\frac{1}{2}$ the length that the road will be when it is finished. How many miles long will the finished road be?

4. A crew is building a road. So far, the crew has completed $\frac{3}{4}$ of the road, and this portion is $\frac{1}{2}$ mile long. How long will the finished road be?

5. If $\frac{3}{4}$ cup of flour makes $\frac{1}{2}$ a batch of cookies, then how many cups of flour are required for a full batch of cookies?

6. If $\frac{1}{2}$ cup of flour makes a batch of cookies, then how many batches of cookies can you make with $\frac{3}{4}$ cup of flour?

7. If $\frac{3}{4}$ cup of flour makes a batch of cookies, then how much flour is in $\frac{1}{2}$ of a batch of cookies?

6.6 Dividing Decimals

Class Activity 6W: Quick Tricks for Some Decimal Division Problems

1. Describe a quick way to calculate $32.5 \div 0.5$ mentally. *Hint:* Think in terms of fractions or in terms of money.

2. Describe a quick way to calculate $1.2 \div 0.25$ mentally.

3. Describe a quick way to estimate $7.2 \div 0.333$ mentally.

Class Activity 6X:
Decimal Division

1. Write one "how many groups?" story problem and another "how many in one group?" story problem for $23.45 \div 2.7$.

2. The problem

   "How many $0.25 are in $12.37?"

   is a story problem for the division problem

   $$12.37 \div 0.25$$

Explain how to think about the same story problem in a different way, so that it is also a story problem for

$$1237 \div 25$$

What can you conclude about how the two division problems

$$0.25\overline{)12.37} \quad \text{and} \quad 25\overline{)1237}$$

are related?

3. Explain how the accompanying figure can be interpreted as the following:

$$0.06 \div 0.02 = ?$$

Explain how the same figure can be interpreted as:

$0.6 \div 0.2 = ?$ or as $6 \div 2 = ?$ or as $6,000,000 \div 2,000,000 = ?$

What other division problems can the figure illustrate?

How many ⬜⬜ are in ⬜⬜⬜⬜⬜⬜ ?

What's the moral here?

4. Fran must calculate $2.45 \div 1.5$ longhand, but she can't remember what to do about decimal points. Instead, Fran solves the division problem $245 \div 15$ longhand and gets the answer 16.33. Fran knows that she must shift the decimal point in 16.33 somehow to get the correct answer to $2.45 \div 1.5$. Explain how Fran could reason about the sizes of the original numbers to determine where to put the decimal point.

Combining Multiplication and Division: Proportional Reasoning

7.1 The Meanings of Ratio, Rate, and Proportion

Class Activity 7A: Comparing Mixtures

1. There are two containers, each containing a mixture of 1 cup red punch and 3 cups lemon-lime soda. The first container is left as it is, but somebody adds 2 cups red punch and 2 cups lemon-lime soda to the second container.

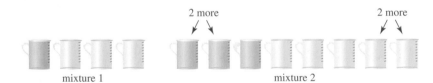

Do you think the two punch mixtures taste the same? Why or why not? Try to think about these questions in the way that a child who has not yet studied ratios might. What ideas do you think such a child might have?

If the mixtures are available, try them to see if they taste the same or not.

2. There are two containers, each containing a mixture of 2 parts blue paint and 5 parts yellow paint. (All parts are the same size.) The first container is left as it is, but somebody adds 3 parts blue paint and 3 parts yellow paint to the second container.

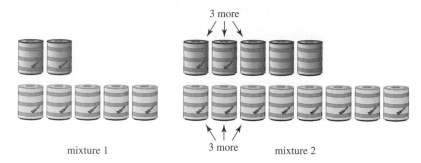

Do you think the two paint mixtures are the same shade of green? Why or why not?

Try to think about these questions in the way that a child who has not yet studied ratios might. What ideas do you think such a child might have?

Class Activity 7B: Using Strip Diagrams, Ratio Tables, and Double Number Lines to Describe Equivalent Ratios

1. For a certain shade of pink paint, the ratio of white paint to red paint is 5 to 2. Explain how to use the strip diagram shown next to find at least 6 different quantities of white and red paint that will be in the ratio 5 to 2 (and so will make the same shade of pink). In each case, describe the amount of pink paint that will be made. Include at least 3 mixtures where the quantities of paint are not both whole numbers of units. (You may choose any units you like, such as gallons, liters, pails, or something else.)

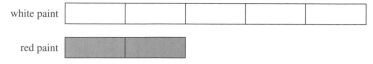

2. Driving at a constant speed, you drove 14 miles in 20 minutes. On the double number line that follows, show different distances and times that would give you the same speed. Use simple, logical reasoning to determine these equivalent rates.

3. One batch of a certain shade of green paint is made by mixing 2 pails of blue paint with 3 pails of yellow paint.

a. Show equivalent ratios of blue and yellow paint in the ratio table:

# of batches	1	2	3	4	5	6	7	8	9	10
# pails blue paint	2									
# pails yellow paint	3									
# pails green paint produced	5									

b. Describe the patterns in the 2nd, 3rd, and 4th rows as you go to the right in the ratio table. Explain why those patterns are present.

Where else have you seen rows like the rows in this ratio table?

c. Describe how the entries in the 6th column of the table are related to the entries in the 1st column of the table.

Describe how entries in the 8th column of the table are related to the entries in the 1st column of the table.

If the table were to continue in the same pattern, how would the entries in the 100th column be related to the entries in the 1st column?

How would the entries in the nth column of the table be related to entries in the 1st column of the table? Explain your reasoning.

d. Describe multiplicative relationships (relationships that use multiplication) among the entries within a single column. Do the same relationships hold for other columns?

Class Activity 7C: Using Ratio Tables to Compare Two Ratios

A ratio table shows a collection of equivalent ratios. If you have two different ratio tables, say for two different punch mixtures, then you can use the ratio tables to compare the mixtures in several different ways.

1. Make ratio tables for the two punch mixtures of Class Activity 7A, and use your ratio tables to compare the drink mixtures in several different ways. Will the mixtures taste the same? If not, which mixture will taste more like red punch?

2. Katie says that the two punch mixtures of Class Activity 7A (that you just compared in part 1) should taste the same because an equal amount of red punch and lemon-lime soda was added to the first mixture to make the second mixture.

   Doug says the two punch mixtures of Class Activity 7A should taste the same because in each case there are 2 more cups of lemon-lime soda than red punch.

   Discuss Katie's and Doug's reasoning.

3. A box of Brand A laundry detergent washes 20 loads of laundry and costs $6. A box of Brand B laundry detergent washes 15 loads of laundry and costs $5.

   In the ratio tables that follow, fill in equivalent rates of loads washed per dollar. Include some examples where the number of loads washed is less than 15 and the cost is less than $5. Explain your reasoning.

Brand A								
loads washed	20							
cost	$6							

Brand B								
loads washed	15							
cost	$5							

   Use your tables in several different ways to make a statement comparing the two brands of laundry detergent.

4. Referring to the laundry detergents in the previous part, Robert says that Brand B is less expensive than Brand A because it costs $5 instead of $6. Discuss Robert's reasoning.

7.2 Solving Proportion Problems by Reasoning with Multiplication and Division

Class Activity 7D: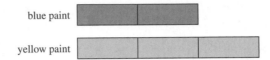
Using Strip Diagrams to Solve Ratio Problems

1. Suppose a certain shade of green paint is made by mixing blue paint with yellow paint in a ratio of 2 to 3.

blue paint [|]

yellow paint [| |]

   For each of parts (a), (b), and (c), use the same shade of green paint as above, which is made by mixing blue paint with yellow paint in a ratio of 2 to 3. Explain how to solve the problems by using the strip diagram.

   a. If you will use 40 pails of blue paint, how many pails of yellow paint will you need?

   b. If you will use 48 pails of yellow paint, how many pails of blue paint will you need?

   c. If you want to make 100 pails of green paint, how many pails of blue paint and how many pails of yellow paint will you need?

2. At lunch, there was a choice of pizza or a hot dog. Three times as many students chose pizza as chose hot dogs. All together, 160 students got lunch. How many students got pizza and how many got a hot dog? Draw a strip diagram to help you solve this problem. Explain your reasoning.

3. The ratio of Shauntay's cards to Jessica's cards is 5 to 3. After Shauntay gives Jessica 15 cards, both girls have the same number of cards. How many cards do Shauntay and Jessica each have now? Draw a strip diagram to help you solve this problem. Explain your reasoning.

4. The ratio of Shauntay's cards to Jessica's cards is 5 to 2. After Shauntay gives Jessica 12 cards, both girls have the same number of cards. How many cards do Shauntay and Jessica each have now? Draw a strip diagram to help you solve this problem. Explain your reasoning.

5. Make a new problem for your students by modifying part 5 or part 6. Change the ratio and change the number of cards that Shauntay gives to Jessica. When you make these changes, which ratios will make the problem easier, and which ratios will make it harder? Once you have chosen a ratio, can the number of cards that Shauntay gives to Jessica be any number, or do you need to take care in choosing this number? Explain.

6. If you mix fruit juice and bubbly water in a ratio of 3 to 5 to make a punch, then how many liters of fruit juice and how many liters of bubbly water will you need to make 24 liters of punch? What if you only want to make 10 liters of punch? Draw a strip diagram to help you solve both versions of this problem.

Class Activity 7E: Solving Proportions by Reasoning about How Quantities Compare

For each of the following, solve the proportions by reasoning about how the quantities compare.

1. Blue and red paint is mixed in a ratio of 2 to 3 to make purple paint. Fill in the blank entries in the next ratio table for paint mixed in this ratio. In doing so, is it easier to compare like quantities or unlike quantities?

# pails blue paint	2	100			
# pails red paint	3		45		
# pails purple paint produced				1000	85

2. At the store, you bought 12 ounces of cheese for $3. Fill in the blank entries in the next ratio table for cheese priced at this rate. In doing so, is it easier to compare like quantities or unlike quantities?

# ounces of cheese	12		20		18	1
$		3	2		7		

3. Traveling at a constant speed, a scooter is going $\frac{3}{4}$ of a mile in 4 minutes. Answer the next questions by reasoning about how quantities compare. Make a ratio table or a double number line to assist you.

    a. How far did the scooter go in the following amounts of time:

        8 minutes?   12 minutes?   2 minutes?   1 minute?

    b. How long did it take the scooter to go 3 miles? 1 mile?

4. If 2 meters of wire weigh 24.8 grams, how much do 6 meters of wire weigh? Try to find several different ways to solve this problem.

5. What if the problem in part 4 is changed to ask how much 10 meters of wire weigh? Will any of the methods you found be suitable for this case?

Class Activity 7F: "Going Through 1"

1. If you mix fruit juice and bubbly water in a ratio of 3 to 5 to make a punch, how many liters of fruit juice and how many liters of bubbly water will you need to make 10 liters of punch?

    a. Use multiplication, division, and logical reasoning to explain how to fill in the blanks in the following table of equivalent ratios, thereby solving this punch problem:

# liters juice	3		
# liters bubbly water	5		
# liters punch	8	1	10

b. Describe the strategy for solving the punch problem that the table in part (a) helps you use. What is the idea behind the way the table was created?

2. If you mix $\frac{3}{4}$ cup of red paint with $\frac{2}{3}$ cup of yellow paint to make an orange paint, then how many cups of red paint and how many cups of yellow paint will you need if you want to make 15 cups of the same shade of orange paint?

   a. Use multiplication, division, and logical reasoning to explain how to fill in the blanks in the following table with equivalent ratios, thereby solving this paint problem:

# cups red	$\frac{3}{4}$			
# cups yellow	$\frac{2}{3}$			
# cups orange		17	1	15

   b. Describe the strategy for solving the paint problem that the table in part (a) helps you use. What is the idea behind the way the table was created?

Class Activity 7G: More Ratio Problem Solving

1. Chandra made a milkshake by mixing $\frac{1}{2}$ cup of ice cream with $\frac{3}{4}$ cup of milk. Use the most elementary reasoning you can to determine how many cups of ice cream and milk Chandra should use if she wants to make the same milkshake (i.e., using the same ratios) in the following amounts:

   a. using 3 cups of ice cream

   b. to make 3 cups of milkshake

2. Russell was supposed to mix 3 tablespoons of weed killer concentrate with $1\frac{3}{4}$ cups of water to make a weed killer. By accident, Russell put in an extra tablespoon of weed killer concentrate, mixing 4 tablespoons of weed killer concentrate with $1\frac{3}{4}$ cups of water. How much water should Russell add to his mixture so that the ratio of weed killer concentrate to water will be the same as in the correct mixture? Use the most elementary reasoning you can to solve this problem.

7.3 Connecting Ratios and Fractions

Class Activity 7H: Connecting Ratios, Fractions, and Division with Unit Rates

For a certain shade of orange paint, the ratio of red to yellow is 3 to 5.

1. Fill in the ratio table for the orange paint:

# cups red	3			1
# cups yellow	5		1	
# cups orange		1		

2. For each of the following fractions and division problems, describe each fraction or division problem as a unit rate and say what that means in terms of the orange paint.

a. $\frac{3}{8}$ or 3 ÷ 8

b. $\frac{5}{8}$ or 5 ÷ 8

c. $\frac{3}{5}$ or 3 ÷ 5

d. $\frac{5}{3}$ or 5 ÷ 3

e. $\frac{8}{3}$ or $8 \div 3$

f. $\frac{8}{5}$ or $8 \div 5$

Class Activity 7I: Solving Proportions by Cross-Multiplying Fractions

Read the following recipe problem:

A recipe that serves 6 people calls for $2\frac{1}{2}$ cups of flour. How much flour will you need to serve 10 people, assuming that the ratio of people to cups of flour remains the same?

One familiar way to solve this problem is by setting up and solving a proportion, as follows: First, we let x be the amount of flour we need to serve 10 people. Then we set two fractions equal to each other:

$$\frac{x}{10} = \frac{2\frac{1}{2}}{6}$$

In setting these fractions equal to each other, we may say "x is to 10 as $2\frac{1}{2}$ is to 6." Next, we cross-multiply to obtain the equation

$$6 \cdot x = 10 \cdot 2\frac{1}{2}$$

Finally, we solve for x by dividing both sides of the equation by 6. Therefore,

$$x = \frac{10 \cdot 2\frac{1}{2}}{6} = \frac{10 \cdot \frac{5}{2}}{6} = \frac{25}{6} = 4\frac{1}{6}$$

We need $4\frac{1}{6}$ cups of flour to serve 10 people.

This class activity will help you understand the rationale for this method of solving proportions.

1. In the solution we just found, we worked with two fractions:

$$\frac{x}{10} \quad \text{and} \quad \frac{2\frac{1}{2}}{6}$$

Interpret the meaning of these fractions in terms of the recipe problem at the beginning of this activity. Explain why these two fractions should be equal.

2. After setting two fractions equal to each other, the next step in solving the proportion was to cross-multiply. Why does it make sense to cross-multiply? What is the rationale behind the procedure of cross-multiplying?

3. In the preceding solution, we set up the proportion

$$\frac{x}{10} = \frac{2\frac{1}{2}}{6}$$

What is another way to set up a proportion so that the unknown amount of flour, x, is in the numerator of one of the fractions? Interpret the two fractions in your new proportion in terms of the recipe problem. Use your interpretations to explain why the two fractions should be equal.

4. Now solve the recipe problem in a different way by using logical thinking and by using the most elementary reasoning you can. Explain your reasoning clearly.

7.4 When You Can Use a Proportion and When You Cannot

Class Activity 7J:
Can You Always Use a Proportion?

Sometimes a problem that looks as if it could be solved by setting up a proportion actually can't be solved that way. Before you set up a proportion to solve a problem, ask the following question about quantities in the problem: If I double one of the quantities, should the other quantity also double? If the answer is no, then you cannot solve the problem by setting up a proportion.

1. Ken used 3 loads of stone pavers to make a circular (i.e., circle-shaped) patio with a radius of 10 feet. Ken wants to make another circular patio with a radius of 15 feet, so he sets up the proportion

$$\frac{3 \text{ loads}}{10 \text{ feet}} = \frac{x \text{ loads}}{15 \text{ feet}}$$

Is this correct? If not, why not? Is there another proportion that Ken could set up to solve the problem? (The area of a circle that has radius r units is πr^2 square units.)

2. In a cookie factory, 4 assembly lines make enough boxes of cookies to fill a truck in 10 hours. How long will it take to fill the truck if 8 assembly lines are used? Is the proportion

$$\frac{10 \text{ hours}}{4 \text{ lines}} = \frac{x \text{ hours}}{8 \text{ lines}}$$

appropriate for this situation? Why or why not? If not, can you solve the problem another way? (Assume that all assembly lines work at the same steady rate.)

3. In the cookie factory of part 2, how long will it take to fill a truck if 6 assembly lines are used? (If you get stuck here, move on to the next problem and come back.)

4. Robyn used the following reasoning to solve the previous problem:

Since 4 assembly lines fill a truck in 10 hours, 8 assembly lines should fill a truck in half that time, namely, in 5 hours. Since 6 assembly lines is halfway between 4 and 8, it ought to take halfway between 10 hours and 5 hours, or $7\frac{1}{2}$ hours, to fill a truck.

Robyn's reasoning seems quite reasonable, but is it really correct? Let's look carefully.

Fill in the following table by using logical thinking about the assembly lines:

# of assembly lines	# of hours to fill a truck
1	
2	
4	10 hours
8	
16	
32	

Now apply Robyn's reasoning again, but this time to 1 assembly line versus 32. Sixteen assembly lines is approximately halfway between 1 and 32. But is the number of hours it takes to fill a truck by 16 assembly lines approximately halfway between the number of hours it takes to fill a truck by 1 assembly line versus by 32 assembly lines?

What can you conclude about Robyn's reasoning?

Class Activity 7K: Who Says You Can't Do Rocket Science?

Problem: A rocket can use two different types of fuel. Rocket scientists know that it takes 30 minutes to fill the fuel tank with type A fuel from a type A hose, whereas it takes 45 minutes to fill the same fuel tank with type B fuel from a type B hose. (The type B hose is smaller than the type A hose.) The rocket's fuel tank will now be filled simultaneously with type A and type B fuels, each flowing out of its own hose at a constant rate. How long will it take to fill the fuel tank?

1. Before you attempt to find an exact answer, determine *approximately* how long it should take for the fuel tank to fill. Answer this by saying, "It will take less than ___ minutes, but more than ___ minutes, to fill the tank." Explain briefly.

2. Use logical reasoning about the quantities to determine how long it will take to fill the fuel tank.

7.5 Percent Revisited: Percent Increase and Decrease

Class Activity 7L: How Should We Describe the Change?

A store raised some of its prices:

- A carton of milk went from $2 to $3
- A box of laundry detergent went from $5 to $6
- A small tube of makeup went from $10 to $15
- A large tube of makeup went from $20 to $30

The milk and the laundry detergent each went up by $1. But does that $1 increase seem equally significant in both cases?

The small tube of makeup went up by $5 and the large tube went up by $10. Does that mean that the price of the large tube of makeup went up more?

Discuss!

Class Activity 7M:
Calculating Percent Increase and Decrease

Throughout this activity, use a variety of methods to calculate percents. Recall that to calculate percents you can

- work with equivalent fractions (either with or without cross-multiplying);
- use a percent table (you may want to "go through 1");
- set up and solve an equation that derives from "P% of Q is R";
- (sometimes) use a picture to help you calculate a percent.

1. Brand A cereal used to be sold in a 20-ounce box. Now Brand A cereal is sold in a 23-ounce box.

   a. Calculate the increase in the weight of cereal in a Brand A box as a percentage of the original weight. This percentage is the percent increase in the weight of a Brand A box of cereal.

   b. Now calculate the new weight of a Brand A box of cereal as a percentage of the original weight, and subtract 100%.

   c. Draw a strip diagram to show the old and new weights of a box of Brand A cereal. Use your strip diagram to explain why part (b) must also produce the percent increase that you calculated in (a).

2. There were 80 gallons of gas in a tank. Now there are only 50 gallons left.

   a. Calculate the decrease in the amount of gas in the tank as a percentage of the original. This percentage is the percent decrease in the amount of gas in the tank.

b. Now calculate the new amount of gas in the tank as a percentage of the original, and subtract it from 100%.

c. With the aid of a strip diagram, explain why part (b) must also produce the percent decrease that you calculated in (a).

3. Whoopiedoo makeup used to be sold in 4-ounce tubes. Now it's sold in 5-ounce tubes for the same price. Ashlee says the label should read "25% more free," whereas Carolyn thinks it should read "20% more free." Who is right, who is wrong, and why? Help the person with the incorrect answer understand her error and how to correct it.

4. The Film Club increased from 63 members to 214 members. By what percent did membership in the Film Club increase?

Class Activity 7N:
Calculating Amounts from a Percent Increase or Decrease

1. A Loungy Chair had cost $400. The price of the Loungy Chair just went up by 20%.

   a. Calculate the new price of the Loungy chair, explaining your reasoning.

   b. Now complete the next percent table (fill in steps as needed):

   $$100\% \rightarrow \$400$$

   $$120\% \rightarrow \underline{}$$

    c. With the aid of a strip diagram, explain why the blank in part (b) must be equal to your answer in (a).

2. A set of sheets was $60. The sheets are now on sale for 15% off.

    a. Calculate the new price of the sheets, after the reduction.

    b. Now complete the next percent table (fill in steps as needed):

$$100\% \to \$60$$

$$85\% \to \underline{\hspace{1cm}}$$

    c. With the aid of a strip diagram, explain why the blank in part (b) must be equal to your answer in (a). Where does the 85% in the percent table come from?

3. The price of a comforter just went up by 15%. The new price, after the increase, is $60.

    a. Explain why you can use the next percent table to calculate the price of the comforter before the increase (fill in steps as needed).

$$115\% \to \$60$$

$$100\% \to \underline{\hspace{1cm}}$$

Where does the 115% come from, and why is it equated with $60?

    b. Explain why you *can't* calculate the price of the comforter before the increase by decreasing $60 by 15%.

4. The price of a sofa went down by 20%. The new reduced price is $400.

   a. Explain why you can use the next percent table to calculate the price of the sofa before the reduction. (Fill in steps as needed.)

   $$80\% \rightarrow \$400$$

   $$100\% \rightarrow \underline{\hspace{1cm}}$$

   Where does the 80% come from, and why is it equated with $400?

   b. Explain why you *can't* calculate the price of the sofa before the reduction by increasing $400 by 20%.

Class Activity 7O: Percent *of* versus Percent Increase or Decrease

1. The price of an oven was marked up from $539 to $639. Fill in the blanks, and justify your answers. Simple drawings may be helpful.

   a. The new price is ____% of the old price.

   b. The new price is ____% more than the old price.

   c. The old price is ____% lower than the new price.

   d. The old price is ____% of the new price.

e. Compare your answers to part (b) and part (c). Why does it make sense that they are *not* the same? (If your answers are the same, go back and rethink your methods.)

2. Explain the difference between the following concepts, and give examples to illustrate each one.

- 200% of an amount

- a 200% increase in an amount

Class Activity 7P: Percent Problem Solving

Strip diagrams may help you solve some of these problems.

1. At first, Prarie had 10% more than the cost of a computer game. After Prarie spent $7.50, she had 15% less than the cost of the computer game. How much did the computer game cost? How much money did Prarie have at first? Explain your reasoning.

2. One mouse weighs 20% more than another mouse. Together, the two mice weigh 66 grams. How much does each mouse weigh? Explain your reasoning.

3. There are two vats of orange juice. After 10% of the orange juice in the first vat is poured into the second vat, the first vat has 3 times as much orange juice as the second vat. By what percent did the amount of juice in the second vat increase when the juice from the first vat was poured into it? Explain your reasoning.

Class Activity 7Q: Percent Change and the Commutative Property of Multiplication

Which, if either, of the following two options will result in the lower price for a pair of pants?

- The price of the pants is marked up by 10% and then marked down by 20% from the increased price.

- The price of the pants is marked down by 20% and then marked up by 10% from the discounted price.

Both options involve marking up by 10% and marking down by 20%. The difference is the order in which the marking up and marking down occur.

1. Before you do any calculations, make a guess about which of the two options should result in a lower price.

2. Determine which of the two options will result in a lower price by using these facts: If a price increases by 10%, then you can find the increased price by multiplying by 1.10 (which is 100% + 10% = 110%). If a price decreases by 20%, then you can find the decreased price by multiplying by 0.80 (which is 100% − 20% = 80%).

3. Explain how the commutative property of multiplication is relevant to the question of which, if either, of the two options results in a lower price for the pair of pants.

Number Theory

8.1 Factors and Multiples

Class Activity 8A:
Factors, Multiples, and Rectangles

1. Elsie has 24 square tiles that she wants to arrange in the shape of a rectangle in such a way that the rectangle is completely filled with tiles. How many different rectangles can Elsie make? Consider this question from two perspectives on the rectangles: (a) the abstract case, and (b) the rectangles representing gardens that have one side along the wall of a house.

   Write one or more statements about factors or multiples that are related to this problem.

2. What if Elsie has only 13 tiles? Now how many rectangles can she make?

3. If Elsie has more than 24 square tiles, will she necessarily be able to make more rectangles than she could in part 1? Try some experiments.

4. John has many 1-inch-by-1-inch square tiles. John will use his tiles to make rectangles (in such a way that each rectangle is filled with tiles), each of which has a side that is 4 inches long. What are the areas of the rectangles that John can make?

Write one or more statements about factors or multiples that are related to this problem.

Class Activity 8B: Problems about Factors and Multiples

1. For each of the situations listed, write a problem about the items or the scenario. In each case, solving your problem should require finding all the factors or several multiples of a number. Solve each problem.

   a. At the store, pencils come in packages of 12.

   b. Amy has a collection of 45 marbles.

   c. The children in a class are clapping, snapping, and stomping to a steady beat in the following pattern: clap, clap, snap, stomp, clap, clap, snap, stomp, ….

2. For each of the situations listed, describe an activity involving the items. In each case, your activity should require finding all the factors or several multiples of a number.

   a. Beads in several different colors and string with which to make necklaces

   b. Graph paper and markers (optional: scissors)

   c. A drum and a tambourine

3. Consider the following problem:

   A rectangular garden has an area of 64 square feet. What could its length and width be?

   Why can you not solve the problem just by finding all the factors of 64? What must you add to the statement of the problem so that it *can* be solved by finding the factors of 64?

Class Activity 8C: Finding All Factors

1. Tyrese is looking for all the factors of 156. So far, Tyrese has divided 156 by all the counting numbers from 1 to 13, listing those numbers that divide 156 and listing the corresponding quotients. Here is Tyrese's work so far:

1, 156	$1 \times 156 = 156$
2, 78	$2 \times 78 = 156$
3, 52	$3 \times 52 = 156$
4, 39	$4 \times 39 = 156$
6, 26	$6 \times 26 = 156$
12, 13	$12 \times 13 = 156$
13, 12	$13 \times 12 = 156$

   Should Tyrese keep checking to see if numbers larger than 13 divide 156, or can Tyrese stop dividing at this point? If so, why? What are all the factors of 156?

2. Find all the factors of 198 in an efficient way.

Class Activity 8D: Do Factors Always Come in Pairs?

Carmina noticed that factors always seem to come in pairs. For example,

$$48 = 1 \times 48, 1 \text{ and } 48 \text{ are a pair of factors of 48.}$$
$$48 = 2 \times 24, 2 \text{ and } 24 \text{ are a pair of factors of 48.}$$
$$48 = 3 \times 16, 3 \text{ and } 16 \text{ are a pair of factors of 48.}$$
$$48 = 4 \times 12, 4 \text{ and } 12 \text{ are a pair of factors of 48.}$$
$$48 = 6 \times 8, 6 \text{ and } 8 \text{ are a pair of factors of 48.}$$

The number 48 has 10 factors that come in 5 pairs. Carmina wants to know if every counting number always has an even number of factors. Investigate Carmina's question carefully. When does a counting number have an even number of factors, and when does it not?

8.2 Greatest Common Factor and Least Common Multiple

Class Activity 8E:
Finding Commonality

1. Follow the instructions on the next page.

2. You have 24 pencils, 30 stickers, and plenty of goodie bags.

    a. List all the ways you could distribute the pencils to goodie bags so that each goodie bag has the same number of pencils and there are no pencils left over.

    b. List all the ways that you could distribute the stickers to goodie bags so that each goodie bag has the same number of stickers and there are no stickers left over.

    c. Now suppose you want to use the same set of goodie bags for both the pencils—as in part (a)—and the stickers—as in part (b). List all your options. What is the largest number of goodie bags you could use?

    d. Describe the options in part (c) in mathematical terms. Describe the largest number of goodie bags in part (c) in mathematical terms.

Shade the squares at the multiples of 4 on strip A, and shade the multiples of 6 on strip B. Predict when the shaded squares on both strips will line up.

A | 1 2 3 4 5 6 7 8 9 10 11 12 13 14 15 16 17 18 19 20 21 22 23 24 25 26 27 28 29 30 31 32 33 34 35 36 37 38 39 40

B | 1 2 3 4 5 6 7 8 9 10 11 12 13 14 15 16 17 18 19 20 21 22 23 24 25 26 27 28 29 30 31 32 33 34 35 36 37 38 39 40

At which numbers do the shaded squares in both strips line up? Describe these locations in mathematical terms. What is the first place the shaded squares line up? Describe this location in mathematical terms.

Shade the squares at the multiples of 4 on strip C, and shade the multiples of 10 on strip D. Predict when the shaded squares on both strips will line up.

C | 1 2 3 4 5 6 7 8 9 10 11 12 13 14 15 16 17 18 19 20 21 22 23 24 25 26 27 28 29 30 31 32 33 34 35 36 37 38 39 40

D | 1 2 3 4 5 6 7 8 9 10 11 12 13 14 15 16 17 18 19 20 21 22 23 24 25 26 27 28 29 30 31 32 33 34 35 36 37 38 39 40

At which numbers do the shaded squares in both strips line up? Describe these locations in mathematical terms. What is the first place the shaded squares line up? Describe this location in mathematical terms.

Class Activity 8F: The Slide Method

1. Examine the initial and final steps of a "slide," which was used to find the GCF and LCM of 900 and 360. Try to determine how it was made. Then make another slide to find the GCF and LCM of 900 and 360.

   A Slide

   initially: $\underline{\qquad|\,900,\,360\qquad}$ final:

10	900, 360
2	90, 36
3	45, 18
3	15, 6
	5, 2

   GCF $= 10 \times 2 \times 3 \times 3 = 180$

   LCM $= 10 \times 2 \times 3 \times 3 \times 5 \times 2 = 1800$

2. Use the slide method to find the GCF and LCM of 1080 and 1200 and to find the GCF and LCM of 675 and 1125.

3. Why does the slide method work?

Class Activity 8G:
Problems Involving Greatest Common Factors
and Least Common Multiples

1. Pencils come in packages of 18; erasers that fit on top of these pencils come in packages of 24. What is the smallest number of pencils and erasers that you can buy so that each pencil can be matched with an eraser? How many packages of pencils will you need and how many packages of erasers? (Assume that you must buy whole packages—you can't buy partial packages.)

   Solve the problem, explaining your solution. Does this problem involve the GCF or the LCM? Explain.

2. Ko has a bag with 45 red candies and another bag with 30 green candies. Ko wants to make snack bags so that each snack bag contains the same number of red candies and each bag contains the same number of green candies (which may be different from the number of red candies) and so that all his candies will be used up in the snack bags. What is the largest number of snack bags that Ko can make this way? How many red candies and how many green candies will go in each snack bag?

   Solve the problem, explaining your solution. Does this problem involve the GCF or the LCM? Explain.

3. Sam has many 8-inch sticks that he is placing end-to-end to make a line of sticks. Becky has many 12-inch sticks that she is placing end-to-end to make a line of sticks. If Sam and Becky want their lines of sticks to be equally long, how long could they be? What is the shortest such length?

   Solve the problem, explaining your solution. Does this problem involve the GCF or the LCM? Explain.

4. Explain how a least common multiple is relevant to the following situation: A class is clapping and snapping to a steady beat. Half of the class uses the pattern

   snap, snap, clap, snap, snap, clap, ...

   The other half of the class uses the pattern

   snap, clap, snap, clap, snap, clap, ...

5. Mary will make a small 8-inch-by-12-inch rectangular quilt for a doll house out of identical square patches. Each square patch must have side lengths that are a whole number of inches and no partial squares are allowed in the quilt. Other than using 1-inch-by-1-inch squares, what size squares can Mary use to make her quilt? Show Mary's other options below. What are the largest squares that Mary can use? How is this question related to GCFs or LCMs?

 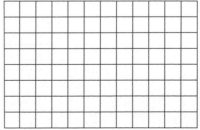

6. Two gears are meshed, as shown in the next figure, with the stars on each gear aligned. The large gear has 36 teeth, and the small gear has 15 teeth. Each gear rotates around a pin through its center. How many revolutions will the large gear have to make and how many revolutions will the small gear make in order for the stars to be aligned again? How is this question related to GCFs or LCMs?

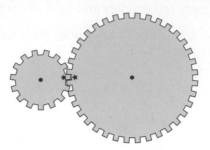

Class Activity 8H: Spirograph Flower Designs

If you're ever had a Spirograph drawing toy, you know it can make designs similar to the flower designs on the next page. This activity explores some of the mathematics of these "spirograph designs."

Examine the flower designs on the next page. Each flower design is created by starting with a number of dots in a circle. Then a fixed "jump number," N, is chosen. Starting at one dot, petals are formed by connecting each subsequent Nth dot until returning to the starting dot, at which point the flower design closes up.

1. Examine the first four flower designs in Figure 8H.1. Try to find relationships between the number of dots at the center of the flower, the jump number, which describes how the petals were made (e.g., by connecting every 8th dot or every 15th dot), and the number of petals in the flower design. These numbers are listed in the following table:

design	number of dots	"Jump Number" a petal connects every ____th dot	number of petals
design 1	36	8	9
design 2	36	15	12
design 3	36	16	9
design 4	30	14	15
design 5	30	4	
design 6	30	12	

2. Predict the number of petals that the 5th and 6th flower designs will have. Then complete the designs to see if your prediction was correct. (To complete the designs, you might find it easiest to count dots forward and then draw the petal backwards.)

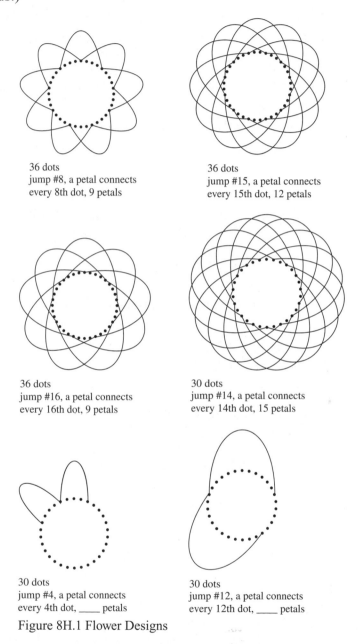

36 dots
jump #8, a petal connects
every 8th dot, 9 petals

36 dots
jump #15, a petal connects
every 15th dot, 12 petals

36 dots
jump #16, a petal connects
every 16th dot, 9 petals

30 dots
jump #14, a petal connects
every 14th dot, 15 petals

30 dots
jump #4, a petal connects
every 4th dot, ____ petals

30 dots
jump #12, a petal connects
every 12th dot, ____ petals

Figure 8H.1 Flower Designs

Class Activity 8I: Relationships Between the GCF and the LCM and Explaining the Flower Designs

1. By experimenting with a number of pairs of counting numbers A and B, discover one or more relationships among A, B, GCF, and LCM, where GCF stands for the greatest common factor of A and B and LCM stands for the least common multiple of A and B.

For example,

- If $A = 6$ and $B = 8$, then GCF $= 2$ and LCM $= 24$.
- If $A = 8$ and $B = 12$, then GCF $= 4$ and LCM $= 24$.
- If $A = 3$ and $B = 5$, then GCF $= 1$ and LCM $= 15$.

In these and other examples, how are A, B, GCF, and LCM related?

2. Refer to Class Activity [8H] on flower designs.

   a. Describe the number of petals in flower designs in terms of the "jump number" and the LCM of the number of dots in the design and the jump number. By considering how the flower designs were made, explain why this relationship must hold for every flower design.

   b. Describe the number of petals in flower designs in terms of the number of dots in the design and the GCF of the number of dots in the design and the jump number. Use parts 1 and 2 (a) to explain why this relationship must hold for every flower design.

Class Activity 8J: Using GCFs and LCMs with Fractions

1. Show how to determine the simplest form of
$$\frac{36}{90}$$
by first finding the GCF of 36 and 90.

2. Show how to determine the simplest form of
$$\frac{36}{90}$$
without finding the GCF of 36 and 90 first.

3. Compare your work in parts 1 and 2. Which method did you prefer? Why?

4. Show how to add

$$\frac{1}{6} + \frac{1}{10}$$

in two ways: using the least common denominator and using the denominator that is the product of the two denominators. Which method did you prefer? Why?

5. If we use the least common denominator to add two fractions, is the resulting sum necessarily in simplest form?

8.3 Prime Numbers

Class Activity 8K:
The Sieve of Eratosthenes

1. Use the Sieve of Eratosthenes to find all the prime numbers up to 120. Start by circling 2 and crossing off every 2nd number after 2. Then circle 3 and cross off every 3rd number. (Cross off a number even if it already has been crossed off.) Continue in this manner, going back to the beginning of the list, circling the next number N that hasn't been crossed off, and then crossing off every Nth number until every number in the list is either circled or crossed off. The numbers that are circled at the end are the prime numbers from 2 to 120.

	2	3	4	5	6	7	8	9	10
11	12	13	14	15	16	17	18	19	20
21	22	23	24	25	26	27	28	29	30
31	32	33	34	35	36	37	38	39	40
41	42	43	44	45	46	47	48	49	50
51	52	53	54	55	56	57	58	59	60
61	62	63	64	65	66	67	68	69	70
71	72	73	74	75	76	77	78	79	80
81	82	83	84	85	86	87	88	89	90
91	92	93	94	95	96	97	98	99	100
101	102	103	104	105	106	107	108	109	110
111	112	113	114	115	116	117	118	119	120

2. Explain why the circled numbers must be prime numbers and why the numbers that are crossed off are not prime numbers.

Class Activity 8L:
The Trial Division Method for Determining Whether a Number Is Prime

You will need the list of prime numbers from Class Activity [8K] on the Sieve of Eratosthenes for this activity.

1. Using the trial division method and your list of primes from the Sieve of Eratosthenes, determine whether the 3 numbers listed are prime numbers. Record the results of your trial divisions below the number. (The first few are done for you.) You will need these results for part 3.

239	323	4001
$239 \div 2 = 119.5$	$323 \div 2 = 161.5$	$4001 \div 2 = 2000.5$
$239 \div 3 = 79.67\ldots$	$323 \div 3 = 107.67\ldots$	$4001 \div 3 = 1333.67\ldots$

2. How do you know when to stop with the trial division method? To help you answer, look at the list of divisions you did in part 1. As you go down each list, what happens to the divisor and the quotient? If your number *was* divisible by some whole number (other than 1), at what point would that whole number be known?

3. In the trial division method, you determine only whether your number is divisible by *prime* numbers. Why is this legitimate? Why don't you also have to find out if your number is divisible by other numbers such as 4, 6, 8, 9, 10, and so on?

Class Activity 8M: Factoring Into Products of Primes

1. Make a factor tree for 240 and use it to write 240 as a product of prime numbers.

2. Compare your factor tree for 240 to a classmate's (or try to make a factor tree for 240 in another way). Are the factor trees identical in all respects? Do they produce the same end result?

   Will it be obvious to children that the end result must be the same, no matter how you make your factor tree? Discuss!

3. Lindsay factored 637 as $637 = 7 \times 7 \times 13$. When Lindsay was then asked to factor 637^2 as a product of prime numbers, she first multiplied $637 \times 637 = 405,769$; then she divided $405,769$ by 2, then by 3, then by 5, and so on, in order to factor $405,769$. Is there an easier way for Lindsay to factor 637^2 into a product of prime numbers? Explain.

4. Given that $527 = 17 \times 31$, is there a way to check if 77 is a factor of 527 without actually dividing 527 by 77? Explain.

8.4 Even and Odd

Class Activity 8N:
Why Can We Check the Ones Digit to Determine Whether a Number Is Even or Odd?

Remember that a counting number is called *even* if that number of objects can be divided into groups of 2 with none left over:

Why is it valid to determine whether a number of objects can be divided into groups of 2 with none left over by checking the ones digit of the number? We will investigate this question in this Class Activity.

1. Recall that we can represent the expanded form of a whole number with bundled toothpicks (or other bundled or grouped objects) as in Figure 8N.1. Using Figure 8N.1, explain why 134 toothpicks can be divided into groups of 2 with

none left over, but there will be 1 toothpick left over when 357 toothpicks are divided into groups of 2. Explain why we have to consider only the ones digit to determine if there will be a toothpick left over by describing what happens with each bundle of 100 toothpicks and each bundle of 10 toothpicks when we divide the toothpicks into groups of 2.

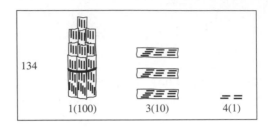

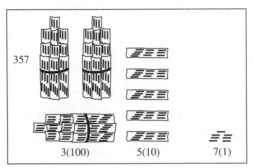

Figure 8N.1 Representing 134 and 357 with bundled toothpicks.

2. Working more generally, let *ABC* be a 3-digit whole number with *A* hundreds, *B* tens, and *C* ones. Use the idea of representing *ABC* with bundled toothpicks to help explain why *ABC* is divisible by 2 exactly when *C* is either 0, 2, 4, 6, or 8. What can we say about each of the *B* bundles of 10 toothpicks and each of the *A* bundles of 100 toothpicks when we divide the toothpicks into groups of 2?

Class Activity 8O:
Questions about Even and Odd Numbers

1. If you add an odd number and an odd number, what kind of number do you get? Investigate this question by working out examples. Then explain why your answer is always correct. Try to find several different explanations by working with the various equivalent ways of saying that a number is even or odd.

2. If you multiply an even number and an odd number, what kind of number do you get? Investigate this question by working out examples. Then explain why your answer is always correct. Try to find several different explanations by working with the various equivalent ways of saying that a number is even or odd.

Class Activity 8P: Extending the Definitions of Even and Odd

We have defined even and odd only for counting numbers. What if we wanted to extend the definition of even and odd to other numbers?

1. If we extend the definitions of even and odd to all the integers, then what should 0 be, even or odd? What should −5 be, even or odd? Explain.

2. Give definitions of even and odd that apply to all integers, not just to the counting numbers.

3. Would it make sense to extend the definitions of even and odd to fractions? Why or why not?

8.5 Divisibility Tests

Class Activity 8Q:
The Divisibility Test for 3

1. Is it possible to tell if a whole number is divisible by 3 just by checking its last digit? Investigate this question by considering a number of examples. State your conclusion.

2. The divisibility test for 3 says that you can determine whether a counting number is divisible by 3 by adding its digits and checking to see if this sum is divisible by 3. If the sum is divisible by 3, then the original number is, too; if the sum is not divisible by 3, then the original number is not either.

For each of the numbers listed, see if the divisibility test for 3 accurately predicts which numbers are divisible by 3. That is, for each number, check its divisibility by 3 by using long division or a calculator, and then add the digits of the number and see if that sum is divisible by 3. The two conclusions should agree.

Example: 1437 is divisible by 3 because $1437 \div 3 = 479$, with no remainder.

$1 + 4 + 3 + 7 = 15$ also indicates that 1437 is divisible by 3, because $15 \div 3 = 5$, with no remainder.

2570

123

14,928

7213

555,555

11,111

3. Explain why the divisibility test for 3 is valid for 3-digit counting numbers. In other words, explain why you can determine whether a 3-digit counting number, ABC, is divisible by 3 by adding its digits, $A + B + C$, and determining if this sum is divisible by 3.

To develop your explanation, consider the following:

a. A counting number is divisible by 3 exactly when that many objects can be divided into groups of 3 with none left over.

divisible by 3 ||| ||| ||| ||| ||| ||| ||| |||

not divisible by 3 ||| ||| ||| ||| ||| ||| ||| ||| |

not divisible by 3 ||| ||| ||| ||| ||| ||| ||| ||| ||

b. Think about representing 3-digit numbers with bundled toothpicks. For example, we can represent the number 247 by using 2 bundles of 100 toothpicks, 4 bundles of 10 toothpicks, and 7 individual toothpicks, as shown in Figure 8Q.1. The number ABC is represented by A bundles of 100 toothpicks, B bundles of 10 toothpicks, and C individual toothpicks.

c. Consider starting to divide bundled toothpicks into groups of 3 by dividing *each individual bundle* of 10 and *each individual bundle* of 100 into groups of 3. Determine how many toothpicks will be left over if you divide the bundles this way and if you do no further dividing into groups of 3.

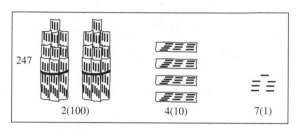

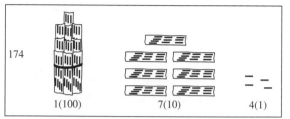

Figure 8Q.1 Representing 247 and 174 with bundled toothpicks.

4. Relate your explanation in part 3 to the following equations:

$$ABC = A \cdot 100 + B \cdot 10 + C$$
$$= (A \cdot 99 + B \cdot 9) + (A + B + C)$$
$$= (A \cdot 33 + B \cdot 3) \cdot 3 + (A + B + C)$$

8.6 Rational and Irrational Numbers

Class Activity 8R:
Decimal Representations of Fractions

1. The decimal representations of the following fractions are shown to 16 decimal places, with no rounding:

$\frac{1}{12} = 0.0833333333333333$ $\qquad$ $\frac{1}{4} = 0.25$

$\frac{1}{11} = 0.9090909090909090$ $\qquad$ $\frac{2}{5} = 0.4$

$\frac{113}{33} = 3.4242424242424242$ $\qquad$ $\frac{37}{8} = 4.625$

$\frac{491}{550} = 0.8927272727272727$ $\qquad$ $\frac{17}{50} = 0.34$

$$\frac{14}{37} = 0.3783783783783783 \qquad \frac{1}{125} = 0.008$$

$$\frac{35}{101} = 0.3465346534653465 \qquad \frac{9}{20} = 0.45$$

$$\frac{1}{41} = 0.0243902439024390 \qquad \frac{19}{32} = 0.59375$$

$$\frac{5}{7} = 0.7142857142857142 \qquad \frac{1}{3200} = 0.0003125$$

$$\frac{1}{14} = 0.0714285714285714 \qquad \frac{1}{64,000} = 0.000015625$$

$$\frac{1}{21} = 0.0476190476190476 \qquad \frac{1}{625} = 0.0016$$

In what way are the decimal representations in the first column similar? In what way are the decimal representations of the fractions in the second column similar?

2. Complete the next set of calculations, using longhand division (not a calculator!) to find the decimal representations of $\frac{2}{55}$ and $\frac{1}{101}$. At each step in the long-division process, write down the remainder you obtain.

<pre>
        0.0   0.0
    55)2.0000000   remainder 2   101)1.0000000   remainder 1
      -0   -0
      ──   ──
       20   remainder 20   10   remainder 10
      ──   ──

                   remainder ___   remainder ___
      ──   ──

                   remainder ___   remainder ___
      ──   ──

                   remainder ___   remainder ___
      ──   ──

                   remainder ___   remainder ___
      ──   ──

                   remainder ___   remainder ___
      ──   ──

                   remainder ___   remainder ___
</pre>

3. Use longhand division to calculate the decimal representations of $\frac{3}{8}$ and $\frac{1}{7}$. As in part 2, write down the remainder you get at each step.

4. Answer the following questions for the decimal representations of the fractions in parts 2 and 3:

   • What happened to the decimal representation of the fraction when you got a remainder of 0?

   • What happened to the decimal representation of the fraction when you got a remainder that you had before?

5. Without actually carrying it out, imagine doing longhand division to find the decimal representation of $\frac{7}{31}$.

   a. What remainders could you possibly get in the longhand division process when finding $7 \div 31$? For example, could you possibly get a remainder of 45 or 73 or 32? How many different remainders are theoretically possible?

   b. If you were doing longhand division to find $7 \div 31$ and you got a remainder of 0 somewhere along the way, what would that tell you about the decimal representation of $\frac{7}{31}$?

   c. If you were doing longhand division to find $7 \div 31$ and you got a remainder you had gotten before, what would then happen in the decimal representation of $\frac{7}{31}$?

   d. Now use your answer to parts (a), (b), and (c) to explain why the decimal representation of $\frac{7}{31}$ must either terminate or eventually repeat after at most 30 decimal places.

6. In general, suppose that $\frac{A}{B}$ is a proper fraction, where A and B are whole numbers. Explain why the decimal representation of $\frac{A}{B}$ must either terminate or begin to repeat after at most $B - 1$ decimal places.

7. Could the number

$$0.10100100010000100000100000001\ldots$$

where the decimal representation continues forever with the pattern of more and more 0s in between 1s, be the decimal representation of a fraction of whole numbers? Explain your answer.

Class Activity 8S: Writing Terminating and Repeating Decimals as Fractions

1. By using denominators that are suitable powers of 10, show how to write the following terminating decimals as fractions:

$$0.137 = \qquad 0.25567 =$$

$$13.89 = \qquad 329.2 =$$

2. Write the following fractions as decimals, and observe the pattern:

$$\frac{1}{9} =$$

$$\frac{1}{99} =$$

$$\frac{1}{999} =$$

$$\frac{1}{9999} =$$

$$\frac{1}{99,999} =$$

3. Using the decimal representations of $\frac{1}{9}, \frac{1}{99}, \ldots$, that you found in part 2, show how to write the following decimals as fractions:

$$0.\overline{2} = 0.222222\ldots = \qquad 0.\overline{08} = 0.080808\ldots =$$

$$0.\overline{003} = 0.003003\ldots = \qquad 0.\overline{52} = 0.525252\ldots =$$

$$0.\overline{1234} = \qquad 0.\overline{123456} =$$

4. Use the fact that

$$0.\overline{49} = \frac{49}{99}$$

to write the next four repeating decimals as fractions. *Hint*: Shift the decimal point by dividing by suitable powers of 10.

$$0.0\overline{49} = \qquad 0.00\overline{49} =$$

$$0.000\overline{49} = \qquad 0.0000\overline{49} =$$

5. Use the results of part 4, together with the fact that

$$0.3\overline{49} = 0.3 + 0.0\overline{49} \quad 0.12\overline{49} = 0.12 + 0.00\overline{49}$$

and other similar facts, to determine how to write the following repeating decimals as fractions:

$$7.3\overline{49} = \qquad 0.12\overline{49} =$$

$$1.2\overline{49} = \qquad 0.111\overline{49} =$$

Class Activity 8T: What Is 0.9999...?

1. Use the fact that $\frac{1}{9} = 0.\overline{1} = 0.111111111 \dots$ to determine the decimal representations of the following fractions:

$$\frac{2}{9} = \qquad\qquad \frac{6}{9} =$$

$$\frac{3}{9} = \qquad\qquad \frac{7}{9} =$$

$$\frac{4}{9} = \qquad\qquad \frac{8}{9} =$$

$$\frac{5}{9} = \qquad\qquad \frac{9}{9} =$$

What can you conclude about $0.\overline{9}$?

2. Add longhand:

$$0.9999999999\ldots$$
$$+\ 0.1111111111\ldots$$

Note that the nines and ones repeat forever.

Now subtract longhand: $-\ .1111111111\ldots$

Look back at what you just did: Starting with $0.\overline{9}$, you added and then subtracted $0.\overline{1}$. What does this tell you about $0.\overline{9}$?

3. Let N stand for the number $0.\overline{9} = 0.999999\ldots$:

$$N = 0.999999999\ldots$$

Write the decimal representation of $10N$:

$$10N =$$

Now subtract N from $10N$ in two ways—in terms of N and as decimal numbers:

in terms of N: as decimals:

$$\begin{array}{r} 10N \\ -N \end{array} \qquad \begin{array}{r} \\ -0.999999999\ldots \end{array}$$

What can you conclude about $0.\overline{9}$?

4. Given that the number 1 has two different decimal representations, namely, 1 and $0.\overline{9}$, find different decimal representations of the following numbers:

$$17 =$$

$$23.42 =$$

$$139.8 =$$

Class Activity 8U: The Square Root of 2

1. If the sides of a square are 1 unit long, then how long is the diagonal of the square?

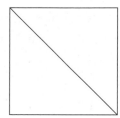

2. Use a calculator to find the decimal representation of $\sqrt{2}$. Based on your calculator's display, does it look like $\sqrt{2}$ is rational or irrational? Why? Can you tell *for sure* just by looking at your calculator's display?

3. What is the decimal representation of

$$\frac{1{,}414{,}213{,}562}{999{,}999{,}999} ?$$

Is this number rational or irrational? Compare with part 2.

4. Suppose that it were somehow possible to write the square root of 2 as a fraction $\frac{A}{B}$, where A and B are counting numbers:

$$\sqrt{2} = \frac{A}{B}$$

Show that, in this case, we would get the equation

$$A^2 = 2 \times B^2$$

5. Suppose A is a counting number, and imagine factoring it into a product of prime numbers. For example, if A is 30, then you factor it as

$$A = 2 \times 3 \times 5$$

Now think about factoring A^2 as a product of prime numbers. For example, if $A = 30$, then

$$A^2 = 2 \times 3 \times 5 \times 2 \times 3 \times 5$$

Could A^2 have an odd number of prime factors? Make a general qualitative statement about the number of prime factors that A^2 has.

6. Now suppose that B is a counting number, and imagine factoring the number $2 \times B^2$ into a product of prime numbers. For example, if $B = 15$, then

$$2 \times B^2 = 2 \times 3 \times 5 \times 3 \times 5$$

Could $2B^2$ have an even number of prime factors? Make a general qualitative statement about the number of prime factors that $2 \times B^2$ has.

7. Now use your answers in parts 5 and 6 to explain why a number in the form A^2 can never be equal to a number in the form $2 \times B^2$, when A and B are counting numbers.

8. What does part 7 lead you to conclude about the assumption in part 4 that it is somehow possible to write the square root of 2 as a fraction, where the numerator and denominator are counting numbers? Now what can you conclude about whether $\sqrt{2}$ is rational or irrational?

Class Activity 8V: Pattern Tiles and the Irrationality of the Square Root of 3

You will need a set of pattern tiles like the ones shown in the next figure for this activity. If a set of pattern tiles is not available, cut out the paper pattern tiles that appear at the end of this manual on pages 677, 679, and 681.

One fascinating aspect of mathematics is that there are connections between simple kindergarten activities and much more advanced ideas that students might not encounter until high school or college math classes. This Class Activity shows one such connection involving pattern tiles.

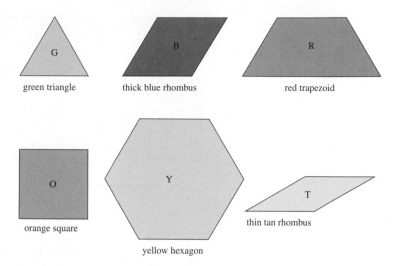

green triangle   thick blue rhombus   red trapezoid

orange square   yellow hexagon   thin tan rhombus

1. In early elementary school, children sometimes use pattern tiles to fill shapes. Find several different ways to fill each of the shapes in Figures 8V.1 and 8V.2 with pattern tiles.

Even though there are many different ways to fill the shapes, can any of the shapes in Figure 8V.1 be filled by the use of one or more squares or thin rhombuses?

Can any of the shapes in Figure 8V.2 be filled without either squares or thin rhombuses?

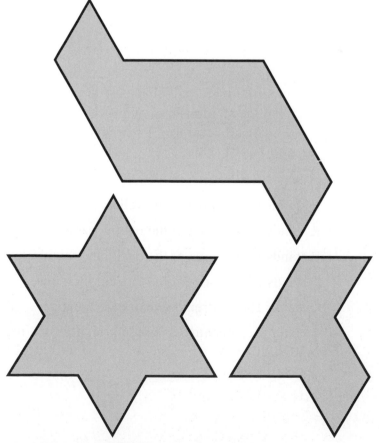

Figure 8V.1 Fill these shapes with pattern tiles.

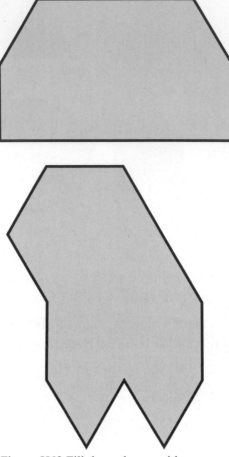

Figure 8V.2 Fill these shapes with pattern tiles.

2. When children try to fill shapes with pattern tiles in different ways, they may begin to notice relationships among the different tiles. Find as many relationships among the tiles as you can. Express these relationships by using the symbols G, Y, R, B, T, and O, where

    • G stands for the area of the green triangle.

    • Y stands for the area of the yellow hexagon.

    • R stands for the area of the red trapezoid.

    • B stands for the area of the thick blue rhombus.

    • T stands for the area of the thin tan rhombus.

    • O stands for the area of the orange square.

    For example, because 2 green triangles fit together to make a thick blue rhombus, 2G = B.

3. If you have not yet done so, find a relationship between T and O, the areas of the thin tan rhombus and the orange square. *Hint*: Use triangles in addition to the thin tan rhombus and the orange square.

4. Can you find any way to relate G, Y, R, and B with O, the area of the orange square?

   Can you find any way to relate G, Y, R, and B with T, the area of the thin tan rhombus?

Figure 8V.3 The green triangle.

5. Use the Pythagorean theorem and Figure 8V.3 to help you determine the area, in square inches, of the green triangle. Your answer should involve a square root of 3.

6. Using the relationships that you found in part 2, and the area of the green triangle that you found in part 5, determine Y, R, and B—the areas of the yellow hexagon, the red trapezoid, and the thick blue rhombus. All these areas will involve the square root of 3. Fill in the values for G, Y, R, and B in Figure 8V.4.

7. The orange square is 1 inch wide and 1 inch long; therefore, its area is 1 square inch. Use the relationship between O and T that you found in part 3 to determine T. Fill in the values for O and T in Figure 8V.4.

8. Looking at the values you wrote in Figure 8V.4, how are the areas of the green triangle, the yellow hexagon, the red trapezoid, and the thick blue rhombus qualitatively different from the areas of the orange square and the thin tan rhombus? Given this, and the fact that $\sqrt{3}$ is irrational, is it surprising that you could not find a relationship between G, Y, R, B, and O or G, Y, R, B, and T in part 4?

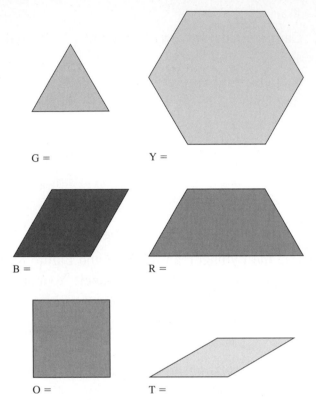

Figure 8V.4 Fill in the areas of these shapes.

Algebra

9.1 Mathematical Expressions and Formulas

Class Activity 9A:
Writing Expressions and a Formula for a Flower Pattern

1. For each flower design in Figure 9A.1, write an expression for the total number of dots in the design. Each expression should involve both multiplication and addition.

2. Fill like parts in the large flower in Figure 9A.2 with the same number of dots. Then write an expression for the total number of dots in your flower design. Write equations in which you evaluate this expression, determining the total number of dots in your flower design.

3. Now consider general flower designs like the ones in Figure 9A.1 and the one you created in part 2? If M, N, and P are any counting numbers, we can imagine a flower design that has M dots in the center circle, N dots in each of the circles surrounding the center circle, and P dots in each of the petals of the flower. Write a formula, in terms of M, N, and P, for the number of dots in the flower design.

4. Create a design that illustrates the formula

$$M + 2N + 2P$$

by imagining different portions of the design filled with different numbers of dots. Explain why your design illustrates the formula $M + 2N + 2P$.

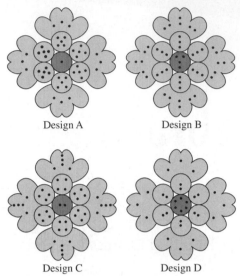

Design A   Design B

Design C   Design D

Figure 9A.1 Write expressions for the total number of dots in each flower.

Figure 9A.2 Fill like parts with equal numbers of dots and write an expression for the total number of dots.

Class Activity 9B: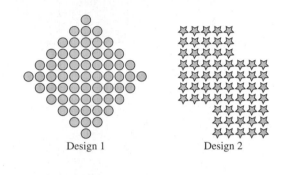
Expressions for Dot and Star Designs

For each of the next designs, write at least two different expressions for the total number of small shapes that the design is made of.

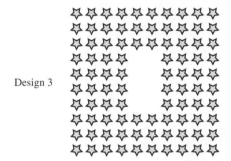

Design 1   Design 2

Design 3

Design 4

Class Activity 9C: Expressions with Fractions

1. For each of the next two rectangles, write an expression using multiplication and addition (or subtraction) for the fraction of the area of the rectangle that is shaded. You may assume that parts that appear to be the same size really are the same size.

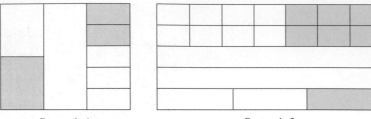

Rectangle 1   Rectangle 2

2. Shade

$$\frac{2}{3} \cdot \frac{4}{5} + \frac{1}{4} \cdot \frac{1}{10}$$

of a rectangle in such a way that you can tell the correct amount is shaded without evaluating the expression.

Class Activity 9D: Evaluating Expressions with Fractions Efficiently and Correctly

1. In order to evaluate

$$\frac{8}{35} \cdot \frac{35}{61}$$

we can cancel thus:

$$\frac{8}{\cancel{35}} \cdot \frac{\cancel{35}}{61} = \frac{8}{61}$$

Discuss the following equations and explain why they demonstrate that the canceling shown previously is legitimate:

$$\frac{8}{35} \cdot \frac{35}{61} = \frac{8 \cdot 35}{35 \cdot 61} = \frac{8 \cdot 35}{61 \cdot 35} = \frac{8}{61} \cdot \frac{35}{35} = \frac{8}{61}$$

2. Write equations to demonstrate that the canceling shown in the following equations is legitimate:

$$\frac{\overset{2}{\cancel{18}}}{5} \cdot \frac{7}{\underset{11}{\cancel{99}}} = \frac{2}{5} \cdot \frac{7}{11} = \frac{14}{55}$$

3. Which of the cancelations in parts (a) through (d) are correct, and which are incorrect? Explain your answers.

a. $\dfrac{\overset{6}{\cancel{36}} \cdot \overset{16}{\cancel{96}}}{\underset{1}{\cancel{6}}} = \dfrac{6 \cdot 16}{1} = 96$

b. $\dfrac{\overset{6}{\cancel{36}} \cdot 96}{\underset{1}{\cancel{6}}} = \dfrac{6 \cdot 96}{1} = 576$

c. $\dfrac{\overset{6}{\cancel{36}} + \overset{16}{\cancel{96}}}{\underset{1}{\cancel{6}}} = \dfrac{6 + 16}{1} = 22$

d. $\dfrac{\overset{6}{\cancel{36}} + 96}{\underset{1}{\cancel{6}}} = \dfrac{6 + 96}{1} = 102$

Class Activity 9E: Expressions for Story Problems

1. Write a story problem so that some quantity in the story situation can be expressed as $4x + 2$. Explain why $4x + 2$ is the appropriate formula for the quantity. Be sure to say what x stands for.

2. Write a story problem so that some quantity in the story situation can be expressed as $4x - 2$. Explain why $4x - 2$ is the appropriate formula for the quantity. Be sure to say what x stands for.

3. There are T tons of sand in a pile initially.

    a. Assume that $\frac{1}{4}$ of the sand in the pile is removed from the pile and, after that, another $\frac{2}{3}$ of a ton of sand is dumped onto the pile. Write a formula in terms of T for the number of tons of sand that are in the pile now.

    b. Starting with T tons of sand, assume that $\frac{2}{3}$ of a ton of sand is dumped onto the pile and, after that, $\frac{1}{4}$ of the sand in the new, larger pile is removed. Write a formula in terms of T for the number of tons of sand that are in the pile now. Is this formula the same as the formula in part (a)?

    c. Evaluate your formulas from parts (a) and (b) when $T = 1\frac{2}{3}$.

4. At a store, the price of an item is $\$P$. Consider three different scenarios:

    First scenario: Starting at the price $\$P$, the price of the item was lowered by $A\%$. Then the new price was lowered by $B\%$.

    Second scenario: Starting at the price $\$P$, the price of the item was lowered by $B\%$. Then the new price was lowered by $A\%$.

Third scenario: Starting at the price P, the price of the item was lowered by $(A + B)$%.

For each scenario, write an expression for the final price of the item. Are any of the final prices the same?

9.2 Equations

Class Activity 9F: How Many High-Fives?

The *high-five problem* (traditionally known as the *handshake problem*): There are 20 students in a class. If every student high-fives with every other student, how many high-fives will there be?

1. Try to find two different expressions for the total number of high-fives among 20 students. One expression should involve addition, and the other expression should involve multiplication. Explain why each expression stands for the total number of high-fives.

2. Formulate an equation that is based on part 1. Solve the high-five problem.

   Which side of the equation is easiest to use to solve the high-five problem?

3. What if there were 50 students in the class? Write an equation for the high-five problem in this case; feel free to use an ellipsis (. . .) in your equation! Explain why the equation holds. Then solve the high-five problem in this case.

   Which side of the equation is easiest to use to solve the high-five problem?

4. What if there were N students in the class? Write an equation for the high-five problem in this case and explain why the equation holds.

Class Activity 9G: Sums of Counting Numbers

Is there a quick way to add a bunch of consecutive counting numbers? This activity will help you find a way by formulating and using equations that come from rectangular designs.

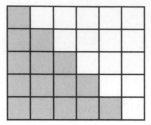

1. Use the rectangular design above to complete the equation below so that the right-hand side is an expression involving multiplication. Explain.

$$1 + 2 + 3 + 4 + 5 =$$

2. Describe a rectangular design that would give rise to an equation you could use to calculate the sum below in an efficient way. Calculate the sum. Explain.

$$1 + 2 + 3 + 4 + \cdots + 198 + 199 + 200$$

3. Write an equation that shows two different ways to express the sum of the first N counting numbers. Explain why your equation is true for all counting numbers.

Class Activity 9H: Sums of Odd Numbers

Is there a quick way to add a bunch of consecutive odd numbers? This activity will help you find and explain another way to express a sum of odd numbers.

1. Calculate each of the next sums.

$$1 + 3 = \text{\underline{\hspace{2cm}}}$$

$$1 + 3 + 5 = \text{\underline{\hspace{2cm}}}$$

$$1 + 3 + 5 + 7 = \text{\underline{\hspace{2cm}}}$$

$$1 + 3 + 5 + 7 + 9 = \text{\underline{\hspace{2cm}}}$$

$$1 + 3 + 5 + 7 + 9 + 11 = \text{\underline{\hspace{2cm}}}$$

$$1 + 3 + 5 + 7 + 9 + 11 + 13 = \text{\underline{\hspace{2cm}}}$$

2. What is special about the solutions to the sums in part 1?

3. Based on your answer in part 2, predict the sum of the first 100 odd numbers.

4. Based on your answer in part 2, predict the next sum:
    $$1 + 3 + 5 + 7 + 9 + \cdots + 91 + 93 + 95 + 97 + 99 = \text{\underline{\hspace{2cm}}}$$

5. Use the next sequence of square designs to find and explain an equation that helps calculate sums of consecutive odd numbers. Imagine the sequence of square designs continuing indefinitely. To get the next square design in the sequence, always add a row and column of small squares of a new color along the bottom and right.

Write an equation that is associated with the Nth square design. One side of the equation should involve a sum of odd numbers. The other side should involve multiplication. Explain.

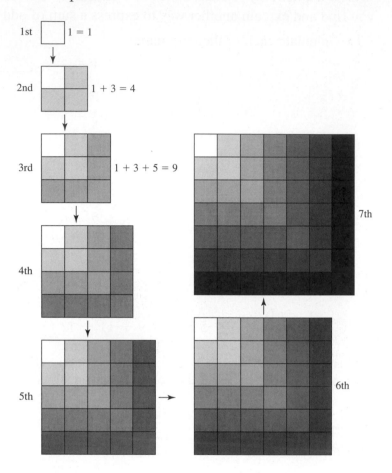

Class Activity 9I: Equations Arising from Rectangular Designs

1. Explain why design (a) gives rise to the equation

$$4 \cdot 4 + 4 \cdot 3 + 2 \cdot 4 + 2 \cdot 3 = 6 \cdot 7$$

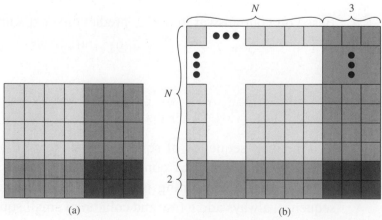

(a)   (b)

2. Design (b) represents an enlarged version of design (a). Find an equation in terms of *N* that design (b) gives rise to. Explain.

3. Other than using a rectangular design to explain why your equation in part 2 is true, how else can you see that the equation is true? (Think back to properties of arithmetic you have studied.)

4. By determining the total number of small squares in design (c) in two different ways, find an equation that design (c) gives rise to.

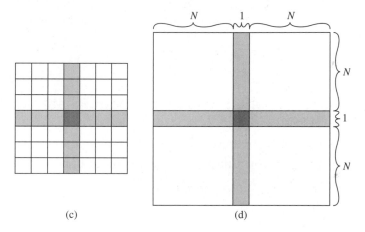

(c)   (d)

5. Design (d) represents an enlarged version of design (c). Find an equation in terms of *N* that design (d) gives rise to. Explain.

6. Other than using a square design to explain why your equation in part 5 is true, how else can you see that the equation is true?

7. Draw, label, and shade a square so that it gives rise to the equation

$$(N + 1)^2 = N^2 + 2N + 1$$

Explain briefly. Other than using your square, how else can you see that the equation is true?

8. Draw, label, and shade a rectangle so that it gives rise to the equation

$$(A + 1) \cdot (B + 2) = AB + 2A + B + 2$$

Explain briefly. Other than using your rectangle, how else can you see that the equation is true?

Class Activity 9J: Equations about Related Quantities

1. To make concrete, you need 3 times as much sand as cement. When Aaron was asked to formulate an equation about concrete, here's what he wrote:

$S =$ sand, $C =$ cement

$3S = C$

Discuss Aaron's work. How should he revise it?

2. Describe quantities that are related by the equation

$$y = 2x$$

State clearly the meaning of y and of x and explain briefly why the equation applies.

Class Activity 9K: Equations for Story Problems

1. For each of the following story situations, write the corresponding equation:

   a. Markus had M dollars in his bank account. After removing $\frac{1}{5}$ of the money in the account and then putting in another $200, Markus now has $800.

   b. Keisha had K dollars in her bank account. After removing $200 and then removing $\frac{1}{5}$ of the remaining money, Keisha now has $800.

   c. Originally, there were L liters of liquid in a container. After $\frac{2}{3}$ of the liquid was poured out, another $2\frac{1}{2}$ liters of liquid was poured into the container. When $\frac{1}{4}$ of the liquid was poured out, 4 liters remained.

2. For each of the following equations, write a corresponding story problem. Be sure to define x in each case.

   a. $x - \dfrac{1}{4}x + 30 = 150$

   b. $x - \dfrac{1}{4} + 30 = 150$

   c. $(x + 30) - \dfrac{1}{4}(x + 30) = 150$

   d. $\dfrac{2}{3}(x - 60) + 20 = 80$

9.3 Solving Equations

Class Activity 9L: Solving Equations Using Number Sense

Solve each of the equations by using your understanding of numbers and operations. Do not use any standard algebraic techniques for solving equations that you may know. Explain your reasoning in each case.

1. $382 + 49 = x + 380$

2. $12 \cdot 84 = 2 \cdot 84 + A$

3. $14Z = 7 \cdot 48$

4. $7 \cdot 36 + T = 8 \cdot 37$

Class Activity 9M: Solving Equations Algebraically and with a Pan Balance

Solve $5x + 1 = 2x + 7$ in two ways, with equations and with pictures of a pan balance. Relate the two methods.

with equations   with a pan balance

$5x + 1 = 2x + 7$

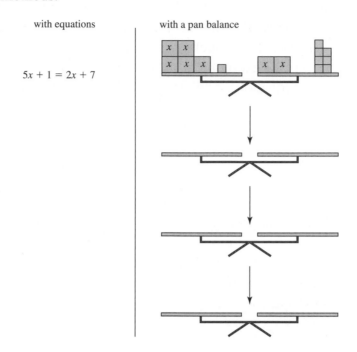

9.4 Solving Algebra Story Problems with Strip Diagrams and with Algebra

Class Activity 9N: How Many Pencils Were There?

In the morning, Ms. Wilkins put some pencils for her students in a pencil box. After a while, Ms. Wilkins found that $\frac{1}{2}$ of the pencils were gone. A little later, Ms. Wilkins found that $\frac{1}{3}$ of the pencils that were left from when she checked before were gone. Still later, Ms. Wilkins found that $\frac{1}{4}$ of the pencils that were left from the last time she checked were gone. At that point there were 15 pencils left. No pencils were ever added to the pencil box. How many pencils did Ms. Wilkins put in the pencil box in the morning?

Solve this problem in as many different ways as you can think of, and explain each solution. Try to relate your different solution methods to each other.

Class Activity 9O: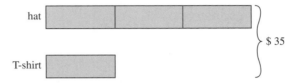
Solving Story Problems with Strip Diagrams and with Equations

The problems in this activity were inspired by problems in the mathematics textbooks used in Singapore in grades 4–6 (see [12], volumes 4A–6B).

1. At a store, a hat costs 3 times as much as a T-shirt. Together, the hat and T-shirt cost $35. How much does the T-shirt cost?

    Solve this problem in two ways: by using the strip diagram shown here and with equations. Explain both solution methods, and discuss how they are related.

2. There are 180 blankets at a shelter. The blankets are divided into two groups. There are 30 more blankets in the first group than in the second group. How many blankets are in the second group?

    Solve this problem in two ways: by using the strip diagram shown here and with equations. Explain both solution methods, and discuss how they are related.

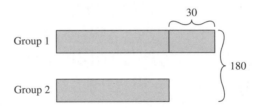

3. On a farm, $\frac{1}{7}$ of the sheep are grey, $\frac{2}{7}$ of the sheep are black, and the rest of the sheep are white. There are 36 white sheep. How many sheep in all are on the farm?

    Solve this problem in two ways: by using the strip diagram shown here and with equations. Explain both solution methods, and discuss how they are related.

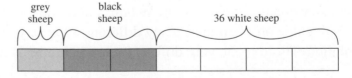

4. Ms. Jones gave $\frac{1}{4}$ of her money to charity and $\frac{1}{2}$ of the remainder to her mother. Then Ms. Jones had \$240 left. How much money did Ms. Jones have at first?

   Solve this problem in two ways: by using the strip diagram shown here and with equations. Explain both solution methods, and discuss how they are related.

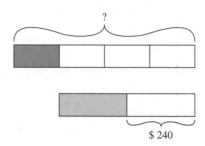

5. When a box of chocolates was full, it weighed 1.1 kilograms. After $\frac{1}{2}$ of the chocolates were eaten, the box (with the remaining chocolates) weighed 0.7 kilograms. How much did the box weigh without the chocolates?

   Solve this problem in two ways: with the aid of a strip diagram and with equations. Explain both solution methods, and discuss how they are related.

6. Quint had 4 times as many math problems to do as Agustin. After Quint did 20 problems and Agustin did 2 problems, they each had the same number of math problems left to do. How many math problems did Quint have to do at first?

   Solve this problem in two ways: by using the strip diagram shown here and with equations. Explain both solution methods, and discuss how they are related.

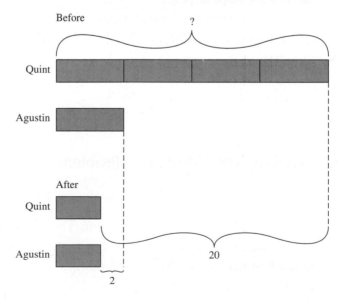

7. Carmen spent $\frac{1}{6}$ of her money on a CD. Then Carmen had $45 left. How much money did Carmen have at first?

   Solve this problem in two ways: with the aid of a strip diagram and with equations. Explain both solution methods, and discuss how they are related.

8. There were 25 more girls than boys at a party. All together, 105 children were at the party. How many boys were at the party? How many girls were at the party?

   Solve this problem in two ways: with the aid of a strip diagram and with equations. Explain both solution methods, and discuss how they are related.

9. There were 10% more girls than boys at a party. All together, 168 children were at the party. How many boys were at the party? How many girls were at the party?

   Solve this problem in two ways: with the aid of a strip diagram and with equations. Explain both solution methods, and discuss how they are related.

10. A bakery sold $\frac{3}{5}$ of its muffins. The remaining muffins were divided equally among the 3 employees. Each employee got 16 muffins. How many muffins did the bakery have at first?

   Solve this problem in two ways: with the aid of a strip diagram and with equations. Explain both solution methods, and discuss how they are related.

Class Activity 9P: Modifying Problems

1. Recall part 2 from Class Activity 9O:

   There are 180 blankets at a shelter. The blankets are divided into two groups. There are 30 more blankets in the first group than in the second group. How many blankets are in the second group?

a. Suppose you want to modify the blanket problem for your students by changing the numbers 180 and 30 to different numbers. Can you change the numbers any way you want and still have a sensible problem? Explain.

b. Suppose you want to modify the blanket problem for your students so that the blankets will be divided into 3 unequal groups instead of 2 groups. Write such a modified problem, making sure that it can be solved. Show two different ways to solve your problem.

2. Recall the pencil problem from Class Activity 9N:

In the morning, Ms. Wilkins put some pencils for her students in a pencil box. After a while, Ms. Wilkins found that $\frac{1}{2}$ of the pencils were gone. A little later, Ms. Wilkins found that $\frac{1}{3}$ of the pencils that were left from when she checked before were gone. Still later, Ms. Wilkins found that $\frac{1}{4}$ of the pencils that were left from the last time she checked were gone. At that point there were 15 pencils left. No pencils were ever added to the pencil box. How many pencils did Ms. Wilkins put in the pencil box in the morning?

a. Suppose you want to modify the pencil problem for your students by changing the number 15 to a different number. Which numbers could you replace the 15 in the problem with and still have a sensible problem (without changing anything else in the problem)? Explain.

b. Experiment with changing some or all of the fractions—$\frac{1}{2}$, $\frac{1}{3}$, and $\frac{1}{4}$—in the problem to some other "easy" fractions. When you make a change, do you also need to change the number 15? Which changes make the problem harder? Which changes make the problem easier?

Class Activity 9Q: Solving Story Problems

The story problems in this activity are taken from Class Activity 9K. Solve each problem, either with the aid of a diagram or by using equations. Explain your reasoning.

1. Markus had M dollars in his bank account. After removing $\frac{1}{5}$ of the money in the account and then putting in another $200, Markus now has $800. How much money did Markus have initially?

2. Keisha had K dollars in her bank account. After removing $200 and then removing $\frac{1}{5}$ of the remaining money, Keisha now has $800. How many dollars did Keisha have in her bank account before removing any money?

3. Originally, there were L liters of liquid in a container. After $\frac{2}{3}$ of the liquid was poured out, another $2\frac{1}{2}$ liters of liquid was poured into the container. When $\frac{1}{4}$ of the liquid was poured out, 4 liters remained. What was the original amount of liquid in the container?

9.5 Sequences

Class Activity 9R:
Arithmetic Sequences of Numbers Corresponding to Sequences of Figures

1. In the following sequence of figures made up of small squares, assume that the sequence continues by adding 4 shaded squares to the top of a figure in order to get the next figure in the sequence:

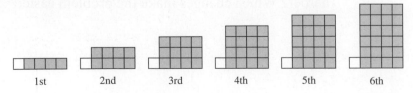

1st   2nd   3rd   4th   5th   6th

a. In the next table, write the number of small squares making up each figure. Imagine that the sequence of figures continues forever, so that for each counting number N, there is an Nth figure. What is a formula for the number of small squares in the Nth figure? Add this information to the table.

Position of Figure	Number of Small Squares in Figure
1st	
2nd	
3rd	
4th	
5th	
6th	
7th	
⋮	⋮
Nth	

b. Relate the structure of the formula you found in part (a) to the structure of the previous figures. Explain why your formula makes sense by relating your formula to the structure of the figures.

c. How many small squares will make up the 25th figure in the sequence? How can you tell?

d. Will there be a figure in the sequence that is made of 250 small squares? If yes, which one? If no, why not? Answer these questions in two ways: with algebra and in a way that a student in elementary school might be able to understand.

e. Will there be a figure in the sequence that is made of 85 small squares? Will there be a figure in the sequence that is made of 403 small squares? If yes, which one? If no, why not? Answer these questions in two ways: with algebra and in a way that a student in elementary school might be able to understand.

2. In the following sequence of figures made of small circles, assume that the sequence continues by adding a white circle to the end of each of the three "arms" of a figure in order to get the next figure in the sequence.

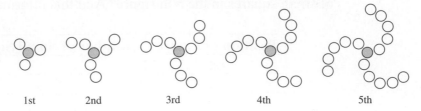

| 1st | 2nd | 3rd | 4th | 5th |

a. In the next table, write the number of small circles that the previous figures are made of.

Imagine that the sequence of figures continues forever, so that for each counting number N, there is an Nth figure. What is a formula for the number of small circles in the Nth pattern? Add this information to your table.

Position of Figure	Number of Small Circles in Figure
1st	
2nd	
3rd	
4th	
5th	
6th	
⋮	⋮
Nth	

b. Relate the structure of the formula you found in part (a) to the structure of the figures. Explain why your formula makes sense by relating your formula to the structure of the figures.

c. How many small circles will the 38th figure in the sequence be made of? How can you tell?

d. Will there be a figure in the sequence that is made of 100 small circles? If yes, which one? If no, why not? Answer these questions in two ways: with algebra and in a way that a student in elementary school might be able to understand.

e. Will there be a figure in the sequence that is made of 125 small circles? If yes, which one? If no, why not? Answer these questions in two ways: with algebra and in a way that a student in elementary school might be able to understand.

Class Activity 9S: How Are Formulas for Arithmetic Sequences Related to the Way Sequences Start and Grow?

This activity will help you notice an interesting connection between the way an arithmetic sequence starts and grows and the formula for the Nth term of the sequence (In the next activity, you'll explain why arithmetic sequences must always have formulas of a specific type.)

1. For each of the next arithmetic sequences, guess a formula for the Nth entry. Then check your guesses.

   First sequence, increasing by 4

   5, 9, 13, 17, . . . Nth entry

   Second sequence, increasing by 4

   7, 11, 15, 19, . . . Nth entry

   Third sequence, increasing by 5

   7, 12, 17, 22, . . . Nth entry

2. For each sequence in part 1, compare the formula you guessed with the way the sequence increases. What relationship do you notice?

3. For each sequence in part 1, compare the formula you guessed with the first entry of the sequence. What relationship do you notice?

4. Based on your observations in parts 2 and 3, guess the formulas for the Nth entries of the next sequences. Then check your guesses.

Fourth sequence, increasing by 3

1, 4, 7, 10, . . . Nth entry

Fifth sequence, decreasing by 4

7, 3, −1, −5, . . . Nth entry

Class Activity 9T:
Explaining Formulas for Arithmetic Sequences

1. The next table shows some entries for an arithmetic sequence whose first entry is 5 and that increases by 3.

Entry Number	Entry
1st	5
2nd	8
3rd	11
4th	14
5th	17
Nth	

  a. If there were a 0th entry, what would it be? Put it in the previous table.

  b. Fill in the blanks to describe how to get entries in the sequence by *starting from the 0th entry*.

   • To find the 1st entry: Start at ___ and add___1 time.

   • To find the 2nd entry: Start at ___ and add ___ 2 times.

   • To find the 3rd entry: Start at ___ and add ___ 3 times.

   • To find the 4th entry: Start at ___ and add ___ 4 times.

   • To find the 5th entry: Start at ___ and add ___ 5 times.

   • To find the Nth entry: Start at ___ and add ___ N times.

  c. For each bullet in part (b), write an expression (using addition and multiplication) that corresponds to the description for finding the entry in the sequence.

   1st entry =

   2nd entry =

   3rd entry =

   4th entry =

   5th entry =

   Nth entry =

2. The next table shows some entries for an arithmetic sequence whose first entry is 1 and that increases by 4.

Entry Number	Entry
1st	1
2nd	5
3rd	9
4th	13
5th	17
Nth	

a. If there were a 0th entry, what would it be? Put it in the previous table.

b. Fill in the blanks to describe how to get entries in the sequence by *starting from the 0th entry.*

   • To find the 1st entry: Start at ____ and add ____ 1 time.

   • To find the 2nd entry: Start at ____ and add ____ 2 times.

   • To find the 3rd entry: Start at ____ and add ____ 3 times.

   • To find the 4th entry: Start at ____ and add ____ 4 times.

   • To find the 5th entry: Start at ____ and add ____ 5 times.

   • To find the Nth entry: Start at ____ and add ____ N times.

c. For each bullet in part (b), write an expression (using addition and multiplication) that corresponds to the description for finding the entry in the sequence.

   1st entry =

   2nd entry =

   3rd entry =

   4th entry =

   5th entry =

   Nth entry =

Class Activity 9U: Geometric Sequences

1. Write a formula for a sequence whose first few entries are the number of small squares in the next sequence of figures. Explain why you wrote your formula as you did.

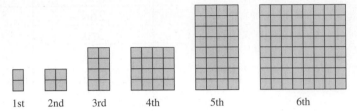

1st   2nd   3rd   4th   5th   6th

2. Write a formula for a sequence whose first few entries are the number of small squares in the next sequence of figures. Explain why you wrote your formula as you did.

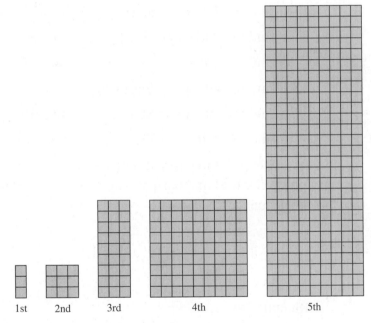

1st   2nd   3rd   4th   5th

3. Suppose you owe $1000 on your credit card and that the credit card company charges you 1.4708% interest every month. That is, at the end of each month an additional 1.4708% of the amount you owe is added to the amount you owe. (This is what would happen if your credit card charged an annual percentage rate of 17.6496%.) Let's assume that you do not pay off any of this debt or the interest that is added to it. Let's also assume that you don't add any more debt other than the interest that you are charged.

a. Fill in the next table to show how much you owe at the end of 1 month, 2 months, and so on, up to 12 months. Explain why you can get each entry from the previous entry by multiplying by 1.014708.

Month	Amount You Owe at End of Month	Month	Amount You Owe at End of Month
1		7	
2		8	
3		9	
4		10	
5		11	
6		12	

b. Determine how much you will owe at the end of 24 months without finding how much you will owe at the end of 13 months, 14 months, 15 months, and so on.

c. Write a formula for the amount of money you will owe at the end of N months. Explain why your formula is valid.

d. Use your formula from part (c) to determine how much money you will owe after 4 years.

Class Activity 9V:
Repeating Patterns

1. Even very young children can work with repeating patterns. For example, see the activities in *Navigating Through Algebra in Prekindergarten–Grade 2* by the National Council of Teachers of Mathematics [8]. Some of the problems that follow are similar to some of the problems described in that publication.

   a. Assume that the following pattern of a square followed by 3 circles and 2 triangles continues to repeat:

   What will be the 100th shape in the pattern? Explain how you can tell.

b. How many circles will there be among the first 150 entries of the given sequence? Explain your reasoning.

c. To answer part (b), Amanda says that since there are 6 circles among the first 10 shapes, and since 150 is 15 sets of 10, there will be $15 \times 6 = 90$ circles among the first 150 entries. Is Amanda's reasoning correct? Why or why not?

2. On a train, the seats are numbered as indicated below. Assume the numbering of the seats continues in this way and that all rows are arranged in the same way. Will seat number 43 be a window seat or an aisle seat? What about seat number 137? What about seat number 294? Describe different ways that you can figure out the answers to these questions.

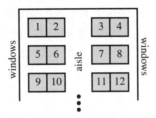

3. What day of the week will it be 100 days from today? Determine the answer with math. Explain your reasoning. How is this problem related to repeating patterns?

4. Five friends are sitting in a circle as shown. Antrice sings a song that has 22 syllables and, starting with Benton, and going clockwise, points to one person for each syllable of the song. The last person that Antrice points to will be "it."

a. Who will be "it"? Explain how to predict the answer by using math.

b. If Fran comes and sits between Ellie and Antrice before Antrice sings her song, who will be "it"?

    c. Antrice switches to a song that has 24 syllables. Now who will be "it"? Use math to predict!

5. What is the digit in the ones place of 2^{100}? Explain how you can tell.

Class Activity 9W: Comparing and Contrasting Sequences

This activity concerns the following three sequences:

        The first sequence is the one whose Nth entry is $2N$.

        The second sequence is the one whose Nth entry is 2^N.

        The third sequence is the one whose Nth entry is N^2.

1. Write the first 7 numbers in each of the 3 sequences.

2. Informally discuss the following: How do the sequences grow? In other words, how do these sequences change in going from one entry to the next? Contrast the way the sequences grow.

3. Draw a sequence of figures made of small circles so that the Nth figure in the sequence is made of $2N$ small circles.

Draw another sequence of figures made of small circles or small squares so that the Nth figure in the sequence is made of N^2 small circles or small squares.

4. How is the structure of the figures you drew in part 3 related to the formulas for the sequences and the way the sequences grow?

Class Activity 9X:
The Fibonacci Sequence in Nature and Art

You will need pine cones or pineapples for part 1. You will need a ruler for parts 2 and 3. You will need graph paper for part 4.

The Fibonacci sequence is

$$1, \quad 1, \quad 2, \quad 3, \quad 5, \quad 8, \quad 13, \quad 21, \quad 34, \ldots$$

Each entry in the sequence is obtained by adding the previous two entries.

1. Look closely at a pine cone or pineapple. You should see two sets of "swirls." One set swirls around clockwise; the other set swirls around counterclockwise. Count the number of swirls in each set. These numbers are usually consecutive Fibonacci numbers.

2. Measure the lengths of the indicated bones in your body, rounded to the nearest inch, and record the results in the next table. Use the same finger for all finger measurements.

Bone Connecting	Length of Bone
shoulder and elbow	
elbow and wrist	
wrist and first knuckle	
first knuckle and second knuckle	
second knuckle and third knuckle	
third knuckle and fingertip	

Compare the lengths of your bones in inches with the Fibonacci sequence.

3. Draw a rectangle whose proportions are pleasing to your eye. Carefully measure the length and width of your rectangle. Then divide the length (the longer measurement) by the width (the shorter measurement). Is this ratio close to the ratios of the following consecutive Fibonacci numbers?

$$\frac{3}{2} = 1.5, \quad \frac{5}{3} = 1.67, \quad \frac{8}{5} = 1.6, \quad \frac{13}{8} = 1.625$$

4. The beginning of a sequence of rectangles is shown next. The sequence starts with a 1-unit-by-1-unit square. To create the next rectangle in the sequence, attach a square to the previous rectangle. Attach the square either below the rectangle or to the right of the rectangle, alternating between attaching it below and attaching it to the right.

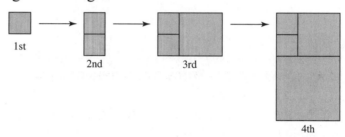

1st   2nd   3rd   4th

a. On graph paper, draw the next two rectangles in the sequence.

b. Do you find the proportions of these rectangles pleasing to your eye?

c. What are the lengths and widths of rectangles in this sequence?

Class Activity 9Y: What's the Next Entry?

For each of the next sequences, find 3 different rules for determining the next 3 entries in the sequence. In each case, describe the rule you use.

1.

    2, 4, 8, ___, ___, ___,
    2, 4, 8, ___, ___, ___,
    2, 4, 8, ___, ___, ___,

2.

2, 5, 11, ___, ___, ___,

2, 5, 11, ___, ___, ___,

2, 5, 11, ___, ___, ___,

3.

2, 3, 6, ___, ___, ___,

2, 3, 6, ___, ___, ___,

2, 3, 6, ___, ___, ___,

9.6 Series ↻

Class Activity 9Z: Sums of Powers of Two

Is there a quick way to add a bunch of consecutive powers of 2? This activity will help you find and explain a formula.

1. Calculate the next sums.

$$1 + 2 = \underline{\hphantom{XX}}$$
$$1 + 2 + 4 = \underline{\hphantom{XX}}$$
$$1 + 2 + 4 + 8 = \underline{\hphantom{XX}}$$
$$1 + 2 + 4 + 8 + 16 = \underline{\hphantom{XX}}$$

2. Based on part 1, predict the sum of the following geometric series without adding all the terms:

$$1 + 2 + 4 + 8 + 16 + 32 + 64 + 128 + 256 + 512$$

3. Based on part 1, predict a formula in terms of N for the following geometric series (fill in the blank with an appropriate expression):

$$1 + 2 + 2^2 + 2^3 + 2^4 + \cdots + 2^N = \underline{\hphantom{XXX}}$$

4. Use Figure 9Z.1 to help you explain why your formula in part 3 should be true.

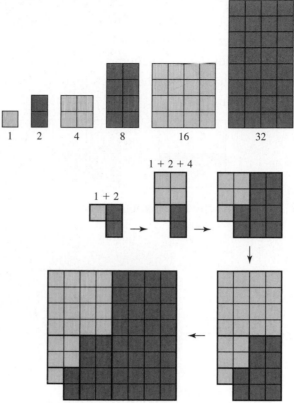

Figure 9Z.1 Sums of powers of 2

5. Here is a systematic way to find a formula for the sum of the geometric series in part 3: Let S be this sum, so that

$$S = 1 + 2 + 2^2 + 2^3 + 2^4 + \cdots + 2^N$$

Use the distributive property to write $2S$ as a series (fill in the blank with a series):

$$2S = 2 \cdot (1 + 2 + 2^2 + 2^3 + 2^4 + \cdots + 2^N)$$

$$= \underline{\hspace{5cm}}$$

Now calculate $2S - S$ in the following two ways, in terms of S and as a series:

$2S - S$ in terms of S: $2S - S$ as a series:

$$2S$$

$$\underline{-S} \qquad\qquad \underline{-1 - 2 - 2^2 - 2^3 - 2^4 + \cdots - 2^N}$$

The two results you get must be equal, so you get an equation. What does this equation tell you about S?

Class Activity 9AA: An Infinite Geometric Series

Is it possible to calculate an infinite sum of numbers? Surprisingly, the answer is yes, as you will see in this activity.

Assume that the next sequence of partially shaded squares continues indefinitely, in such a way that we get the next square in the sequence by shading $\frac{1}{2}$ of the unshaded part of a square.

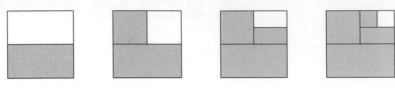

1. Explain why the shaded portions of the 2nd, 3rd, and 4th squares in the sequence are

$$\frac{1}{2} + \left(\frac{1}{2}\right)^2$$

$$\frac{1}{2} + \left(\frac{1}{2}\right)^2 + \left(\frac{1}{2}\right)^3$$

$$\frac{1}{2} + \left(\frac{1}{2}\right)^2 + \left(\frac{1}{2}\right)^3 + \left(\frac{1}{2}\right)^4$$

2. What fraction of the square is shaded in the 2nd, 3rd, and 4th figures? Give each answer in simplest form. Based on your results, predict what fraction of the Nth square is shaded.

3. Based on your work in part 2, when would you reach a square that is at least 99.9% shaded?

4. Based on the sequence of shaded squares, what would you expect the infinite sum

$$\frac{1}{2} + \left(\frac{1}{2}\right)^2 + \left(\frac{1}{2}\right)^3 + \left(\frac{1}{2}\right)^4 + \left(\frac{1}{2}\right)^5 + \cdots$$

to be equal to?

5. Here is a way to calculate the infinite sum in part 4. Let S stand for this sum. In other words,

$$S = \frac{1}{2} + \left(\frac{1}{2}\right)^2 + \left(\frac{1}{2}\right)^3 + \left(\frac{1}{2}\right)^4 + \left(\frac{1}{2}\right)^5 + \cdots$$

Assuming that there is an "infinite distributive property," write $\frac{1}{2}S$ as an infinite sum (fill in the blank):

$$\frac{1}{2}S = \frac{1}{2} \cdot \left(\frac{1}{2} + \left(\frac{1}{2}\right)^2 + \left(\frac{1}{2}\right)^3 + \left(\frac{1}{2}\right)^4 + \cdots \right)$$

$$= \underline{\hspace{8cm}}$$

Now calculate $S - \frac{1}{2}S$ in two ways, in terms of S and as a series:

in terms of S: as a series:

$$S$$ $\frac{1}{2} + (\frac{1}{2})^2 + (\frac{1}{2})^3 + (\frac{1}{2})^4 + (\frac{1}{2})^5 + \cdots$

$$-\frac{1}{2}S$$ $\underline{\hspace{6cm}}$

The two results you get must be equal, so you get an equation. Solve this equation for S.

Class Activity 9BB: Making Payments Into an Account

You will need a calculator for this activity.

Suppose that at the beginning of every month, you make a payment of $200 into an account that earns 1% interest per month. (That is, the value of the account at the end of the month is 1% higher than it was at the beginning of the month.)

1. Make a guess: After making your 12th payment at the beginning of the 12th month, how much money will be in the account? (The remaining parts of this activity will help you calculate this amount exactly.)

2. Explain why the entries shown in the right-hand column in the next table are correct. Then fill in the remaining columns with series similar to those in the first 3 rows. (You may use "…" within your series in the last row.)

Month	Amount at Beginning of Month (After Payment)
1	200
2	$200 + (1.01)200$
3	$200 + (1.01)200 + (1.01)^2 200$
4	
5	
6	
⋮	⋮
12	

3. Let S be the series you wrote in the last row of the right column in part 2. Use the distributive property to write $(1.01)S$ as a series.

4. Calculate $(1.01)S - S$ in two ways: in terms of S and as a series.

5. The two results you get in part 4 must be equal, so you get an equation. Solve this equation for S. Compare the result with your guess in part 1.

9.7 Functions

Class Activity 9CC:
Interpreting Graphs of Functions

1. Items (a) through (f) are hypothetical descriptions of a population of fish. Each description corresponds to a population function, for which the input is time elapsed since the fish population was first measured, and the output is the population of fish at that time. Match the descriptions of these population functions to the graphs in Figure 9CC.1. In each case, explain why the shape of the graph fits with the description of the function.

a. The population of fish rose slowly at first, and then rose more and more rapidly.

b. The population of fish rose rapidly at first, and then rose more and more slowly.

c. The population of fish rose at a steady rate.

d. The population of fish dropped rapidly at first, and then dropped more and more slowly.

e. The population of fish dropped slowly at first, and then dropped more and more rapidly.

f. The population of fish dropped at a steady rate.

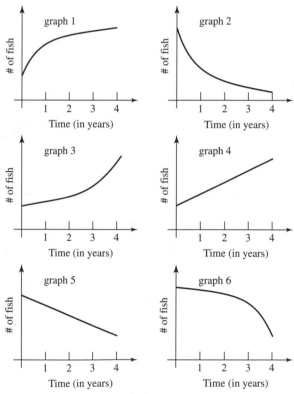

Figure 9CC.1 Fish populations

2. Hot water is poured into a mug and left to cool. This situation gives rise to a temperature function for which the input is the time elapsed since pouring the water into the mug and the output is the temperature of the water at that time. The

graph of this function is one of the three graphs shown next. Which graph do you think it is, and why? For each graph, describe how water would cool according to that graph.

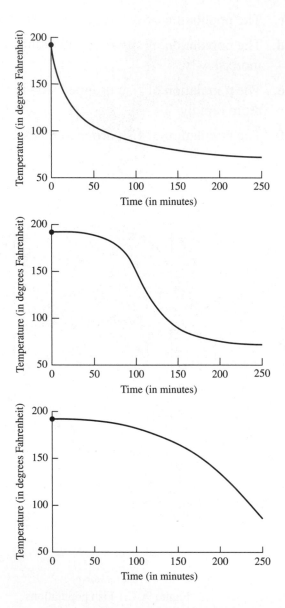

Which graph is the correct one for part 2? See page 224.

3. A tagged manatee swims up a river, away from a dock. Meanwhile, the manatee's tag transmits its distance from the dock. This situation gives rise to a distance function for which the input is the time since the manatee first swam away from

the dock and the output is the manatee's distance from the dock at that time. The graph of this distance function is shown below.

Write a story about the manatee that fits with this graph. Explain how features of the graph fit with your story.

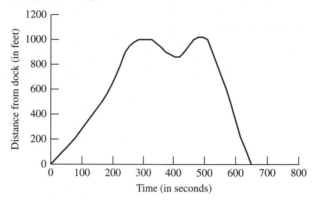

Class Activity 9DD: Are These Graphs Correct?

1. Carl started to drive from Providence to Boston, but after leaving he realized that he had forgotten something and drove back to Providence. Then Carl got back in his car and drove straight to Boston. This scenario gives rise to a distance function whose input is time elapsed since Carl first started to drive to Boston and whose output is Carl's distance from Providence. Could the next graph be the graph of the distance function described? Why or why not? If not, draw a different graph that could be the graph of the distance function. (Boston is 50 miles from Providence.)

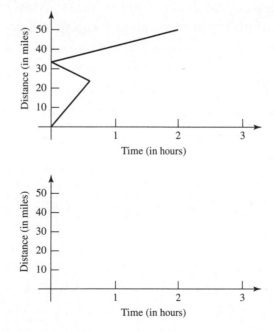

2. Here is what happened when Jenny ran a mile in 10 minutes. She got off to a good start, and ran faster and faster. Then all of a sudden, Jenny tripped. Once Jenny got back up, she started to run again, but at a slower pace. But near the end of her mile run, Jenny picked up some speed.

    The next graph is supposed to fit with the story about Jenny's mile run. What is wrong with this graph?

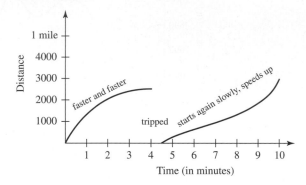

3. Describe two functions that the story about Jenny's mile run in part 2 could give rise to. In each case, describe the inputs and corresponding outputs. Sketch graphs that could be the graphs of these two functions.

    The correct graph on p. 222 is the first graph.

9.8 Linear Functions

Class Activity 9EE:
A Function Arising from Proportions

To make a certain shade of pink paint, for every 2 cups of white paint, you will produce 3 cups of pink paint by adding 1 cup of red paint to the white paint. So the ratio of white paint to pink paint is 2 to 3. This situation gives rise to a "pink-paint function" for which the input is the number of cups of white paint and the output is the number of cups of pink paint produced for that amount of white paint.

1. Make a table, and draw a graph of the pink-paint function described. Be sure to label your axes appropriately.

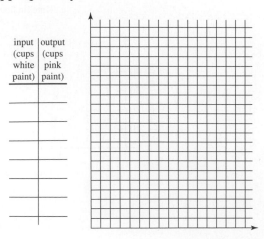

2. Fill in the blank to make a true statement about the pink-paint function:

   "Whenever the input increases by 2, the output _____."

   Explain how this statement is reflected in the table and the graph of the pink-paint function.

3. Fill in the blank to make a true statement about the pink-paint function:

   "Whenever the input increases by 1, the output _____."

   Explain how this statement is reflected in the graph of the pink-paint function.

4. Let x stand for the number of cups of white paint. Let P be the pink-paint function, so that $P(x)$ is the number of cups of pink paint when x cups of white paint are used. Write a formula for $P(x)$, and describe how this formula is related to your answer for part 3.

Class Activity 9FF: Arithmetic Sequences as Functions

Every sequence can be viewed as a function that associates to the input N, the output which is the Nth entry in the sequence. Arithmetic sequences give rise to special kinds of functions.

1. Consider the arithmetic sequence

$$3, 5, 7, 9, 11, 13, \ldots$$

a. Make a table, find a formula, and draw a graph for the function associated with the arithmetic sequence.

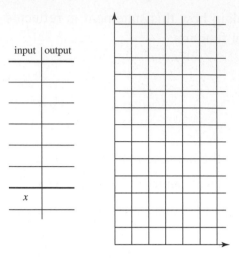

input	output
x	

b. Fill in the blank to make a true statement about the function in part (a):

"Whenever the input increases by 1, the output _____."

How is this statement reflected in the table and the graph of the function?

c. In part (a), how are components of the formula reflected in the graph?

2. Consider the arithmetic sequence

$$2.5, 3, 3.5, 4, 4.5, 5, \ldots$$

a. Make a table, find a formula, and draw a graph for the function associated with the arithmetic sequence.

input	output
x	

b. Fill in the blank to make a true statement about the function in part (a):

"Whenever the input increases by 1, the output _____."

How is this statement reflected in the table and the graph of the function?

c. In part (a), how are components of the formula reflected in the graph?

3. What do you think the graphs of arithmetic sequences all have in common?

Class Activity 9GG: Analyzing the Way Functions Change

1. You will need graph paper for parts of this activity.

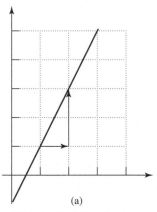

(a)

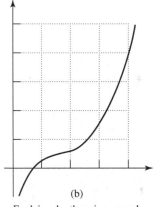

(b)

Fill in the blank to make a
true statement about graph (a):
"Whenever the input increases by 1
the output _____ "
Explain why the statement is true.

Explain why there is no number
you can place in the blank to
make a true statement about
graph (b):
"Whenever the input increases by 1
the output increases by _____"

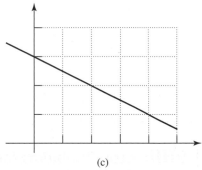

(c)

Fill in the blank to make a true statement about graph (c):
"Whenever the input increases by 1 the output _____ "
Explain why the statement is true.

2. Consider a function that has the following properties:

- When the input is 1, the output is 5.

- Whenever the input increases by 1, the output increases by 3.

    a. Make a table and draw the graph of a function that has the properties described.

    b. Explain how the properties in the previous two bulleted items are reflected in the graph of the function.

    c. Find a formula for a function that has the properties described.

3. Consider a function that has the following properties:
   - When the input is 0, the output is 0.
   - Whenever the input increases by 3, the output increases by 7.

    a. Make a table and draw the graph of a function that has the properties described.

    b. Explain how the properties in the previous two bulleted items are reflected in the graph of the function.

    c. Find a formula for a function that has the properties described.

Class Activity 9HH: Story Problems for Linear Functions

You will need graph paper for part 1(b).

1. There will be a raffle at the fall festival. The fall festival committee spent $45 on prizes for the raffle. Raffle tickets will be sold for $1.50 each.

    a. Describe a function that arises from this situation.

    b. Make a table and draw a graph of your function in part (a).

c. Find a formula for your function in part (a), and explain why your formula is valid.

d. Where does the graph of your function in part (b) cross the x-axis? What is the significance of this point in terms of the raffle?

2. Write a story problem which gives rise to a function, f, that has the formula $f(x) = 3x + 5$. Explain why your function has that formula.

3. Write a story problem which gives rise to a function, g, that has the formula $g(x) = \frac{3}{5}x$.

Class Activity 9II: Deriving the Formula for Temperature in Degrees Fahrenheit in Terms of Degrees Celsius

1. For each pair of numbers, determine the number that is halfway between the two numbers. In each case, explain why your answer is correct.

    a. 0 and 14

    b. 0 and 11

    c. 0 and b

    d. 2 and 14

    e. 2 and 11

    f. 2 and b

    g. a and b

2. For each pair of numbers, determine the number that is $\frac{1}{3}$ of the way between the two numbers (and closer to the first number). In each case, explain why your answer is correct.

    a. 0 and 12

    b. 0 and 11

    c. 0 and b

    d. 2 and 14

    e. 2 and 12

    f. 2 and b

    g. a and b

3. For each pair of numbers, determine the number that is 40% of the way between the two numbers (and closer to the first number). In each case, explain why your answer is correct.

    a. 0 and 120

    b. 0 and b

    c. 20 and 170

    d. 20 and b

    e. a and b

4. Water freezes at 0° Celsius, which is 32° Fahrenheit, and boils at 100° Celsius, which is 212° Fahrenheit. Given that 40° Celsius is 40% of the way between 0° Celsius and 100° Celsius, what is 40° Celsius in degrees Fahrenheit? Answer this question based on your work in part 3.

5. Based on your work in part 3, write an expression for the number that is P% of the way between a and b. Explain why your expression fits with your work in part 3.

6. Based on your work in previous parts of this problem, write a formula to convert C° Celsius to degrees Fahrenheit. Your formula should be in terms of C. Explain why your formula is correct. (You may assume that C is between 0 and 100, but the correct formula will be valid for other values of C as well.)

Geometry

10.1 Visualization

Class Activity 10A: Visualizing Lines and Planes

1. Visualize a line in a plane. The line divides the plane into 2 disjoint pieces—visualize these 2 pieces as well. Visualize a line in space. Does a line in space divide space into disjoint pieces? The word *disjoint* means distinct and not meeting.

2. Visualize 2 lines in a plane. How many disjoint pieces do the 2 lines divide the plane into? The answer depends on how the lines are positioned relative to each other. Explain. Draw pictures to aid your explanation but be sure to also "see" this in your mind's eye.

3. Visualize 3 lines in a plane. How many disjoint pieces do the 3 lines divide the plane into? Again, the answer depends on how the lines are positioned relative to each other. Try to *visualize* the distinct configurations. Then draw pictures to help you show all the different types of configurations and to see how many disjoint pieces there are in each case.

4. Visualize a plane in space. A single plane in three-dimensional space divides space into 2 disjoint regions. If the plane you are thinking of is horizontal, then these 2 regions are the region above the plane and the region below the plane. Visualize a nonhorizontal plane and the 2 distinct regions into which it divides space.

5. Visualize 2 planes in space. Into how many disjoint regions do 2 planes divide space? The answer depends on how the planes are arranged relative to each other. Explain. Use 2 pieces of paper to help you but be sure to try to "see" the planes in your mind's eye.

6. Visualize 3 planes in space. Into how many disjoint regions do 3 planes divide space? As always, the answer depends on how the planes are arranged in space. Describe the different types of configurations, and make paper models to help you. (You will probably want to cut the paper and use tape.) Be sure to also *visualize* these different types of configurations. How can you tell whether you've found all the different possibilities for disjoint regions?

Class Activity 10B: The Rotation of the Earth and Time Zones

A table-tennis ball and a flashlight would be useful for part 2. A larger ball such as a basketball, or better yet, a globe, can be used to demonstrate to the whole class.

The surface of the earth is divided into different time zones. For example, the continental United States has 4 time zones: Eastern, Central, Mountain, and Pacific. This activity will help you explain why it makes sense to have different time zones and how times vary as you move about the world.

1. Visualize the earth in space, rotating about the axis through the North and South Poles. The earth completes a full rotation about its axis every 24 hours (approximately). Visualize the sun, far away, sending light rays to illuminate the portion of the earth that is facing the sun. Figures 10B.1 and 10B.2 may help.

2. If available, a flashlight and a table-tennis ball can be used to simulate the sun and the earth. Hold the table-tennis ball between two fingers, more or less vertically, at points representing the North and South Poles. Shine the flashlight on the side of the ball. If you have a globe, picture the sun rays coming from one side of

the room, illuminating one side of the globe. On your table-tennis ball, or globe, where is it about noon? Where is it about midnight?

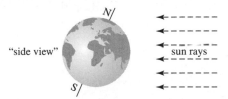

Figure 10B.1 Earth

3. Given that the sun rises in the east, approximately what time of day is it at locations A, B, C, and D in Figure 10B.2, in which the earth is pictured as seen from above the North Pole? Explain.

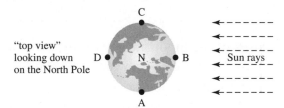

Figure 10B.2 The earth seen from above the North Pole

4. Now go back to your globe or table-tennis ball as in part 2. Where is it sunrise and where is it sunset? Explain.

5. Viewed from outer space, looking down on the North Pole, which way does the earth rotate, clockwise or counterclockwise? Use parts 3 and 4 to explain your answer.

6. Explain why it makes sense that the time on the east coast of the United States should be different from the time on the west coast of the United States. Is it earlier on the west coast than on the east coast, or is it later? Explain why, using your previous work.

Class Activity 10C:
Explaining the Phases of the Moon

Every month the moon goes through phases, waxing from a new moon to a full moon and then waning from a full moon back to a new moon, as shown in the following diagram:

new moon ——————————→ full moon ——————————→ new moon
(invisible)   waxing   (fully visible)   waning

The phases of the moon are caused by its rotation about the earth every month. The moon gives off no light of its own, so we can only see it because light from the sun reflects off the moon. Therefore, *we only see that portion of the moon which faces both toward the sun and toward us on the earth*. As the moon rotates about the earth, different portions of the moon become visible to people on the earth, depending on the positions of the earth, moon, and sun.

1. Imagine floating far above the earth and moon in outer space, looking straight down at the plane of the path of the moon around the earth, as in Figure 10C.1 parts (A) and (B). Explain why the shaded portion of the moon shown in part (B) represents the part of the moon that is visible from the earth. Use the dashed lines to help you explain.

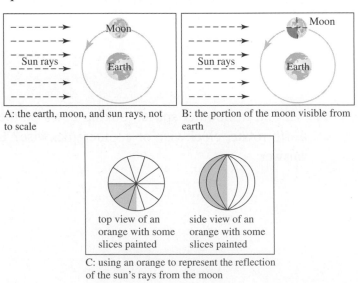

A: the earth, moon, and sun rays, not to scale

B: the portion of the moon visible from earth

top view of an orange with some slices painted

side view of an orange with some slices painted

C: using an orange to represent the reflection of the sun's rays from the moon

Figure 10C.1 In what phase is the moon?

2. Describe how the moon appears to a person on the earth when the earth, moon, and sun rays are positioned as shown in Figure 10C.1, parts (A) and (B). To help you, use the idea of looking down on the top of an orange and at the side of an orange, as indicated in part (C).

3. Describe how the moon appears to a person on the earth in each of the diagrams in Figure 10C.2. In each case, explain why the moon appears that way. Parts (A) through (D) are not to scale, but part (E) shows the earth and moon, and the distance between them, to scale.

4. Determine the phase of the moon in Figure 10C.1 (A) and in Figure 10C.2 (A–D). In which diagram is the moon new? In which is it full? In which is it waxing? In which is it waning? Explain your answers.

Sun rays are not in the plane of the page; they come from slightly above (or below) this plane.

Figure 10C.2   In what phase is the moon?

You might be wondering why there aren't eclipses at every new moon and full moon. A solar eclipse occurs when the moon passes right in front of the sun, as observed from the earth, temporarily obscuring our view of the sun. A lunar eclipse occurs when the earth is directly between the sun and moon and casts a shadow on the moon. At a new moon, the moon is between the sun and the earth. At a full moon, the earth is between the sun and the moon. So why isn't there a solar eclipse at every new moon and lunar eclipse at every full moon? The reason is that the sun is not in the plane in which the moon revolves around the earth, so that the earth, moon, and sun rarely lie in a straight line. Think of the sun rays shown in Figure 10C.2 as coming from slightly *above* (or below) the plane formed by the page.

10.2 Angles

Class Activity 10D: Angle Explorers

1. An "angle explorer" is made by fastening 2 cardboard strips with a brass fastener, as shown in the next figure. Discuss how to use an angle explorer to relate the two ways of describing an angle: as an amount of turning or as 2 rays (or line segments) meeting.

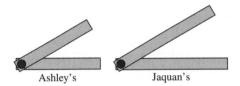

Ashley's   Jaquan's

2. Ashley and Jaquan make angle explorers, as shown in the preceding figure, but Ashley uses shorter cardboard strips than Jaquan. Ashley says that her angle explorer shows a smaller angle than Jaquan's. What is Ashley's misconception, and how could you help her correct it?

3. When we show an angle, do we have to make one of the rays or line segments horizontal, or is it okay to show an angle as on the angle explorer here?

Class Activity 10E:
Angles Formed by Two Lines

1. The next figure shows 3 pairs of lines meeting (or you may wish to think of this as showing 1 pair of lines in three situations, when the lines are moved to different positions). In each case, how do angles *a* and *c* appear to be related, and how do angles *b* and *d* appear to be related?

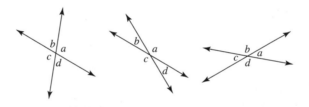

2. Do you think the same phenomenon you observed in part 1 will hold for *any* pair of lines meeting at a point? Do you have a convincing reason why or why not?

3. Explain *why* what you observed in part 1 must always be true by using the fact that an angle formed by a straight line is 180°. What does this fact tell you about several pairs of angles?

Class Activity 10F: Angles Formed When a Line Crosses Two Parallel Lines

A pair of lines marked with arrows indicates that the lines are parallel.

Given 2 parallel lines and a transversal line that crosses the 2 parallel lines, as shown below, the Parallel Postulate states that $a = a'$, $b = b'$, $c = c'$, and $d = d'$ (this is one version of the Parallel Postulate). Assume that the Parallel Postulate is true.

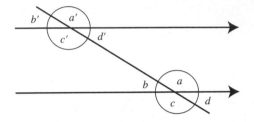

1. Use the Parallel Postulate to explain why $e = f$ (alternate interior angles are equal).

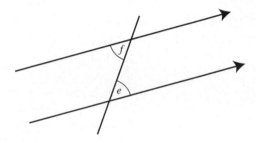

2. Use the Parallel Postulate to explain why $g + h = 180°$.

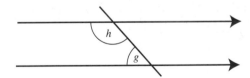

Class Activity 10G: Seeing That the Angles in a Triangle Add to 180°

You will need a ruler and scissors for this activity.

1. Work with a group of people. Each person in your group should do the following:

    a. Using a ruler, draw a large triangle that looks different from the triangles of other group members. Cut out your triangle.

b. Tear (do not cut) all 3 corners off your triangle. Then put the corners together point to point, without overlaps or gaps. What do you notice? What does this tell you about the angles of the triangle?

2. Work with a group of people. Each person in your group should do the following:

a. Using a ruler, draw a large triangle that looks different from the triangles of other group members. Cut out your triangle.

b. As indicated next, fold the corner that is opposite the longest side (or a longest side) of your triangle down to meet the longest side. Do this in such a way that the fold line is parallel to the longest side of the triangle.

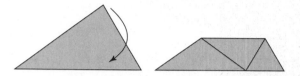

c. Fold the other two corners of the triangle in to meet the corner that is now along the longest side of the triangle.

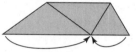

d. What does this way of folding the triangle show you about the angles of the triangle? Do the other people in your group reach the same conclusion, even though they started with different triangles?

These are neat ways to see that the angles in a triangle add to 180°, but it is not so easy to explain *why* they must always work.

Class Activity 10H: Using the Parallel Postulate to Prove That the Angles in a Triangle Add to 180°

This activity will show you a way to prove that the angles in a triangle add to 180°.

1. Given any triangle with corner points A, B, and C, let *a*, *b*, and *c* be the angles of the triangle at A, B, and C, respectively. Consider the line through A parallel to the side BC that is opposite A.

What can you say about the 3 adjacent angles at A that are formed by the triangle and the line through A?

What can you conclude about the sum of the angles in the triangle?

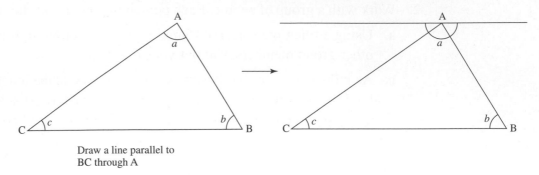

Draw a line parallel to
BC through A

2. What if you used a different triangle in part 1? Would you still reach the same conclusion?

Class Activity 10I: Describing Routes Using Distances and Angles

You will need a protractor and a ruler for this activity.

1. The map in the next figure shows a route that you must program Dave, a robot, to "walk." On the map, 1 inch represents 5 of Dave's paces. Dave starts at point A, facing the route, so that he is ready to start walking along it. Use a protractor to help you describe how Dave should get to point H. For example, here's what Dave should do to get from point A to point C:

Starting at A, go 5 paces to B. At B, turn clockwise (to your right) 60°. Go another 10 paces to C.

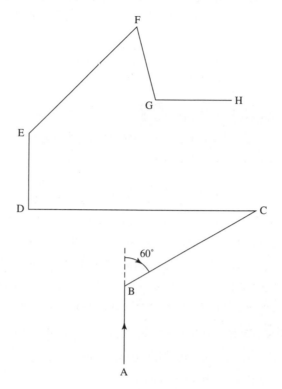

2. For each of the routes in the next figure, describe how Dave, the robot, should move and turn to "walk" around the route. The shortest line segments on the map represents 5 of Dave's paces. In each case, Dave will start at the point labeled A, facing the route, so that he is ready to start walking along it.

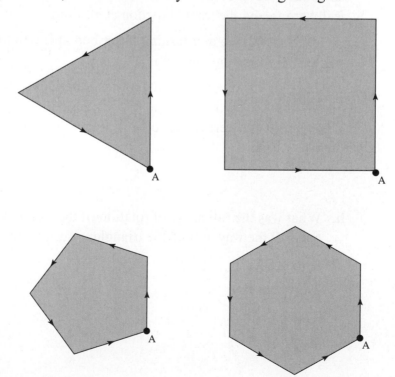

3. For each route in part 2, determine Dave's total amount of turning along the route if he returns to point A and *turns to face the same direction in which he started.*

Class Activity 10J:
Explaining Why the Angles in a Triangle Add to 180° by Walking and Turning

You will need sticky notes and, if available, masking tape.

This activity will show you a way to understand why the angles in a triangle add to 180°. It is best done as a demonstration for the whole class.

1. Put 3 "dots" (sticky notes) labeled *A*, *B*, and *C* on the floor to create the corners of a triangle. If possible, connect them with masking tape to make a triangle you can see. Label a point *P* on the line segment between *A* and *B*.

2. Pick two people: one to be a *walker* and one to be a *turner*. The rest are *observers*.

   The walker's job: Stand at point *P*, facing point *B*. Walk all the way around the triangle, returning to point *P*.

   The turner's job: Stand at one fixed spot, and face the same direction that the walker faces at all times. This means that when the walker turns at a corner, you should turn in the same way.

   The observers' job: Observe the walker and the turner, and make sure that they really are facing the same direction at all times.

   Repeat the walking and turning described above until everyone can confidently answer the following questions:

   a. Let's say that the walker and turner were facing north when the walker began walking around the triangle. Which directions did the turner face during the experiment? Were any directions left out? Were any directions repeated?

   b. What was the full angle of rotation of the turner when the walker walked once all the way around the triangle, returning to point *P*?

3. On the next diagram, show which angles the walker turned through at the corners of the triangle. Label these angles d, e, and f.

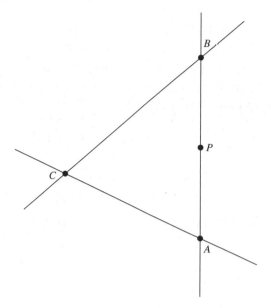

4. Based on your answer to part 2(b), what can you say about the value of $d + e + f$?

5. Check your answer to the previous problem by using a protractor to find the angles d, e, f and adding them.

　　What if you used a different triangle? The values of d, e, and f might be different, but what about $d + e + f$?

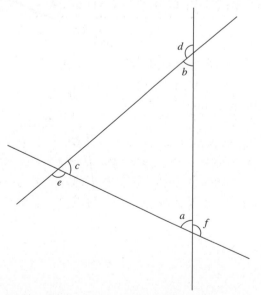

Figure 10J.1 The exterior angles of a
triangle add to 360°

6. You should have just found that the sum of the **exterior angles** of a triangle is 360°. In other words, $d + e + f = 360°$, where d, e, and f are the exterior angles, as shown in Figure 10J.1.

Use the formula $d + e + f = 360°$ to explain why the sum of the **interior angles** in a triangle is equal to 180°. In other words, show that $a + b + c = 180°$, where a, b, and c are the interior angles of a triangle, as shown in Figure 10J.1.

Hint: What do you notice about $a + f$, $b + d$, and $c + e$? Can you use this somehow?

7. What if you used a different triangle in this activity? Would you still reach the same conclusion?

Class Activity 10K:
Angle Problems

In some (but not all) of these problems, it will be helpful to add or to extend one or more line segments.

1. Determine a formula for angle x in terms of angles a and b. Explain why your formula is valid (without measuring any angles).

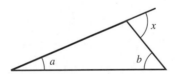

2. Determine the sum of the angles, $a + b + c + d + e + f$. Explain why your answer is valid (without measuring any angles). See if you can find two explanations!

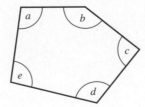

3. Given that the lines marked with arrows are parallel, determine the sum of the angles $a + b + c + d$. Explain why your answer is valid (without measuring any angles). See if you can find more than one explanation!

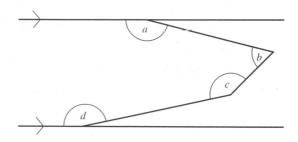

Class Activity 10L: Students' Ideas and Questions about Angles

Discuss the next ideas and questions that students had about angles.

1. Harry has learned that the angles in a triangle add to 180° and that there are 360° in a circle. Harry wonders about the next picture: "Shouldn't the circle be less than 180° because it is inside the triangle?"

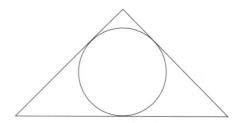

2. Sam says that a circle has infinitely many degrees because you can think of a degree as being like a little wedge. By making the wedges smaller, you can fit more and more wedges in the circle.

    Kaia counters that you can't have an angle smaller than 1°.

Sam's drawing

10.3 Angles and Phenomena in the World

Class Activity 10M: Angles of Sun Rays

1. How are the following related? Draw diagrams to help you describe and explain the relationships.

   a. The height of the sun in the sky

   b. The length of the shadows of telephone poles (or other objects)

   c. The angle that sun rays make with horizontal ground

2. Because the sun is so far away, light rays coming from the sun form virtually parallel straight lines near the earth. When light rays from the sun strike a location on the earth, they form an angle with the horizontal ground. Figure 10M.1 shows a diagram of a portion of the earth seen from above the North Pole, marked N, and sun rays traveling toward the earth. Assume that these sun rays are parallel to the page.

   a. At each location A, B, C, and D in Figure 10M.1, show the angle that a sun ray makes with the horizontal ground there.

   b. At each location A, B, C, and D in Figure 10M.1, describe how the sun would appear to a person standing there. Is the sun high in the sky or low in the sky? Is the sun in the east, in the west, or directly overhead?

c. At each location A, B, C, and D in Figure 10M.1, describe how long the shadow of a telephone pole would be. Is the shadow of a telephone pole long or short compared to the other locations? Show the shadows of the telephone poles on Figure 10M.2.

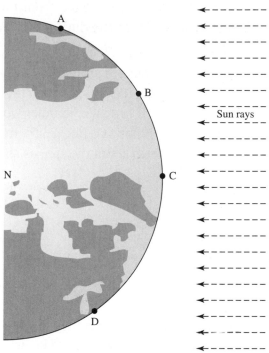

Figure 10M.1 Parallel sun rays traveling toward the earth

Figure 10M.2 Show the shadows formed by the telephone poles at points A, B, C, D in Figure 10M.1.

Class Activity 10N: How the Tilt of the Earth Causes Seasons

If available, a globe or a ball with labels representing the North and South Poles would be useful for this activity.

What causes the seasons? Some people mistakenly believe that the seasons are caused by the earth's varying distance from the sun. In fact, the distance from the earth to the sun varies only a little during the year. The seasons are caused by the tilt of the earth's axis.

1. Visualize the earth rotating around the sun over the course of a year. As the earth travels around the sun, the axis between the North and South Poles of the earth remains parallel to itself in space; in other words, the tilt of the earth's axis does not change. The earth's axis is tilted 23.5° from the perpendicular to the plane in which the earth rotates about the sun, as shown in the following diagram:

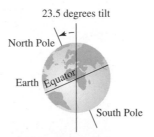

Simulate the earth's yearly journey around the sun either with a globe or as follows: Make a fist around a pencil. The pencil represents the earth's axis (through the North and South Poles), and your fist represents the earth. Imagine the sun in front of you. Move your fist around your imagined sun, keeping your pencil tilted to represent the tilt of the earth. *Keep the pencil parallel to its original position* as you move your "earth" around the "sun." Notice that as the earth travels around the sun, the North Pole is sometimes tilted toward the sun and sometimes tilted away from the sun.

2. The following diagram shows the earth at two different times of year. In diagram 1, the North Pole is tilted directly toward the sun. In diagram 2, the South Pole is tilted directly toward the sun, and the North Pole is tilted directly away from the sun. In both diagrams, assume that the sun rays are parallel to the page. To picture other times of year, visualize sun rays coming from outside of the plane of the page.

   a. Points A and B in diagrams 1 and 2 are both shown at around noon. In diagram 1, is the sun higher in the sky at point A or point B? In diagram 2, is the sun higher in the sky at point A or point B?

   b. During the day, the earth rotates on its axis. In both diagrams 1 and 2, visualize how the locations of points A and B will change throughout the day. Which of the points, A or B, will receive more sunlight over the course of a day in diagram 1? Which of the points, A or B, will receive more sunlight over the course of a day in diagram 2?

   c. What season is it in the northern hemisphere in diagram 1? What season is it in the northern hemisphere in diagram 2? Why?

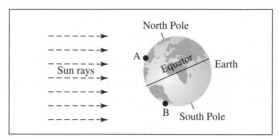

Diagram 1

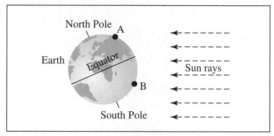

Diagram 2

Figure 10N.1 Earth's position around the sun at different times of year

Class Activity 10O:
How Big Is the Reflection of Your Face in a Mirror?

You will need a mirror and a ruler for the first part of this activity.

   How big is the reflection of your face in a mirror? Is it the same size as your face, or is it larger or smaller, and if so, how much? The answers to these questions may surprise you.

   1. Use a ruler to measure the length of your face from the top of your forehead to your chin. Now hold a mirror *parallel* to your face and measure the length of your face's reflection in the mirror, from the top of the forehead to the chin. Measure carefully!

       Hold the mirror closer to your face or farther away (but always *parallel* to your face), and repeat the measuring processes just described. The *position* of your reflection will probably change, but does the *size* of your reflection change or not? The answer may surprise you.

       Compare the length of your face and the length of your reflected face in the mirror. How do these lengths appear to be related?

   2. Figure 10O.1 shows a side view of a person looking into a mirror. Using the laws of reflection, determine what the person will see at each of the points A, B, and C. We see objects by seeing the light that travels from the object to our eyes. So a person looking at a particular point sees the light that travels in a straight line from that point to the person's eye. To determine what a person sees at a point in a mirror, you must determine where the light at that point came from. For this you will need the laws of reflection.

3. Use the laws of reflection to show where the person looking into the mirror in Figure 10O.2 will see the top of her forehead and where she will see the bottom of her chin. Measure the length of the person's face and the length of her reflected face in the mirror. How do these lengths appear to be related? Your result should fit with what you discovered in part 1.

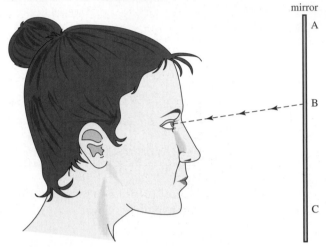

Figure 10O.1 Looking into a mirror

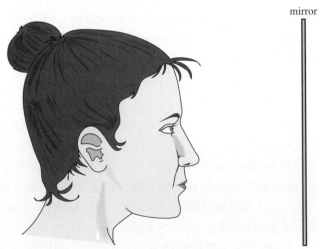

Figure 10O.2 Where is the person's reflection in the mirror?

Class Activity 10P: Why Do Spoons Reflect Upside Down?

A large, reflective spoon would be helpful for this activity.

When you look at your reflection in the bowl of a spoon, you will notice that (in addition to looking quite distorted) your image will appear upside down. Have you ever wondered why? We will explore this now.

Figure 10P.1 is a diagram of a person looking into the bowl of a (very large) spoon. Only a cross-section of the spoon is shown. The lines shown are the *normal lines* to the spoon at the points A, B, and C. Use these normal lines and the laws of reflection to determine what the person sees when she looks at points A, B, and C. (Assume that the person sees light that enters the center of her eye.)

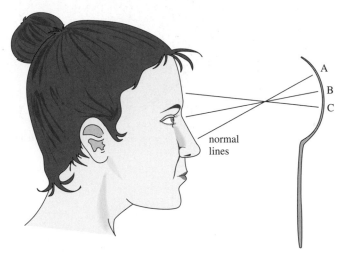

Figure 10P.1 Looking into a spoon

Class Activity 10Q: The Special Shape of Satellite Dishes

Satellite dishes are shaped in a special way so as to efficiently capture incoming radio waves broadcast from a satellite. The top diagram of Figure 10Q.1 shows the cross-section of a satellite dish. The curve formed by this cross-section is called a **parabola**.

1. Verify that all incoming radio waves hitting a parabolic satellite dish (top diagram of Figure 10Q.1) reflect onto the receiver. The receiver is shown as a small circle inside and above the center of the satellite dish. (Actual satellite dishes usually do not extend above their receiver, as this one does, but this exaggerated diagram will be easier to work with.)

2. The cross-section of a cone-shaped satellite dish forms a v-shaped curve, as shown in the bottom diagram of Figure 10Q.1. What kind of receiver would a cone-shaped satellite dish need to capture all the incoming radio waves reflected from the inside of the satellite dish? Could the receiver be as small as the one for a typical parabolic satellite dish? Explain.

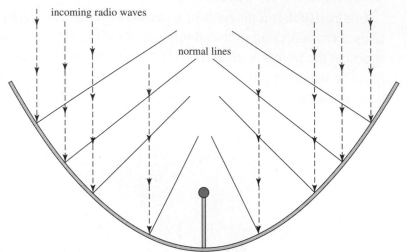

cross-section of a parabolic satellite dish

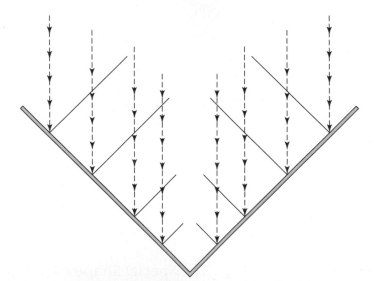

cross-section of a hypothetical cone-shaped satellite dish

Figure 10Q.1 Cross-sections of satellite dishes

10.4 Circles and Spheres

Class Activity 10R:
Points That Are a Fixed Distance from a Given Point

You will need a ruler for this activity.

1. Use a ruler to draw 5 different points that are 1 inch away from the point P:

•
P

   Now draw 5 more points that are 1 inch away from the point P. If you could keep drawing more and more points that are 1 inch away from point P, what shape would this collection of points begin to look like?

2. Ask a person to point to a particular point in space. Call that point P. Using a ruler, find several other locations in space that are 1 ruler-length away from point P. (A ruler-length might be 12 inches or 6 inches, depending on your ruler.) Try to visualize all the points in space that are 1 ruler-length away from your point P. What shape do you see?

Class Activity 10S: Using Circles

You will need a compass for this activity. Some string would also be useful.

1. Use the definition of a circle to explain why a compass draws a circle. How is the radius of the circle related to the compass?

2. Explain how to use a piece of string and a pencil to draw a circle. Use the definition of a circle to explain why your method will draw a circle.

3. Suppose that, 1 hour and 45 minutes ago, a prisoner escaped from a prison located at point P, shown on the map that follows. Due to the terrain and the fact that no vehicles have left the area, police estimate that the prisoner can go no faster than 4 miles per hour. Show all places on the map where the prisoner might be at this moment. Explain.

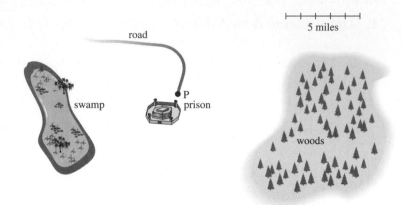

4. The treasure map for this exercise shows an X and an O marking two spots. The treasure is described as buried under a spot that is 30 feet from X and 50 feet from O. Use this information to help you show where the treasure might be buried. Is the information enough to tell you *exactly* where the treasure is buried? Explain.

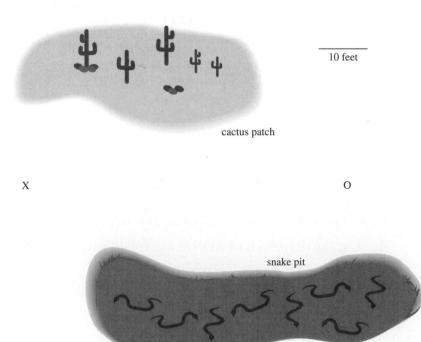

Class Activity 10T: The Global Positioning System (GPS)

You will need string for this activity.

The Global Positioning System (GPS) is a navigation system designed and maintained by the U.S. Department of Defense for military use, but it is also available for civilian use. With a handheld GPS unit, it is possible to determine your location on the earth, accurate to within about 10 meters. The GPS system uses a network of 24 satellites that orbit the earth. Figure 10T.1 shows a GPS satellite. Suppose a GPS unit receives information on its distance from each satellite within its range. The GPS unit can then figure its location by using those distances, based on the geometry of spheres.

Suppose a GPS unit learns that it is a certain distance from satellite 1 and another certain distance from satellite 2. The following activity will help you describe all possible locations for the GPS unit by simulating the situation with people and string.

1. Pick two people to represent satellites 1 and 2, and pick a third person who will show all possible locations of the GPS unit. The GPS person should stand between satellites 1 and 2.

2. Cut two pieces of string, representing the distances from satellites 1 and 2 to the GPS unit.

Figure 10T.1 A GPS satellite

3. Satellites 1 and 2 should each hold one end of their piece of string, and the GPS person should hold the other ends of the two pieces of string in one hand, pulling the strings tight. (Everyone may have to adjust positions so that it is possible to do this. Once suitable positions are found, everyone should stay fixed in his or her position.)

4. The designated GPS person will now be able to show all possible locations of the GPS unit by moving the strings, while keeping them pulled tight and held in one hand (and while satellites 1 and 2 remain fixed in their positions). See Figures 10T.2 and 10T.3.

5. Describe the shape of all possible locations of the GPS unit. How is this related to the intersection of two spheres?

Figure 10T.2 Showing a position of a GPS unit

Figure 10T.3 Showing another position of a GPS unit

6. Now suppose that there is also a third satellite beaming information to the GPS unit. Pick a person to represent sallelite 3, and cut a piece of string to represent the distance of satellite 3 to the GPS unit.

7. Satellite 3 should hold one end of her or his string while the GPS person holds the other end in the same hand with the strings from satellites 1 and 2. By pulling all three strings tight, the GPS person can show all possible locations of the GPS unit. In general, there will be two such locations. See Figures 10T.4 and 10T.5.

Figure 10T.4 One position of a GPS unit, given information from 3 satellites

Figure 10T.5 Another position of a GPS unit, given information from 3 satellites

How is this exercise related to the intersection of three spheres?

As you've seen, with information from three satellites, a GPS unit can narrow its location to one of two points. If one of those two locations can be recognized as being in outer space, and not on the surface of the earth, then the GPS unit can report its location on the earth. This is the idea behind the GPS system.

Class Activity 10U: Circle Designs

You will need various coins for part 1 and a compass for part 2.

1. How many pennies can you place around a single penny, each touching the inner penny? Try it and see. Do the pennies fit snugly around the inner penny or not?

    Now try placing as many pennies as you can around a single nickel so that each penny touches the inner nickel. Do the pennies fit snugly around the inner nickel or not?

    How many nickels can you place around a single nickel, each touching the inner nickel? Do the nickels fit snugly around the inner nickel or not?

2. Although the accompanying design looks complex, it is surprisingly easy to make. Use a compass (or a paper clip) to draw a design like the one below. Say briefly how to draw the design. If you look closely, you will also see the phenomenon you discovered about arranging pennies in part 1.

3. The next design was made by drawing part of the design of part 2. Use a compass (or a paper clip) to draw a design like this one.

10.5 Triangles, Quadrilaterals, and Other Polygons

Class Activity 10V:

Using a Compass to Draw Triangles and Quadrilaterals

You will need a compass and ruler for this activity. Focus on the definition of a circle throughout the activity.

1. Use a compass to help you draw an isosceles triangle. Without measuring any side lengths, explain why your triangle must be isosceles.

2. Try to draw an equilateral triangle by using only a ruler and pencil, no compass. Why does this not work so well?

   Now use a compass to help you draw an equilateral triangle. Without measuring any side lengths, explain why your triangle must be equilateral.

3. To make an equilateral triangle, follow the steps outlined in the next figure. Notice that you really need to draw only the top portions of the circles. Use this method to make examples of several different equilateral triangles.

   Explain *why* this method must always produce an equilateral triangle.

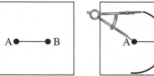

| Step 1: Start with any line segment AB. | Step 2: Draw a circle centered at A, passing through B. | Step 3: Draw a circle centered at B, passing through A. | Step 4: Label one of the two points where the circles meet C. Connect A, B, and C with line segments. |

4. In the next picture, the line segments AB and AC have the same length. Use a ruler and compass to draw a rhombus that has AB and AC as two of its sides. (You may wish to try drawing the rhombus without a compass first. Notice that it is difficult and clumsy to do so.)

   Hint: To create the rhombus, you will need to construct a fourth point, D, such that the distance from D to B is equal to the distance from D to C, and such that these two distances are also equal to the common distance from A to B and A to C. Think about the *definition of circles* to help you figure out how to construct the point D.

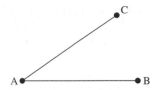

5. The line segment AB shown in the next figure is 4 inches long. Use a ruler and compass to construct a triangle that has AB as one of its sides, has a side that is 3 inches long, and has another side that is 2 inches long. Describe how you constructed your triangle, and explain why your construction must produce the desired triangle. *Hint*: Modify the construction of an equilateral triangle shown in part 4 of Class Activity 10V by drawing circles of different radii.

6. Take a blank piece of paper. Use a ruler and compass to construct a triangle that has one side of length 6 inches, one side of length 5 inches, and one side of length 3 inches.

7. Is it possible to make a triangle that has one side of length 6 inches, one side of length 3 inches, and one side of length 2 inches? Explain.

Class Activity 10W:
Making Shapes by Folding Paper

You will need paper, scissors, and a ruler for this activity.

1. To create an isosceles triangle, follow the next set of instructions.

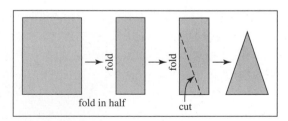

a. By referring to the definition of isosceles triangle, explain *why* the method described must always create an isosceles triangle.

b. What properties does your isosceles triangle have? Find as many as you can. Explain if you can.

2. To create a rhombus, follow the next set of instructions.

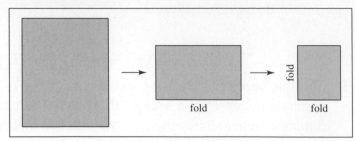

Step 1: Fold a rectangular piece of paper in half and then in half again, creating perpendicular fold lines.

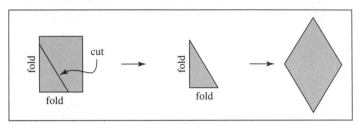

Step 2: Draw a line from anywhere on one fold to anywhere on the perpendicular fold. Cut along the line you drew. When you unfold, you will have a rhombus.

   a. By referring to the definition of rhombus, explain *why* the method described must always create a rhombus.

   b. What properties does your rhombus have? Find as many as you can. Explain if you can.

3. An ordinary rectangular piece of paper is one example of a rectangle. You can create other rectangles out of an ordinary piece of paper as follows: Fold the paper so that one edge of the paper folds directly onto itself. The opposite edge will automatically fold onto itself as well. Now unfold the paper and fold the paper again, this time so that the other two edges fold onto themselves. When you unfold, you can cut along the fold lines to create 4 rectangles.

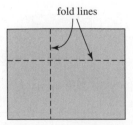

By referring to the definition of a rectangle, explain why the method just described must always create rectangles. What properties do your rectangles have?

4. To create a parallelogram, start with a rectangular piece of paper of any size. Follow the next set of steps.

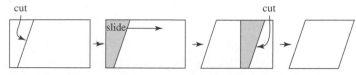

Draw a line segment connecting two opposite sides of a rectangle. Cut along the line segment. Put the piece back (shown shaded) and slide it over as shown. Mark and cut at the leading edge of the slid-over piece.

What properties does your parallelogram have?

Class Activity 10X: Constructing Quadrilaterals with Geometer's Sketchpad

In this activity, you will construct various kinds of quadrilaterals. Save your sketches for use in a subsequent activity.

To do this activity, you must be able to do the following in Geometer's Sketchpad:

- Construct points and line segments with the construction tools.

- Use the *Construct* menu to construct a line segment between two given points.

- Use the *Construct* menu to construct a line that is parallel to another line and goes through a given point.

- Use the *Construct* menu to construct a line that is perpendicular to another line and goes through a given point.

- Use the *Construct* menu to construct a circle that goes through a given point and has a radius of the same length as a given line segment.

- Hide objects by using the *Display* menu.

1. Construct a "general" quadrilateral. You should be able to move the vertices so as to vary the quadrilateral and show (theoretically) all possible quadrilaterals (if your computer screen were infinitely large).

2. Construct a "general" trapezoid. Use the definition of trapezoid so that your construction is guaranteed to be a trapezoid, even when you move the vertices. This means that you will need to use the *Construct* menu to construct a parallel line to a given line segment. By moving the vertices of your trapezoid, you should be able to show (theoretically) all possible trapezoids (if your computer screen were infinitely large).

3. Construct a "general" parallelogram. Use the definition of parallelogram so that your construction is guaranteed to be a parallelogram, even when you move the vertices. By moving the vertices of your parallelogram, you should be able to show (theoretically) all possible parallelograms (if your computer screen were infinitely large).

4. Construct a "general" rectangle. Use the definition of rectangle so that your construction is guaranteed to be a rectangle, even when you move the vertices. By moving the vertices of your rectangle, you should be able to show (theoretically) all possible rectangles (if your computer screen were infinitely large).

5. Construct a "general" square. Use the definition of square so that your construction is guaranteed to be a square, even when you move the vertices. To do this construction, it will help you to remember the definition of a circle. By moving the vertices of your square, you should be able to show (theoretically) all possible squares (if your computer screen were infinitely large).

6. Construct a "general" rhombus. Use the definition of rhombus so that your construction is guaranteed to be a rhombus, even when you move the vertices. To do this construction, it will help you to remember the definition of a circle. By moving the vertices of your rhombus, you should be able to show (theoretically) all possible rhombuses (if your computer screen were infinitely large).

Class Activity 10Y: Relating the Kinds of Quadrilaterals

1. In each of parts (a) through (d), describe the relationships among the given kinds of shapes. In each case, write as many sentences as you can of the following forms:

Every _____ is a _____.

There are _____ that are not _____.

a. Describe the relationship between squares and rectangles.

b. Describe the relationship between squares and rhombuses.

c. Describe the relationship between rectangles and trapezoids.

d. Describe the relationship between rhombuses and parallelograms.

2. a. Explain why squares and rectangles are related the way they are.

  b. Explain why squares and rhombuses are related the way they are.

  c. When you relate rectangles and trapezoids, are you relying *only* on information that is stated directly in the definitions of these shapes, or are you relying on information that is not stated directly in the definitions, such as visual information?

  d. When you relate rhombuses and parallelograms, are you relying *only* on information that is stated directly in the definitions of these shapes, or are you relying on information that is not stated directly in the definitions, such as visual information?

Class Activity 10Z: Venn Diagrams Relating Quadrilaterals

  1. Draw a Venn diagram relating the set of squares and the set of rectangles.

  2. Draw a Venn diagram relating the set of rhombuses, the set of squares, and the set of rectangles.

  3. Draw a Venn diagram relating the set of parallelograms and the set of trapezoids.

4. Our definition of a trapezoid is a quadrilateral with *at least one* pair of parallel sides. Some books define trapezoid as a quadrilateral with *exactly one* pair of parallel sides. How would the Venn diagram relating parallegrams and trapezoids be different if we used this other definition of trapezoid?

Class Activity 10AA: Investigating Diagonals of Quadrilaterals with Geometer's Sketchpad

You will need sketches for a general quadrilateral, rectangle, and rhombus from Class Activity 10X for this activity.

To do this activity, you will need to be able to measure angles and lengths of line segments. Both of these can be done with the *Measure* menu. To measure an angle, you will need to select three points *in the following order*: a point on one line segment, the point where the line segments meet, and a point on the other line segment.

1. Choose a vertex of your general quadrilateral. Construct a diagonal of the quadrilateral that has your chosen point on it. The diagonal splits the angle at your chosen point into two angles. Measure these two angles, and compare them. Observe how these two angles change as you move various vertices of the quadrilateral around to make different quadrilaterals.

    Now choose a vertex of your general rhombus. Construct a diagonal of the rhombus that has your chosen point on it. As before, the diagonal splits the angle at your chosen point into two angles. Measure these two angles, and compare them. Observe how these two angles change as you move various vertices of the rhombus around to make different rhombuses.

    Compare what you observed for the quadrilateral with what you observed for the rhombus.

2. Construct the two diagonals in each of your sketches of a general quadrilateral, rectangle, and rhombus. Now move the vertices in your sketches around in different ways so as to see many different quadrilaterals, rectangles, and rhombuses. As you move the vertices, observe the diagonals, and do the following:

    • Measure the angles that the diagonals make with each other.

    • Find where the diagonals meet—where is this point located on the diagonals?

    • Compare the lengths of the two diagonals.

    What do the diagonals of rectangles all have in common? What do the diagonals of rhombuses all have in common? What about diagonals of general quadrilaterals?

Class Activity 10BB: Investigating Diagonals of Quadrilaterals (Alternate)

1. Figure 10BB.1 shows examples of different kinds of quadrilaterals and their diagonals. Look carefully at the diagonals and do the following:

   - Observe and (if possible) measure the angles that the diagonals make with each other.

   - Observe where the diagonals meet—where is this point located on the diagonals?

   - Compare the lengths of the two diagonals.

   What do the diagonals of rectangles all have in common? What do the diagonals of rhombuses all have in common? What about diagonals of general quadrilaterals?

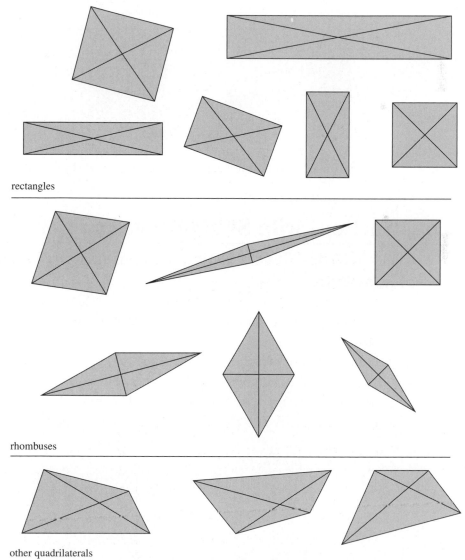

rectangles

rhombuses

other quadrilaterals

Figure 10BB.1 Some quadrilaterals and their diagonals

2. Shown in Figure 10BB.2 are some rhombuses and other quadrilaterals with one of the two diagonals drawn in. The two angles created by the diagonal are labeled *a* and *b*. In each case, compare angle *a* with angle *b*. Compare what you observed for quadrilaterals with what you observed for rhombuses.

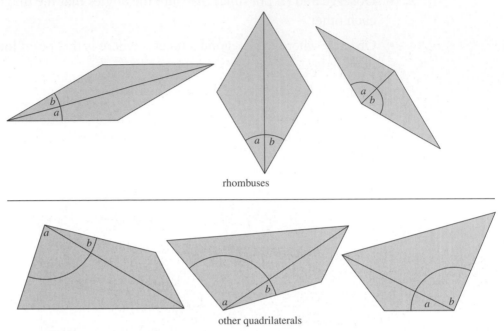

Figure 10BB.2 Some quadrilaterals and the angles made by their diagonals

10.6 Constructions with Straightedge and Compass

Class Activity 10CC: Relating the Constructions to Properties of Rhombuses

1. The next picture shows the result of using a straightedge and compass to construct a line that is perpendicular to a line segment AB and that divides AB in half. There are two circles of the same radius, one centered at A and one centered at B. Draw the rhombus that arises naturally from this construction and that has A and B as vertices. Use the definition of rhombus to explain *why* the quadrilateral that you identify as a rhombus really must be a rhombus.

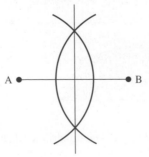

2. Which special properties of rhombuses are related to the construction of a line that is perpendicular to a line segment and divides the line segment in half? Explain.

3. The next picture shows the result of using a straightedge and compass to construct a ray that divides an angle in half. There are three circles of the same radius, one centered at P, one centered at Q, and one centered at R. Draw the rhombus that arises naturally from this construction. Use the definition of rhombus to explain *why* the quadrilateral that you identify as a rhombus really must be a rhombus.

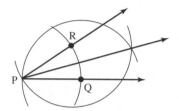

4. Which special properties of rhombuses are related to the construction of a ray that divides an angle in half? Explain.

Class Activity 10DD: Constructing a Square and an Octagon with Straightedge and Compass

Use a straightedge and compass to do the following constructions:

1. Using a straightedge and compass, construct a line that is perpendicular to the line segment AB shown in the next figure and that passes through point A (*not* through the midpoint of AB!). *Hint*: First extend the line segment AB.

   Now use a straightedge and compass to construct a square that has AB as one side.

A •————————————————• B

2. Using a straightedge and compass, construct an octagon whose vertices all lie on the circle in the next figure and whose sides all have the same length.

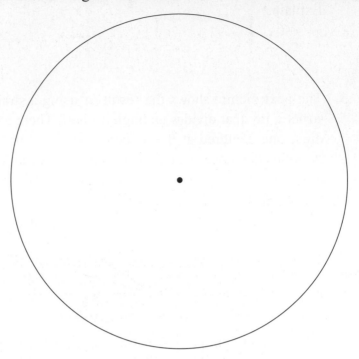

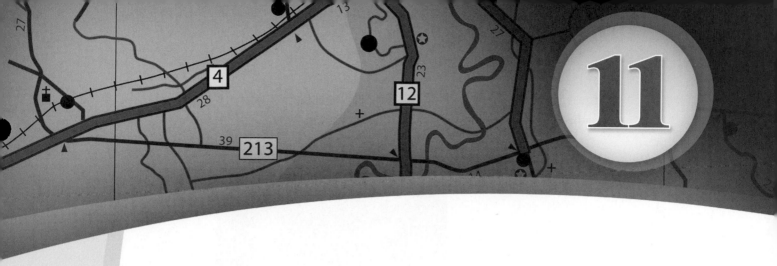

Measurement

11.1 Fundamentals of Measurement

Class Activity 11A:

The Biggest Tree in the World

Listed next are several different trees that could perhaps qualify as the biggest tree in the world. Compare these trees. Why can reasonable people differ about which tree is biggest?

Tree # 1: "General Sherman" is a giant sequoia located in Sequoia National Park in California. (See Figure 11A.1.) According to the National Park Service, General Sherman is 275 feet tall, has a circumference (at its base) of 103 feet, and has a volume of 52,500 cubic feet.

Tree # 2: "General Grant" is a giant sequoia located in Sequoia National Park in California. According to the National Park Service, General Grant is 268 feet tall, has a circumference (at its base) of 108 feet, and has a volume of 46,600 cubic feet.

Tree # 3: "Mendocino tree" is a redwood tree in Montgomery Redwoods State Reserve near Ukiah, California. It is 368 feet tall and has a diameter of 10.4 feet, which means that its circumference should be about 33 feet.

Tree # 4: A Banyan tree in Calcutta, India, has a circumference of 1350 feet (meaning the circumference of the whole tree, not just the trunk) and covers three acres.

Tree # 5: A tree in Santa Maria del Tule near Oaxaca, Mexico, is 130 feet tall and is described as requiring 40 people holding hands to encircle it.

Some Web sites have photos of these large trees. Go to *www.pearsonhighered.com/ beckmann*.

Figure 11A.1 Is General Sherman the biggest tree in the world?

Class Activity 11B: ▨
What Does "6 Square Inches" Mean?

Square tiles that are 1-inch-by-1-inch would be helpful for this activity.

1. **a.** Discuss the following as clearly and concretely as you can:

   What does it mean to say that a shape has an area of 6 square inches? Illustrate concretely with tiles, if available, or use the graph paper in Figure 11B.1.

   b. If we weren't thinking carefully, we might try to illustrate 6 square inches by drawing a square that is 6 inches wide and 6 inches long. Why is it easy to think that such a square has area 6 square inches, and why is this *not correct*?

   c. Discuss the confusion that can arise from the following:

   - Informally, people might refer to a square that is 6 inches by 6 inches as a "6-inch square," but the area of such a square is *not* 6 square inches.
   - The mathematical notation

$$6 \text{ in.}^2$$

   stands for "6 square inches," but it's easy to read it incorrectly as "6 inches squared."

3. People sometimes say, "Area is length times width." Why is it not correct to characterize area this way?

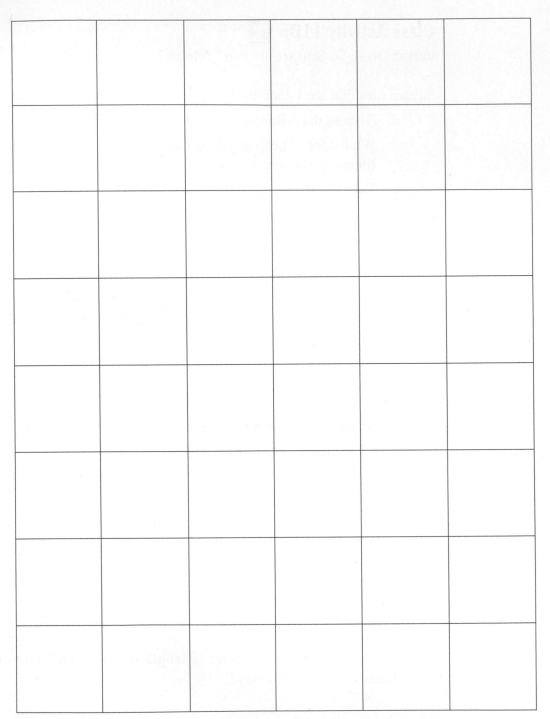

Figure 11B.1 Inch graph paper

Class Activity 11C: Using a Ruler

1. The most primitive way to measure the length of an object in inches is to place inch-long strips (or objects) end-to-end along the object. The number of inch-long strips it takes is the length of the object in inches. On the other hand, when we use a ruler to measure the length of an object, we read a number on a tick mark. Explain how these two processes of measuring are related.

2. Children sometimes try to measure the length of an object by placing one end of the object at the 1 marking instead of the 0 marking, as shown on the centimeter ruler in the figure. How might you help a child understand why the strip below is not 5 cm long, even though the end of the strip is at 5? Why might a child put one end of the strip at the 1 marking? Is it okay to measure by starting at 1 or at another tick mark?

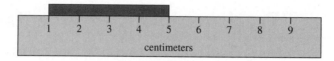

3. When asked how long the dark strip in the next figure is, some children will respond that it is 8 cm long. Others will respond that it is 7 cm long. How do you think children come up with these answers?

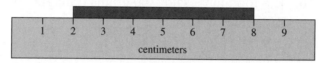

4. Some students might report that the strip measured by the inch ruler shown is 2.3 inches long. Why is this not correct? What is a correct way to report the length of the strip?

11.2 Length, Area, Volume, and Dimension

Class Activity 11D: Dimension and Size

1. Imagine a lake. Describe one-dimensional, two-dimensional, and three-dimensional parts or aspects of the lake. In each case, state how you would measure the size of that part or aspect of the lake—by length, by area, or by volume—and name an appropriate U.S. customary unit and an appropriate metric unit for measuring or describing the size of that part or aspect of the lake. What are practical reasons for wanting to know the sizes of these parts or aspects of the lake?

2. Imagine a house. Describe one-dimensional, two-dimensional, and three-dimensional parts or aspects of the house. In each case, state how you would measure the size of that part or aspect of the house—by length, by area, or by volume—and name an appropriate U.S. customary unit and an appropriate metric unit for measuring or describing the size of that part or aspect of the

house. What are practical reasons for wanting to know the sizes of these parts or aspects of the house?

11.3 Error and Precision in Measurements

Class Activity 11E: Reporting and Interpreting Measurements

1. **a.** Does a food label that says "0 grams trans fat in one serving" mean that the food contains no trans fat? If not, what does it mean?

    b. If a food label said "0.0 grams trans fat" would that mean there is no trans fat in the food?

2. One source says that the average distance from the earth to the sun is 93,000,000 miles, and another source says that the average distance from the earth to the sun is 92,960,000 miles. Can both of these descriptions be correct, or must at least one of them be wrong? Explain.

11.4 Converting from One Unit of Measurement to Another

Class Activity 11F: 🎚
Conversions: When Do We Multiply? When Do We Divide?

1. Julie is confused about why we *multiply* by 3 to convert 6 yards to feet. She thinks we should *divide* by 3 because feet are smaller than yards.

    a. Draw a picture to show Julie how yards and feet are related. Take care that your picture accurately portrays length as a one-dimensional, not a two-dimensional attribute. Use your picture and the meaning of multiplication to explain to Julie why we multiply by 3 to convert 6 yards to feet.

b. Help Julie think about the relationship between the *size* of a unit and the *number* of units it takes to describe the length of an object.

c. Try to think of other ways to help Julie better understand conversions. What problems or questions could you pose to Julie?

2. Nate is confused about why we *divide* by 100 to convert 200 centimeters to meters. He thinks we should *multiply* by 100 because meters are bigger than centimeters. What are some ways you could help Nate better understand conversions?

Class Activity 11G: Conversion Problems

1. Shaquila is 57 inches tall. How tall is Shaquila in feet?
   Should you multiply or divide to solve this problem? Explain. Describe a number of different correct ways to write the answer to the conversion problem. Explain briefly why these different ways of writing the answer mean the same thing.

2. Carlton used identical paper clips to measure the length of a piece of wood. He found that the wood was 35 paper clips long. Next, Carlton will measure the length of the wood, using identical rods. Carlton found that 2 rods are as long as 5 paper clips. How many rods long is the wood? Explain your reasoning.

3. Suppose that the children in your class want to have a party at which they will serve punch to drink. The punch that the children want to serve is sold in half-gallon containers. If 25 people attend the party, and if each person drinks 8 fluid ounces of punch, then how many containers of punch will you need? Describe several different ways that children could correctly solve this problem. For each method of solving the problem, explain simply and clearly why the method makes sense.

Class Activity 11H: Using Dimensional Analysis to Convert Measurements

Methods A and B provide two ways of writing the steps for converting 25 meters to yards with dimensional analysis, using the fact that 1 in. = 2.54 cm.

Method A

$$\frac{25 \text{ m} \mid 100 \text{ cm} \mid 1 \text{ in.} \mid 1 \text{ ft} \mid 1 \text{ yd}}{\mid 1 \text{ m} \mid 2.54 \text{ cm} \mid 12 \text{ in.} \mid 3 \text{ ft}} \qquad 27.3 \text{ yd (approx.)}$$

Method B

$$25 \text{ m} \times \frac{100 \text{ cm}}{1 \text{ m}} \times \frac{1 \text{ in.}}{2.54 \text{ cm}} \times \frac{1 \text{ ft}}{12 \text{ in.}} \times \frac{1 \text{ yd}}{3 \text{ ft}} = 27.3 \text{ yd (approx.)}$$

   To carry out the calculations for method A, multiply the numbers in the top of the table and divide by the numbers in the bottom of the table. To carry out the calculations for method B, multiply the fractions.

1. **a.** Compare methods A and B.

   b. Method B works by starting with a measurement (such as 25 m) and repeatedly multiplying by certain fractions. Discuss the fractions that you multiply by. How are they chosen?

   c. Explain why method B works; in other words, explain why 25 meters really must be equal to 27.3 . . . yards. What is special about the fractions you multiply by that allows you to deduce this?

   d. If you converted 25 meters to yards by reasoning about the meaning of multiplication and division, how would your calculations compare to the calculations you do with dimensional analysis?

2. Use dimensional analysis to convert 1 mile to kilometers, using the fact that 1 in. = 2.54 cm.

Class Activity 11I: Area and Volume Conversions

1. One yard is 3 feet. Does this mean that 1 square yard is 3 square feet? Draw a picture to show how many square feet are in a square yard. Explain why you should multiply to determine the number of square feet in a square yard.

2. A rug is 5 yards long and 4 yards wide. What is the area of the rug in square yards? What is the area of the rug in square feet? Show two different ways to solve this problem. Explain in each case.

3. A room has a floor area of 35 square yards. What is the floor area of the room in square feet? Explain your answer.

4. A compost pile is 2 yards high, 2 yards deep, and 2 yards wide. Does this mean that the compost pile has a volume of 2 cubic yards? Explain.

5. Determine the volume in cubic feet of the compost pile described in the previous part in two different ways. Explain in each case.

Class Activity 11J: Area and Volume Conversions: Which Are Correct and Which Are Not?

1. Analyze the calculations that follow, which are intended to convert 25 square meters to square feet. Which use legitimate methods and are correct, and which are not? Explain.

   a. $25 \text{ m}^2 = 25 \text{ m} \times \dfrac{100 \text{ cm}}{1 \text{ m}} \times \dfrac{1 \text{ in.}}{2.54 \text{ cm}} \times \dfrac{1 \text{ ft}}{12 \text{ in.}} = 82 \text{ ft}^2$

   b.

   $$25 \text{ m}^2 = 25 \text{ m}^2 \times \frac{100 \times 100 \text{ cm}^2}{1 \text{ m}^2} \times \frac{1 \text{ in.}^2}{2.54 \times 2.54 \text{ cm}^2} \times \frac{1 \text{ ft}^2}{12 \times 12 \text{ in.}^2} = 269 \text{ ft}^2$$

   c. $25 \text{ m} = 25 \text{ m} \times \dfrac{100 \text{ cm}}{1 \text{ m}} \times \dfrac{1 \text{ in.}}{2.54 \text{ cm}} \times \dfrac{1 \text{ ft}}{12 \text{ in.}} = 82 \text{ ft}$

   Therefore,

   $$25 \text{ m}^2 = 82^2 \text{ ft}^2 = 6727 \text{ ft}^2$$

   d. 25 square meters is the area of a square that is 5 meters wide and 5 meters long, so

   $$5 \text{ m} = 5 \text{ m} \times \frac{100 \text{ cm}}{1 \text{ m}} \times \frac{1 \text{ in.}}{2.54 \text{ cm}} \times \frac{1 \text{ ft}}{12 \text{ in.}} = 16.404 \text{ ft}$$

   Therefore,

   $$25 \text{ m}^2 = 16.404 \times 16.404 \text{ ft}^2 = 269 \text{ ft}^2$$

2. Use the fact that 1 in. = 2.54 cm to convert 27 cubic feet to cubic meters in at least two different ways.

Class Activity 11K: Problem Solving with Conversions

1. How much water does the typical person drink over a lifetime? What size container would hold this amount of water? Compare this size container with something familiar.

   To answer these questions, first estimate how much a typical person might drink per day. Then do some calculations. Consider working with metric measurements.

2. Suppose you could plant trees in rows that are 10 feet apart and so that the trees are 10 feet apart in each row. How many square miles of land would you need for 1 million trees? For 1 billion trees? For 1 trillion trees? Compare these land areas to familiar areas.

Area of Shapes

12.1 Areas of Rectangles Revisited

Class Activity 12A: Units of Length and Area in the Area Formula for Rectangles

If available, square centimeter tiles would be helpful.

1. What does it mean to say that a shape has an area of 15 square centimeters?

2. The large rectangle shown here is 3 cm by 5 cm. What is a primitive way to determine the area of the rectangle in square centimeters by relying directly on the meaning of area?

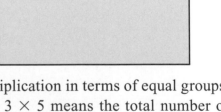

A 1-cm-by-
1-cm square
of area 1 cm²

3. In Chapter 4 we defined multiplication in terms of equal groups. According to our definition, 3×5 means the total number of objects in 3 groups of 5 objects. Using our definition of multiplication, explain why the area of the large rectangle in part 2 is 3×5 cm².

4. The *length times width* area formula for rectangles involves lengths, but doesn't explicitly involve equal groups. Discuss:

   How are the *lengths* 3 cm and 5 cm *linked to* yet *different from* the numbers of groups and numbers of things in each group in your explanation for part 3?

5. **a.** Given that the line segment shown is 1-unit long, use the grid to show a rectangle that is 0.7 units by 0.8 units.

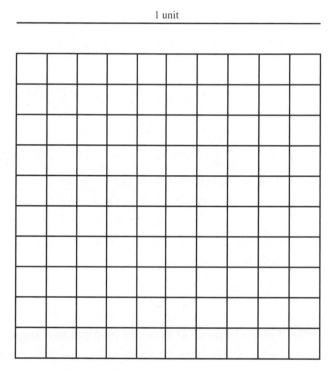

1 unit

   b. Show and describe the 0.7- and 0.8-unit lengths on your rectangle, keeping in mind that length is a one-dimentional attribute. Explain why you should *not* use the small squares to describe these lengths.

   c. Apply the *length times width* formula for the area of the rectangle and verify that the formula gives you the correct area for your rectangle. Attend carefully to units of area.

12.2 Moving and Additivity Principles about Area

Class Activity 12B: Different Shapes with the Same Area

You will need 7 identical small rectangular (but not square) pieces of paper, scissors, and tape for this activity.

1. Either determine the area of your 7 rectangles (in square centimeters or square inches) or call the area A square centimeters.

2. Cut 6 of your 7 rectangles diagonally in half, creating 2 identical triangles, as shown in the middle of the next figure.

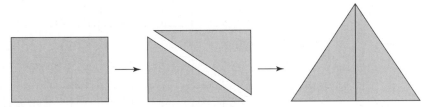

   There are 6 different ways to join a pair of identical edges of the triangles to create a new shape. One of those ways creates the original rectangle. Another way creates a triangle that looks like the one shown on the right in the figure. Find all 6 of these shapes. (By the way, how can you tell, before you make them, that there will be 6 such shapes?)

3. Given that the area of the original rectangle is A square centimeters, determine the areas of the 5 other shapes you created in part 2 *without using any area formulas*, and explain your reasoning.

4. Cut your seventh remaining rectangle into pieces of any size or shape you like. Rearrange those pieces and tape them together, without overlapping, to create a new shape, such as the one in this figure. You can even make a shape that is not flat, if you like. Determine the area of your new shape and explain your reasoning.

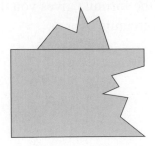

5. Now compare all 7 shapes that you created in parts 2 and 4. What do all the shapes have in common, and what is different about the shapes? Do all the shapes have the same perimeter? Do all the shapes have the same length?

Class Activity 12C: 🏛
Using the Moving and Additivity Principles
You will need blank paper, scissors, and a ruler for part 2 of this activity.

1. Use the moving and additivity principles (one or both) to determine the area of the L-shaped region in several different ways. In each case, explain your reasoning and write and evaluate an algebraic expression that fits with the strategy. Try to find strategies of the following types: a simple subdividing strategy, a takeaway strategy, a move and reattach strategy, a combine two copies and take half strategy.

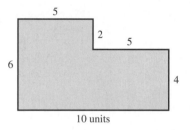

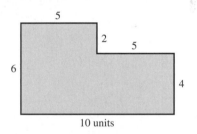

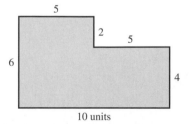

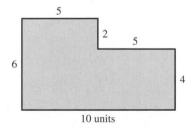

2. Use the moving and additivity principles (one or both) to determine the area of the shaded square, which is inside the 2-unit-by-2-unit square, in several different ways. In each case, explain your reasoning.

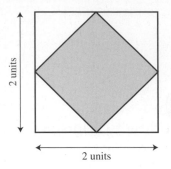

3. Take a piece of paper and fold it into fourths by folding it in half and then in half again, as shown in the next diagram. While the paper is still folded, cut off the "open" corner—so that you cut off four triangles, as indicated on the right. When you unfold the paper, you will have either an octagon, a hexagon, or a rhombus, depending on how you cut. (Can you see how to make each of these shapes?)

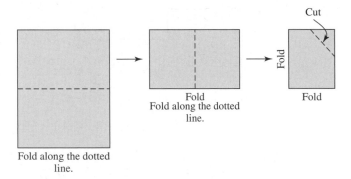

Determine the area of your octagon, hexagon, or rhombus. Use only the moving and additivity principles, actual measurements, and the formula for areas of rectangles to determine the area. Do not use any other formulas.

12.3 Areas of Triangles

Class Activity 12D: Determining Areas of Triangles in Progressively Sophisticated Ways

1. Use the moving and additivity principles to determine the area of the next two triangles in three different ways: (a) by moving small pieces and relying directly

on the definition of area, (b) by moving bigger chunks to create a rectangle, and (c) by viewing the triangle as part of a larger rectangle.

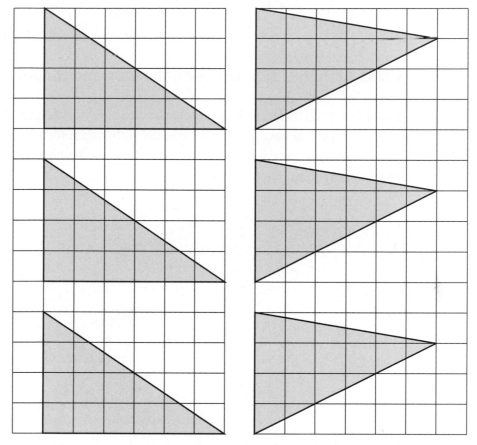

2. The area of the next triangle is difficult to determine by moving small pieces or moving chunks. Instead, view the triangle as part of a larger rectangle. Then use the moving and additivity principles to determine the areas of the extra pieces. Finally, use the moving and additivity principles to take away the extra area and thereby determine the area of the shaded triangle.

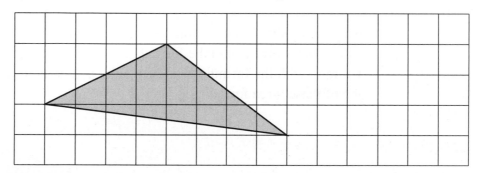

3. Think about some of the methods you used to determine the areas of the triangles in this activity: moving chunks, putting inside a rectangle and taking half, and putting inside a rectangle and taking away. Find arithmetic problems that can be made easy to solve by using numerical strategies that are similar in spirit to these

geometric strategies. Describe how to solve these arithmetic problems and say briefly how the solution methods are roughly similar to the geometric methods.

Class Activity 12E: Choosing the Base and Height of Triangles

Show the three different ways to choose the base and height of the triangles in the next figure. Once you have chosen a base, the right angle formed by the corner of a piece of paper may help you determine where to draw the height, which must be perpendicular to the base (or an extension of the base).

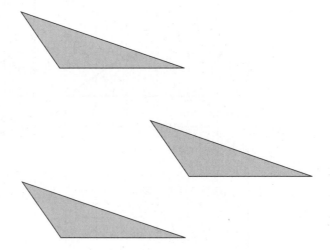

Class Activity 12F: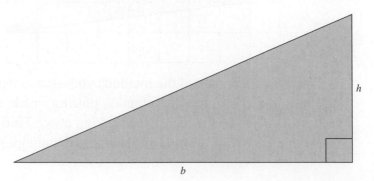
Explaining Why the Area Formula for Triangles Is Valid

1. Use the moving and additivity principles to explain in three ways why the next triangle has area $\frac{1}{2}(b \times h)$ square units for the given choices of b and h. One explanation should fit naturally with the formula $\frac{1}{2}(b \times h)$, another explanation should fit naturally with the formula $(\frac{1}{2}b) \times h$, and a third explanation should fit naturally with the formula $b \times (\frac{1}{2}h)$. Why is it valid to describe the area with any one of these three formulas?

2. Use the moving and additivity principles to explain in two ways why the next triangle has area $\frac{1}{2}(b \times h)$ square units for the given choices of b and h. One explanation should fit naturally with the formula $b \times (\frac{1}{2}h)$ and the other should fit naturally with the formula $\frac{1}{2}(b \times h)$.

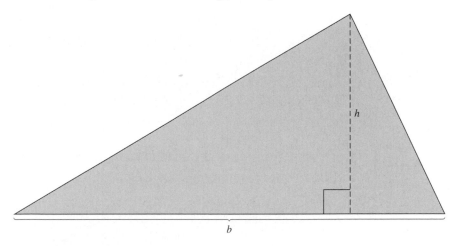

3. The area of the triangle in Figure 12F.1 is still $\frac{1}{2}(b \times h)$ square units for the given choices of b and h. What is wrong with the following reasoning that claims to show that the area of the triangle ABC is $\frac{1}{2}(b \times h)$ square units?

    Draw a rectangle around the triangle ABC, as shown in Figure 12F.2. The area of this rectangle is $b \times h$ square units. The line AC cuts the rectangle in half, so the area of the triangle ABC is half of $b \times h$ square units—in other words, $\frac{1}{2}(b \times h)$ square units.

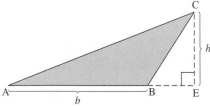

Figure 12F.1 A triangle

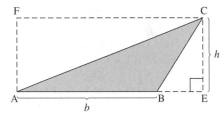

Figure 12F.2 Can you find the area this way?

4. What is a valid way to explain why the triangle in part 3 has area $\frac{1}{2}(b \times h)$ square units for the given choice of b and h?

Class Activity 12G: Determining Areas

1. Determine the area of the shaded triangle that is in the rectangle in the next figure in *two different ways*. Explain your reasoning in each case.

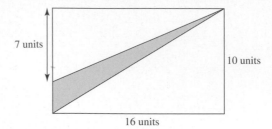

2. Determine the area of the shaded triangle in the next figure in *two different ways*. Explain your reasoning in each case.

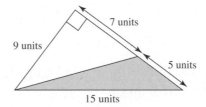

3. Determine the areas of the shaded shapes in the next pair of figures. The figure on the left consists of a 3-unit by 3-unit square and a 5-unit by 5-unit square. Explain your reasoning in each case.

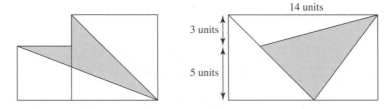

12.4 Areas of Parallelograms and Other Polygons

Class Activity 12H:
Do Side Lengths Determine the Area of a Parallelogram?

1. A rectangle is a special kind of parallelogram. We can calculate the area of a rectangle in terms of the lengths of the sides of the rectangle. Does this mean we can therefore calculate the area of a parallelogram in terms of the lengths of the sides of the parallelogram? Investigate this question as follows:

   The three parallelograms in Figure 12H.1 (the first of which is also a rectangle) all have two sides that are 3 units long and two sides that are 7 units long. The small squares in the grid are 1 unit by 1 unit.

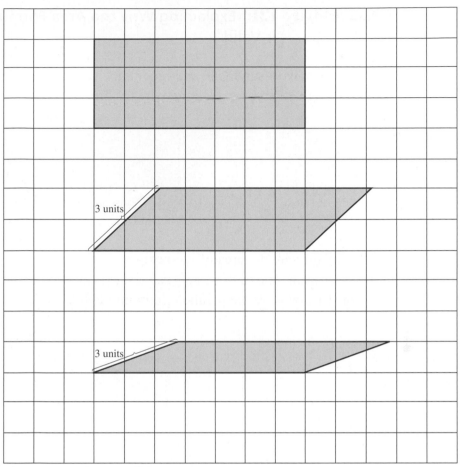

Figure 12H.1 Three parallelograms

    a. Use the moving and additivity principles to determine the areas of the three parallelograms in Figure 12H.1.

    b. Can there be a formula for areas of parallelograms that is only in terms of the lengths of the sides? Explain why or why not.

2. There is no formula for areas of parallelograms that is expressed solely in terms of the lengths of the *sides* of the parallelogram. However, there *is* a formula for areas of parallelograms. Try to find a formula *in terms of lengths of parts of the parallelogram.* Use the following parallelogram to help you explain your formula:

Class Activity 12I: Explaining Why the Area Formula for Parallelograms Is Valid

1. Show how to subdivide and recombine the next parallelogram to form a b by h rectangle, thereby explaining why the area of the parallelogram is $b \times h$.

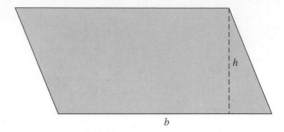

2. Explain why the area of the next shaded parallelogram is $b \times h$. To do so, consider using one of these approaches: (a) enclose the parallelogram in a rectangle, or (b) subdivide the parallelogram into two triangles.

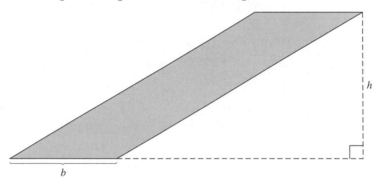

12.5 ⓒ Cavalieri's Principle about Shearing and Area

Class Activity 12J: Shearing a Toothpick Rectangle to Make a Parallelogram

For this activity you will need enough toothpicks to form a rectangle, as shown in the next figure.

1. Stack your toothpicks to form a rectangle, as shown, and determine the area of this rectangle.

2. Now push on the ends of the toothpicks so as to shear your rectangle, forming a parallelogram as shown in the following figure:

3. What happens to the area of the rectangle when it is sheared into the shape of a parallelogram? What is the area of the parallelogram formed by your toothpicks?

4. If a classmate shears her rectangle more than you shear yours, so that her parallelogram is more elongated than yours, will the area of your classmate's parallelogram differ from the area of your parallelogram? Explain.

Class Activity 12K: Is This Shearing?

The next figure shows a rectangle made of toothpicks being sheared into a parallelogram. During the process of shearing, which of the following change and which remain the same?

- Area
- Lengths of the sides
- Height of the stack of toothpicks

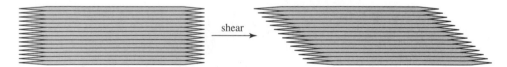

The next figure shows a rectangle made with pieces of drinking straws tied with a string being "squashed" into a parallelogram. During the process of squashing, which of the following change and which remain the same?

- Area
- Lengths of the sides
- "Vertical height" of the straw figure

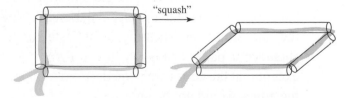

Is the process of squashing the same as shearing? Why or why not?

Class Activity 12L: Shearing Parallelograms

1. Imagine shearing parallelogram ABCD so that side AB remains fixed. Draw the path that the line segment CD could move along during shearing. How is this path related to the line segment AB?

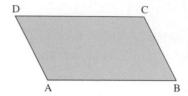

2. Determine the area of the next parallelogram by shearing it into a rectangle. Explain your reasoning. Adjacent dots are 1 cm apart.

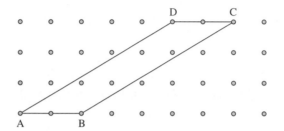

3. Determine the area of the next parallelogram by shearing it into a rectangle. Explain your reasoning. Adjacent dots are 1 cm apart. *Note:* Shearing does not have to be horizontal.

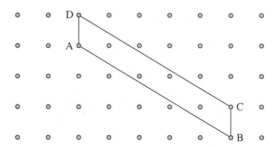

Class Activity 12M: Shearing Triangles

You will need scissors for this activity.

1. Cut a large non-right triangle out of paper and cut it into strips as indicated by the dashed lines on the next triangle on the left. On a flat surface, put the paper strips back together to make the original triangle. Now give your paper strips a push from the side, simulating shearing, as indicated on the right in the next figure. When you shear your paper triangle you can form new shapes that are basically triangles, except that the edges are jagged. (If your paper strips were infinitesimally thin, then the edges would not be jagged.)

By shearing your paper triangle, form various different (jagged) triangles, including a right triangle.

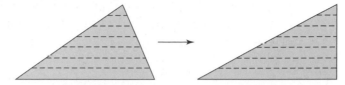

Determine which of the following change during shearing and which remain the same:

- Area

- Lengths of the sides

- Height of the "stack" of paper strips

2. Imagine shearing the triangle ABC so that side AB remains fixed. Draw all the locations to which point C could move during shearing. Describe the nature of these locations; in particular, how are they related to the line segment AB?

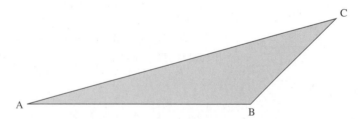

3. Determine the area of the next triangle by first shearing the triangle into a right triangle and then using the moving and additivity principles to determine the area of the right triangle. Explain why you can determine the area of the original triangle by this method. Adjacent dots are 1 cm apart.

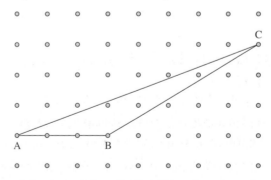

4. Determine the area of the next triangle by first shearing the triangle into a right triangle and then using the moving and additivity principles to determine the area

of the right triangle. Explain why you can determine the area of the original triangle by this method. *Note:* Shearing does not have to be horizontal.

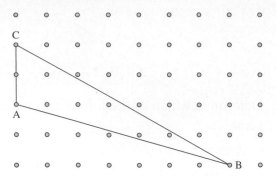

12.6 Areas of Circles and the Number Pi

Class Activity 12N: How Big Is the Number π?

Suppose that the only thing you know about the number π is that it is the circumference of a circle of diameter 1. Explain how you can use the next figure to give information about the size of the number π. (Based on the picture, you should be able to say that π lies between two numbers. Which two numbers?)

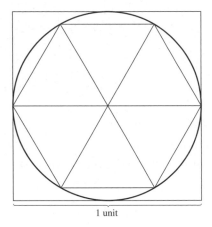

1 unit

Class Activity 12O: A Hands-on Method to Approximate the Value of π

You will need a compass, scissors, and extra paper for this activity. A can or other round container would be helpful.

1. Use a compass to draw a circle on a piece of paper, or place a can on paper and trace around the outside to draw a circle.

2. Cut a long, narrow strip of paper and wrap the strip around your circle (the long edge of your strip should rest on the circle); if you have a can, wrap the strip around the can. Cut the strip of paper so that it is the length of the circumference of your circle.

3. Now use the diameter of your circle as a unit of length and measure how long your circumference-strip is in terms of that unit. What do you find? What does that tell you about the number π?

Class Activity 12P: Overestimates and Underestimates for the Area of a Circle

Scissors might be helpful for this activity.

Use the next figure to explain why the area of a circle that has radius r units is less than $4r^2$ square units and greater than $2r^2$ square units. In other words, explain why

$$2r^2 \text{ units}^2 < \text{area of circle} < 4r^2 \text{ units}^2$$

To explain why the area of the circle is greater than $2r^2$ square units, you may want to trace, cut out, and rearrange the triangles inside the circle.

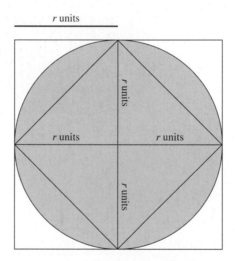

Class Activity 12Q: Why the Area Formula for Circles Makes Sense

You will need scissors for this activity.

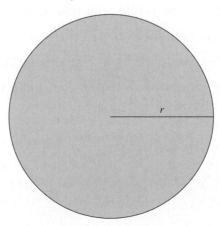

1. Trace the given circle and cut your traced circle into 8 pie pieces. Arrange the 8 pie pieces as shown at the top of Figure 12Q.1.

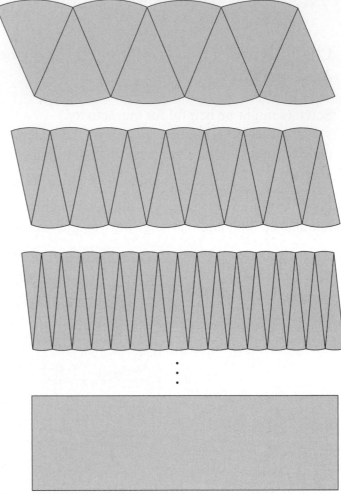

Figure 12Q.1 Rearranging a circle

2. Now cut your traced circle into 16 pie pieces. Arrange the 16 pie pieces as shown in the middle of Figure 12Q.1.

3. Imagine cutting a circle into more and more smaller and smaller pie pieces and rearranging them as in Figure 12Q.1.

   • What shape would your rearranged circle become more and more like?

   • What would the lengths of the sides of this shape be?

   • What would the area of this shape be?

4. Using your answers to part 3, explain why it makes sense that a circle of radius r units has area πr^2 square units, given that the circumference of a circle of radius r is $2\pi r$.

Class Activity 12R: Area Problems

1. A reflecting pool will be made in the shape of the shaded region shown in the next figure. The curves shown are $\frac{1}{4}$ circles. What is the area of the surface of the pool? Explain your reasoning.

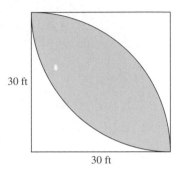

30 ft

30 ft

2. Given an octagon that has perimeter P units and whose distance from the center to a side is r units, find a formula in terms of P and r for the area of the octagon. Explain your reasoning. Is this related to the case of a circle?

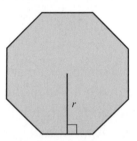

r

12.7 Approximating Areas of Irregular Shapes

Class Activity 12S:
Determining the Area of an Irregular Shape

1. Think about several different ways that you might determine (at least approximately) the surface area of Lake Lalovely shown on the map in Figure 12S.1. Suppose that you have the following items on hand:

   - Many 1-inch-by-1-inch paper or plastic squares
   - Graph paper (adjacent lines separated by $\frac{1}{4}$ inch)
   - A scale for weighing (such as one used to determine postage)
   - String
   - Modeling dough or clay

Which of these items could help you to determine approximately the surface area of the lake. How?

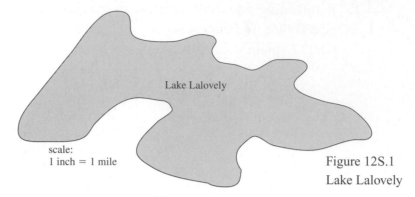

scale:
1 inch = 1 mile

Figure 12S.1
Lake Lalovely

2. Suppose that you have a map with a scale of 1 inch = 100 miles. You trace a state on the map onto $\frac{1}{4}$-inch graph paper. (The grid lines are spaced $\frac{1}{4}$ inch apart.) You count that the state takes up about 100 squares of graph paper. Approximately what is the area of the state? Explain.

3. Suppose that you have a map with a scale of 1 inch = 15 miles. You cover a county on the map with a $\frac{1}{8}$-inch-thick layer of modeling dough. Then you re-form this piece of modeling dough into a $\frac{1}{8}$-inch-thick rectangle. The rectangle is $2\frac{1}{2}$ inches by $3\frac{3}{4}$ inches. Approximately what is the area of the county? Explain.

4. Suppose that you have a map with a scale of 1 inch = 50 miles. You trace a state on the map, cut out your tracing, and draw this tracing onto card stock. Using a scale, you determine that a full $8\frac{1}{2}$-inch-by-11-inch sheet of card stock weighs 10 grams. Then you cut out the tracing of the state that is on card stock and weigh this card-stock tracing. It weighs 6 grams. Approximately what is the area of the state? Explain.

12.8 Contrasting and Relating the Perimeter and Area of a Shape

Class Activity 12T: Calculating Perimeters

String will be helpful for this activity.

1. Imagine you are working with elementary school children. Tell the children what we mean by the term *perimeter.* You may wish to use string to help you.

    If you didn't have string, how would you calculate the perimeter of the polygon in the next figure? Why does it make sense that we can calculate the perimeter by adding? The grid lines are 1 cm apart.

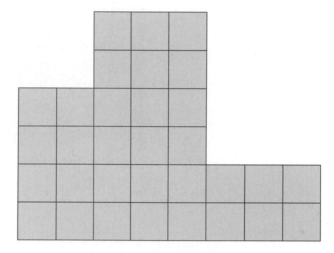

2. There are several different methods for calculating the perimeter of a rectangle. Describe at least two different methods. For each method, write the corresponding expression for the perimeter of an A-cm-by-B-cm rectangle.

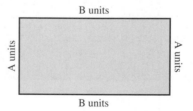

Class Activity 12U: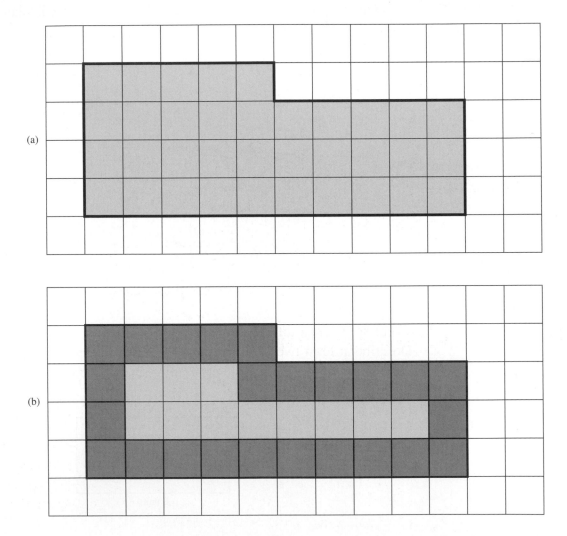
Perimeter Misconceptions

You will need a centimeter ruler for part 2.

1. Johnny wants to calculate the perimeter of the shaded shape in Figure (a). Johnny's method is to shade the squares along the border of the shape, as shown in Figure (b), and to count these border squares. Therefore, Johnny says the perimeter of the shape is 24 cm. Is Johnny's method valid? If not, why not?

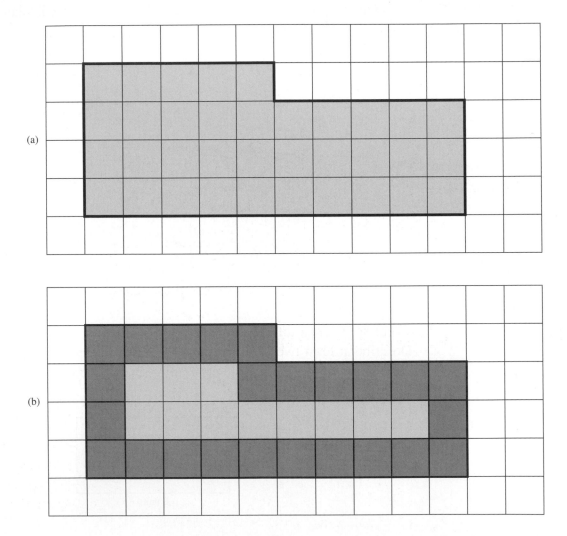

(a)

(b)

2. When Susie was asked to draw a shape with perimeter 15 cm, she drew a shape like the shaded one shown in the next figure on centimeter grid paper.

   a. Carefully measure the diagonal line segment in the shaded shape with a centimeter ruler. Then explain why the shape does not have perimeter 15 cm.

   b. Draw a shape that has perimeter 15 cm on the same graph paper. (The corners of your shape do not have to be located where grid lines meet.) Explain how you figured out how to make your shape.

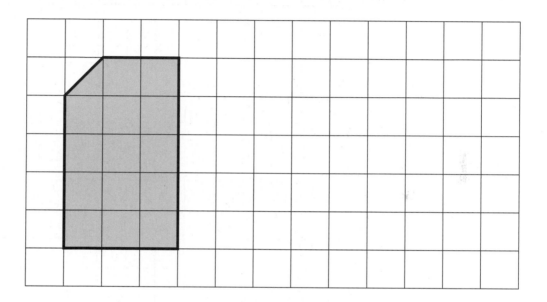

Class Activity 12V:
How Are Perimeter and Area Related?

String would be useful for this activity.

1. Suppose surveyors have determined that a forest on flat terrain has a perimeter of 20 kilometers. What is the area of the forest? Can you answer this question without additional information, or is more than one answer possible? Now suppose that you learn that the forest is in the shape of a rectangle. Can you determine the area now, or is more than one answer possible? Contemplate these questions for a few minutes, then move on to the next part.

2. Figure 12V.1 shows graph paper. The grid lines are 1 unit apart. Draw at least 5 different rectangles of perimeter 20 units on this graph paper. Include some rectangles that have sides whose lengths *aren't whole numbers of units*.

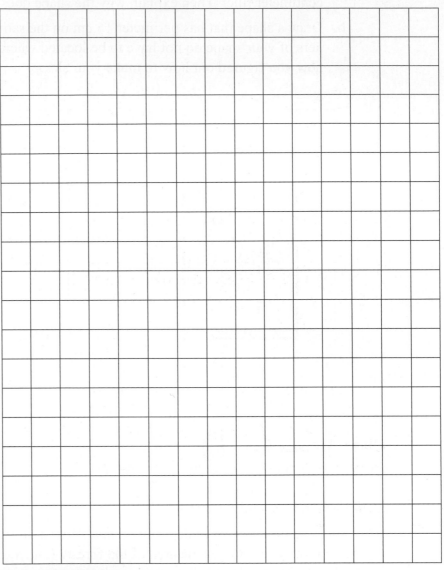

Figure 12V.1 Graph paper

3. Determine the areas of the rectangles you just drew. In the next table, list the areas of your rectangles in decreasing order. Below each area, draw a small sketch showing the approximate shape of the corresponding rectangle.

How are the larger-area rectangles qualitatively different in shape from the smaller-area ones?

area					
shape					

4. Show how two people can use a loop of string and 4 fingers to represent all rectangles of a certain fixed perimeter.

   Now consider all the rectangles of perimeter 20 cm, *including those whose side lengths aren't whole numbers of centimeters*. What are all the theoretical possibilities for the areas of rectangles of perimeter 20 cm? What is the largest possible area, and what is the smallest possible area (if there is one)?

5. Suppose that a forest on flat terrain has perimeter 20 kilometers, but there is no information on the shape of the forest. What can you say about the forest's area? Use a loop of string to help you think about this question.

Class Activity 12W: Can We Determine Area by Measuring Perimeter?

Nick wants to find the area of an irregular shape. Nick cuts a piece of string so that it goes all the way around the outside of the shape. Then Nick forms his piece of string into a square on top of graph paper. Using the graph paper, Nick gets a good estimate for the area of his string square. Nick then uses the square's area as his estimate for the area of the original irregular shape.

Discuss whether Nick's method is a legitimate way to estimate areas of irregular shapes.

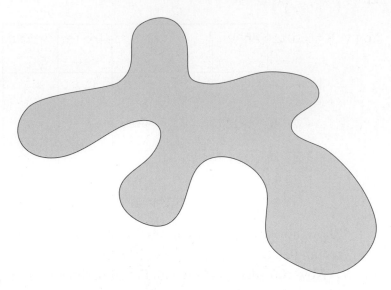

12.9 Using the Moving and Additivity Principles to Prove the Pythagorean Theorem

Class Activity 12X: Using the Pythagorean Theorem

You will need a calculator for part 2 of this activity.

1. What, if anything, does the Pythagorean theorem say about the 3 triangles in the next figure? The letters a, b, c, d, e, f, x, y, and z represent the lengths of the indicated sides (all measured in the same units).

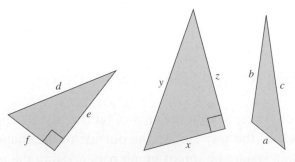

2. Tyler and Sarah measured the distance between two trees and found it to be 18 feet. But when they measured this distance, Tyler held up his end of the tape measure 8 inches higher than Sarah's end. If Sarah and Tyler had measured the distance between the trees by holding the tape measure horizontally, would they get an appreciably different result? Explain.

Class Activity 12Y: Can We Prove the Pythagorean Theorem by Checking Examples?

You will need a ruler with $\frac{1}{4}$-inch markings (or finer) for this activity.

1. For each of the right triangles, measure the lengths of the sides and check that the Pythagorean theorem really is valid in each case. In other words, check that the sum of the squares of the lengths of the two shorter sides really is equal to the square of the length of the hypotenuse.

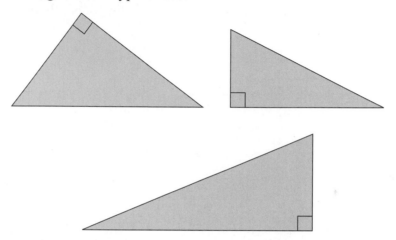

2. Would it be possible to prove that the Pythagorean theorem is true by checking many right triangles, continuing what you did in part 1? Explain.

Class Activity 12Z: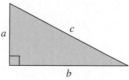
A Proof of the Pythagorean Theorem

Scissors might be helpful for this activity. Start with any arbitrary right triangle. Let a and b be the lengths of the short sides and let c be the length of the hypotenuse. (See Figure 12Z.1). To prove the Pythagorean theorem, we must explain why $a^2 + b^2 = c^2$ is true. Even though we will be working with copies of the *particular* triangle shown in Figure 12Z.1, our explanation for why the Pythagorean theorem is true will be *general* because it would work in the same way for *any* right triangle.

Figure 12Z.1 A right triangle

1. Figure 12Z.2 shows some triangles and some squares. All the triangles shown are copies of our original right triangle with sides of lengths a, b, and c. The square shapes have all 4 sides the same length and 4 angles right angles, making them true squares.

Follow the instructions in Figure 12Z.2 and show two different ways of filling a square that has sides of length $a + b$ with triangles and squares without gaps or overlaps. You may wish to cut out the squares and triangles on page 445 and use these to help you figure out how to fill in the squares of side length $a + b$.

2. Now use part 1 and the moving and additivity principles about areas to explain why $a^2 + b^2 = c^2$. There are several different ways to do this.

   Hint: Notice that *both* of the two ways of filling a square of side length $a + b$ in Figure 12Z. 2 use 4 copies of the original right triangle.

   Summarize your proof of Pythagoras's theorem.

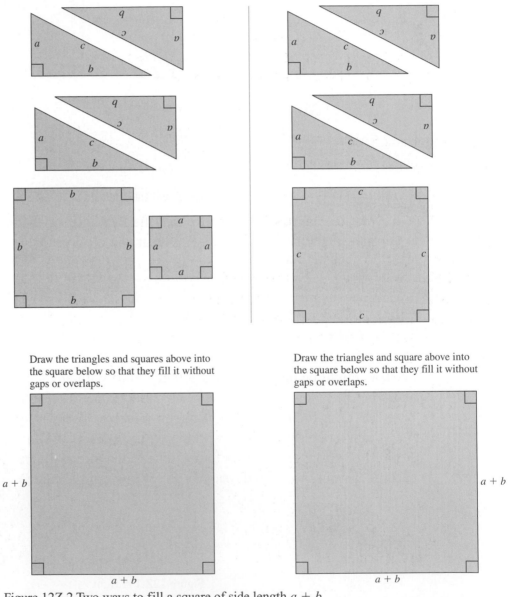

Figure 12Z.2 Two ways to fill a square of side length $a + b$

3. Here is a subtle point in the proof of the Pythagorean theorem: In both of the squares of side length $a + b$ in Figure 12Z.2, there are places along the edges where 3 figures (2 triangles and 1 square) meet at a point. How do we know that the edge formed there really is a straight line and doesn't actually have a small bend in it, such as pictured in the next figure? We need to know that the edge there really is straight in order to know that the assembled shapes really do create large *squares* and not *octagons*. Explain why these edges really are straight. (*Hint*: Consider the angles at the points where a square and two triangles meet.)

Solid Shapes and Their Volume and Surface Area

13.1 Polyhedra and Other Solid Shapes

Class Activity 13A: Making Prisms and Pyramids

You will need toothpicks or straws and gumdrops or modeling clay for this activity. If it is available, you could also use liquid soap.

As in the photograph, stick toothpicks into gumdrops or into small balls of modeling clay to make the shapes listed. To make larger shapes, stick straws into balls of clay. In each case, visualize the shape first and predict how many toothpicks and gumdrops you will need for the following:

1. Rectangular prism

2. Triangular prism

3. Pyramid with a triangle base

4. Pyramid with a square base

Some teachers like to dip these shapes into a liquid soap solution to show the faces of the shapes.

Class Activity 13B:
Analyzing Prisms and Pyramids

1. Answer the next questions *without* using a model. Use your visualization skills and look back at other models. (When you are done, verify with a model if one is available.)

   - How many faces does a pentagonal prism have? Why? Describe the faces of a pentagonal prism. What kinds of shapes are they? How many of each kind of shape are there?

   - How many edges and how many vertices does a pentagonal prism have? Explain.

2. Answer the next questions *without* using a model. Use your visualization skills and look back at other models. (When you are done, verify with a model if one is available.)

   - How many faces does a pyramid with a hexagonal base have, assuming that you count the base? Why? Describe the faces of a pyramid with a hexagonal base. What kinds of shapes are they? How many of each kind of shape are there?

   - How many edges and how many vertices does a pyramid with a hexagonal base have? Explain.

Class Activity 13C: What's Inside the Magic 8 Ball?

You will need a Magic 8 Ball for this activity. (One or more can be shared by a class.) Magic 8 Balls are typically available where popular children's toys are sold. Scissors and tape or snap-together plastic polygons would also be helpful.

1. Play with a Magic 8 Ball for a little while. Generally speaking, how does the Magic 8 Ball work? What sorts of things are inside it? Why do you see different "answers" at different times? Other than breaking the Magic 8 Ball, how might you determine the shape that is inside the Magic 8 Ball?

2. Let's say someone wants to make his or her own version of a Magic 8 Ball. This person would probably put a polyhedron inside that is very uniform and regular all the way around, so that all the answers would be equally likely to appear. Such a shape would have the following properties:

   • The faces are identical copies of one regular polygon; so all faces are equilateral triangles, or all faces are squares, or all faces are regular pentagons, and so forth.

   • The shape has no indentations and protrusions; in other words, the shape is *convex* (as described in the text).

   • All the vertices are identical, so the same number of faces meet at each vertex.

   Make a guess: How many such shapes do you think there can be?

   Try to make some shapes that have the properties described above. Tape paper polygons together or use snap-together plastic polygons. (See page 423.) How many shapes can you find?

3. The actual Magic 8 Ball should contain one of the shapes mentioned in part 2. Which one must it be?

Class Activity 13D: Making Platonic Solids with Toothpicks and Gumdrops

You will need toothpicks and gumdrops or modeling clay for this activity.

Make all five Platonic solids by sticking toothpicks into gumdrops or small balls of clay. (Your dodecahedron may sag a little, but the others will be more stable.) Refer to the following descriptions of the Platonic solids:

Tetrahedron has 4 equilateral triangle faces, with 3 triangles coming together at each vertex.

Cube has 6 square faces, with 3 squares coming together at each vertex.

Octahedron has 8 equilateral triangle faces, with 4 triangles coming together at each vertex.

Dodecahedron has 12 regular pentagon faces, with 3 pentagons coming together at each vertex.

Icosahedron has 20 equilateral triangle faces, with 5 triangles coming together at each vertex.

Use your models to fill in the following table:

Shape	**# and Type of Faces**	**# of Edges**	**# of Vertices**
Tetrahedron	4 equilateral triangles		
Cube	6 squares		
Octahedron	8 equilateral triangles		
Dodecahedron	12 regular pentagons		
Icosahedron	20 equilateral triangles		

Class Activity 13E: Why Are There No Other Platonic Solids?

You will need scissors and tape for this activity. Snap-together plastic triangles, squares, and pentagons could also be helpful.

1. Each vertex of a tetrahedron has 3 equilateral triangles coming together. Each vertex of an octahedron has 4 equilateral triangles coming together. Each vertex of an icosahedron has 5 equilateral triangles coming together. Can there be a convex polyhedron whose faces are equilateral triangles and for which 6 equilateral triangles come together at each vertex? Investigate this by working with paper or plastic equilateral triangles. (Page 423 has triangles you can cut out.) Explain your conclusion.

2. What if there were a polyhedron for which 7 or more equilateral triangles came together at each vertex? Could such a polyhedron be convex? Investigate this by working with paper or plastic equilateral triangles. Explain your conclusion.

3. At each vertex of a cube, 3 squares come together. Can there be a convex polyhedron whose faces are squares and for which 4 squares come together at each vertex? Is it possible to make a convex polyhedron in such a way that 5 or more squares come together at each vertex? Investigate these questions by working with paper or plastic squares. (Page 425 has squares you can cut out.) Explain your conclusions.

4. At each vertex of a dodecahedron, 3 regular pentagons come together. Is it possible to make a convex polyhedron in such a way that 4 or more regular pentagons come together at each vertex? Investigate this question by working with paper or plastic regular pentagons. (Page 425 has pentagons you can cut out.) Explain your conclusions.

5. Can there be a convex polyhedron whose faces are all regular hexagons and for which 3 hexagons come together at each vertex? Investigate this question by working with paper or plastic regular hexagons. (Page 427 has hexagons you can cut out.) Explain your conclusion.

6. Is it possible to make a convex polyhedron whose faces are all regular hexagons? Consider the same question for regular 7-gons, 8-gons, and so on. (Page 427 has hexagons, 7-gons, and octagons that you can cut out.)

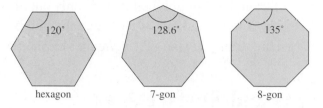

hexagon   7-gon   8-gon

Class Activity 13F:
Relating the Numbers of Faces, Edges, and Vertices of Polyhedra

To do this activity, you will need to have made a polyhedron, either out of paper; out of plastic, snap-together triangles, squares, or pentagons; or out of a combination of these polygons.

1. Count the number of faces, edges, and vertices of your polyhedron. The following table lists numbers of faces, edges, and vertices of shapes that other students have made in the past. Record your data and the data of some of your classmates in the blank spaces.

	# Faces	# Edges	# Vertices
yours			
partner			
partner			
partner			
partner			
partner			
shape 1	14	21	9
shape 2	10	15	7
shape 3	24	36	14
shape 4	4	6	4
shape 5	8	12	6
shape 6	20	30	12

2. There is an interesting relationship between the numbers of faces, edges, and vertices. Can you find it?

   The previously recorded data (for shapes 1–6) are from polyhedra made only out of triangles. For polyhedra made only out of triangles, there is a special relationship between the number of faces and the number of edges that other polyhedra do not share. Can you find it? *Challenge:* Explain why this relationship must hold.

13.2 Patterns and Surface Area

Class Activity 13G: What Shapes Do These Patterns Make?

Scissors and tape would be helpful for this activity.

1. Figure 13G.1 shows small patterns for solid shapes. *Visualize* the shapes that patterns 1, 2, 3, and 4 will make. What shapes are they?

   Compare the patterns and note similarities. Which shapes will be similar, and how will these shapes be similar?

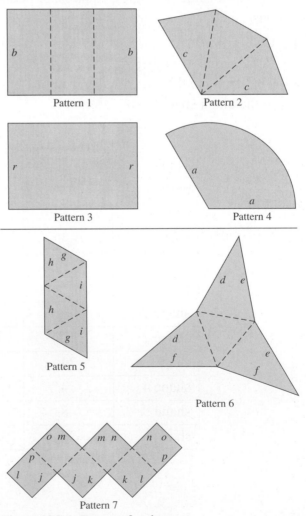

Figure 13G.1 Patterns for shapes

2. Patterns 1, 2, 3, and 4 do not close up because they don't include the bases. Show how you would modify these patterns to include the bases. What are the similarities?

3. *Visualize* the shapes that patterns 5, 6, and 7 will make. What shapes are they? Do any of these patterns make the same shape or the same kind of shape as patterns 1 through 4?

4. Now cut out the patterns on page (413) (or make your own similar patterns), fold along the dotted lines, and join edges with the same labels to make the shapes. Rethink, and possibly revise, your answers to parts 1 through 3.

Class Activity 13H:
Patterns for Prisms and Pyramids

You will need scissors, tape, a compass, a ruler, graph paper, and blank paper for this activity.

1. Examine the patterns in the next set of figures. Try to visualize what would happen if you were to cut these patterns out on the heavy lines, fold them on the dotted lines, and tape various sides together. What kinds of polyhedra would they make? Which parts of the patterns would make the bases?

   Now cut out the large versions of these patterns on pages (415), (417), (419), and (421) by cutting on the heavy lines, fold them on the dotted lines, and tape (or hold) the sides together to form various polyhedra. Were your predictions correct?

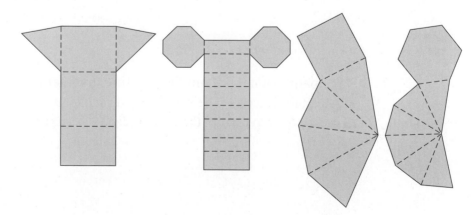

2. Use graph paper to make a pattern for a prism whose bases are a rectangle that is not a square. Include the bases in your pattern. Cut out your pattern and see if it works.

3. Let's say that the width, length, and height of the prism that you made in part 2 are W cm, L cm, and H cm respectively (it's up to you which edge length you call which). Show which lengths on your pattern are W, L, and H. Then find a formula in terms of W, L, and H for the total surface area of the prism and explain your reasoning.

4. Use a ruler and a compass to make a pattern for a pyramid that has a triangle base of side lengths 4 cm, 5 cm, and 6 cm (or divide the numbers by 2 and use inches if your ruler doesn't have centimeter markings).

Class Activity 13I: Patterns for Cylinders

You will need blank paper, scissors, and tape for this activity.

1. Take a standard 8.5-inch-by-11-inch piece of paper, roll it up, and tape it, without overlapping the paper, to make a cylinder without bases, as shown in the next figure. What is the area of the surface of the cylinder not including the bases? Why?

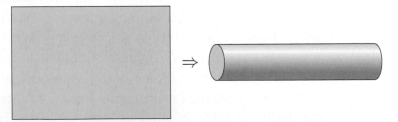

   What is the surface area of the cylinder (including the bases)? Explain.

2. A company wants to manufacture tin cans that are 3 inches in diameter and 4 inches tall. Describe the shape and dimensions of the paper label the company will need to wrap around the side of each can. Explain your reasoning.

3. Predict the shape you will make when you follow the next instructions.
   Cut out the rectangle on page (443). Cut along the curve, then attach the side labeled A to the side labeled B (without overlaps). Attach the side labeled C to the side labeled D (without overlaps).

Class Activity 13J: Patterns for Cones

1. How does one make a pattern for the lateral portion (i.e., the side portion, which does not include the base) of a cone? The pattern should not require the paper to overlap. Describe which edges would be joined to make the cone from the pattern.

2. On a piece of paper, draw half of a circle that has radius 5 inches. (*Suggestion:* Put the point of your compass in the middle of the long edge of the piece of paper.) Cut out the half-circle, and attach the two radii on the straight edge (the diameter) to form a cone without a base. Calculate the radius of the circle that will form a base for your cone. Explain your reasoning. Then draw this circle, and verify that it does form the base of the cone.

3. Make a pattern for a cone such that the base is a circle of radius 2 inches and the cone without the base is made from a half-circle. Determine the total surface area of your cone. Explain your reasoning.

4. Make a pattern for a cone such that the base is a circle of radius 2 inches and the lateral portion of the cone is made from part of a circle of radius 6 inches. What fraction of the 6-inch circle will you need to use? Determine the total surface area of your cone. Explain your reasoning.

Class Activity 13K: Cross-Sections of a Pyramid

Modeling dough or modeling clay and dental floss would be helpful for part 2.

The following picture shows a pyramid with a square base like an Egyptian pyramid:

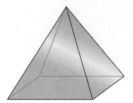

1. Visualize a plane slicing through the pyramid. The places where the plane meets the pyramid form a shape in the plane. Which shapes in the plane can be made this way, as a cross-section of the pyramid?

    List some plane shapes that you think *can* occur as a cross-section of the pyramid.

    List some plane shapes that you think *cannot* occur as a cross-section of the pyramid.

2. If available, use modeling dough or modeling clay to make a pyramid. Slice straight through the pyramid with dental floss, as if you were slicing the pyramid with a plane. Observe the cross-section that you create this way (i.e., the plane shape where the pyramid was cut). Put the pyramid back together and slice it in a different way.

    List the cross-sections you found by slicing the pyramid in various ways.

3. Think more about which plane shapes can and cannot occur as a cross-section of the pyramid. For each of the following shapes, either explain how the shape can occur as a cross-section of the pyramid or explain why it cannot occur: a trapezoid, a pentagon, a hexagon.

Class Activity 13L: Cross-Sections of a Long Rectangular Prism

Modeling clay or modeling dough and dental floss would be helpful for this activity.

Suppose you have a very long 2-inch-by-4-inch board in the shape of a rectangular prism as pictured here:

If you saw through the board with a straight cut, the place where the board was cut makes a shape in a plane (a cross-section). In this activity, consider only cuts that go through the middle of the board, *not through the ends*.

1. Is it possible to saw the board with a straight cut in such a way that the shape formed by the cut is a square? Try to visualize if this is or isn't possible.

2. Is it possible to saw the board with a straight cut in such a way that the shape formed by the cut is *not* a rectangle? (A square *is* a kind of rectangle.) Try to visualize if this is or isn't possible. If the answer is yes, what kind of shape other than a rectangle can you get?

3. Use modeling dough to make a model of a long 2-inch-by-4-inch board. Make a straight slice through your model with dental floss. Describe the plane shape that the cut made. Now restore your model of the board to its original shape and make a different slice through your model. Keep trying different ways to slice your model. Describe all the different shapes you get where the model was cut.

4. Are there any plane shapes that can't arise from slicing the board? Give some examples. How do you know they can't arise? In particular, are these shapes possible: a pentagon? a quadrilateral that is not a parallelogram?

Class Activity 13M: Shadows of Solid Shapes

You will need flashlights or other lights and some solid shapes for this activity. If flashlights are not available, solid shapes can be placed on an overhead projector instead.

1. List two shapes that can be the shadow of a cylinder. If possible, check your answers by holding a cylinder under a light.

2. Give an example of a shape that can make these two shadows: a rectangle and a triangle.

3. Give an example of a shape that can make these two shadows: a triangle and a pentagon.

13.3 Volumes of Solid Shapes

Class Activity 13N: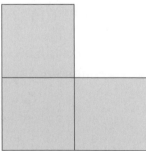
Why the Volume Formula for Prisms and Cylinders Makes Sense

Cubic-inch blocks would be helpful for this activity.

1. What does it mean to say that a solid shape has a volume of 12 cubic inches?

2. Explain why the

$$(height) \times (area\ of\ base)$$

formula gives the correct volume for right prisms and cylinders. Do so by imagining that the prism or cylinder is built with 1-unit-by-1-unit-by-1-unit clay cubes (or other cubes that could be cut into pieces, if necessary). Think about building the shape in layers.

- How many layers would you need?

- How many cubes would be in each layer?

If cubic-inch blocks are available, it may help you to build prisms on the bases shown here, as instructed. Use these models to help you explain why the volume formula is valid.

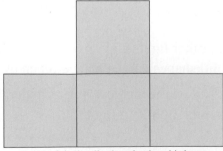

Build a 3-inch-tall prism that has this base.   Build a 4-inch-tall prism that has this base.

3. In the volume formula for prisms and cylinders, the height is a *length* and the area of the base is an *area*. How are this length and area *linked to yet different from* the number of layers and the number of cubes in each layer in your explanation in part 2?

4. Use the result of part 2 and Cavalieri's principle to explain why

$$(\text{height}) \times (\text{area of base})$$

gives the correct volume for an *oblique* prism or cylinder. Explain why the height should be measured perpendicular to the bases, and not "on the slant."

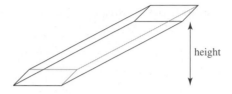

Class Activity 13O: Filling Boxes and Jars

1. How many plastic 2-cm-by-2-cm-by-2-cm cubes can be stacked neatly in an 8-cm-by-10-cm-by-12-cm box? Explain.

2. How many plastic 2-cm-by-2-cm-by-2-cm cubes can be stacked neatly in an 8-cm-by-9-cm-by-12-cm box? Explain.

3. A BerryBombs cereal box is 10 inches tall, $7\frac{1}{2}$ inches wide, and $2\frac{1}{2}$ inches deep. Give the length, width, and height of a cardboard box that could hold exactly 12 BerryBombs cereal boxes, leaving no extra space. Now find the dimensions of another box that could hold 12 BerryBombs cereal boxes with no extra space.

4. A 9-inch-by-9-inch-by-12-inch jar in the shape of a rectangular prism is completely filled with gum balls of diameter $\frac{3}{4}$ inches. Estimate the number of gum balls in the jar, and explain your reasoning.

5. A jar in the shape of a 9-inch-tall cylinder with a circular base of diameter 6 inches is completely filled with gum balls of diameter $\frac{3}{4}$ inches. Estimate the number of gum balls in the jar, and explain your reasoning.

Class Activity 13P: Comparing the Volume of a Pyramid with the Volume of a Rectangular Prism

You will need scissors, tape, and dry beans or rice for this activity.

1. Cut out, fold, and tape the patterns on pages 447 and 447A to make an open rectangular prism and an open pyramid with a square base.

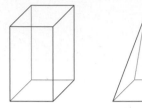

2. Verify that the prism and the pyramid have bases of the same area and have equal heights.

3. Just by looking at your shapes, make a guess: How do you think the volume of the pyramid compares with the volume of the prism?

4. Now fill the pyramid with beans, and pour the beans into the prism. Keep filling and pouring until the prism is full. Based on your results, fill in the blanks in the equations that follow:

$$\text{volume of prism} = \underline{\ \ } \times \text{volume of pyramid}$$
$$\text{volume of pyramid} = \underline{\ \ } \times \text{volume of prism}$$

Class Activity 13Q: The $\frac{1}{3}$ in the Volume Formula for Pyramids and Cones

You will need scissors and tape for this activity.

According to the volume formula, a right pyramid that is 1 unit high and has a 1-unit-by-1-unit square base has volume

$$\frac{1}{3} \times 1 \times (1 \times 1) \text{ unit}^3 = \frac{1}{3} \text{ unit}^3$$

Now pretend that you *don't yet* know the volume formula for pyramids and cones. This class activity will help you use principles about volumes to explain where the $\frac{1}{3}$ comes from.

1. Cut out three of the four patterns on pages 449 and 451. (The fourth is a spare.) Fold these patterns along the *undashed* line segments, and glue or tape them to make three *oblique* pyramids. Make sure the dashed lines appear on the outside of each oblique pyramid.

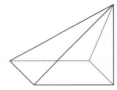

2. Fit the three oblique pyramids together to make a familiar shape. What shape is it? What is the volume of the shape formed from the three oblique pyramids? Therefore, what is the volume of one of the oblique pyramids?

3. Use your answers to parts 2 and 3, and Cavalieri's principle, to explain why a *right* pyramid that is 1 unit high and has a 1-unit-by-1-unit square base has volume $\frac{1}{3}$ cubic units. (The dashed lines on the model oblique pyramids are meant to help you see how to shear the oblique pyramid. Imagine that the oblique pyramids are made out of a stack of small pieces of paper, where each dashed line going around the oblique pyramid represents a piece of paper.)

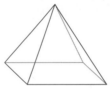

Class Activity 13R: Volume Problem Solving

1. A cone without a base is made from a half-circle of radius 10 cm. Determine the volume of the cone. Explain your reasoning.

2. Consider the block pictured next.

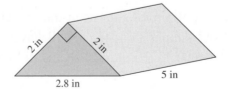

   a. Which of the following can be applied to determine the volume of the block: the pyramid volume formula, the prism volume formula, both, or neither? Explain, and determine the volume of the block with a formula if it is possible to do so.

   b. Determine the volume of the block in another way and explain your reasoning.

3. Determine the volume of the staircase pictured next in two different ways.

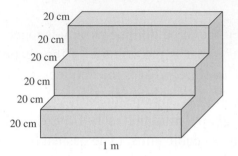

Class Activity 13S: 🗘
The Volume of a Rhombic Dodecahedron

1. Cut out the patterns on page 453 and use them to make 6 pyramids.

2. Cut out the pattern on the bottom of page 455 and use it to make a cube.

3. Let's say the cube is 1 unit wide, 1 unit deep, and 1 unit high. Determine the volumes of the pyramids. You may put shapes together to do so.

4. Cut out the two patterns at the top of page 455 and put them together to make a closed shape. The shape will have 12 faces, each of which is a rhombus. The shape is called a **rhombic dodecahedron.**

5. Determine the volume of the rhombic dodecahedron. You may put shapes together to do so.

6. One interesting property of rhombic dodecahedra is that they can be stacked and fit together to fill up space without any gaps. If you have a number of rhombic dodecahedra, try this out. Cubes can also be stacked and fit together to fill up space without any gaps, but ordinary dodecahedra (with pentagon faces) cannot.

Class Activity 13T: Volume versus Surface Area and Height

You will need several blank pieces of paper (including graph paper if available), a ruler, scissors, and tape for parts of this activity.

1. Young children sometimes think that taller containers necessarily hold more than shorter ones. Make or describe two open-top boxes such that the taller box has a smaller volume than the shorter box.

2. Students sometimes get confused between the volume and surface area of a solid shape and about how to calculate volume and surface area.

    a. Discuss the distinction between volume and surface area.

    b. Discuss the differences and similarities in the way we calculate the volume and surface area of a rectangular prism.

3. *A cylinder volume contest*: Each team may use no more than one ordinary piece of paper to make a cylinder with no bases. The paper may be cut apart and taped to make the cylinder. The team that makes the cylinder of largest volume wins the contest.

    a. Would it be possible to make a cylinder of even larger volume than the winning team's cylinder?

    b. What is the area of the side surface of the winning cylinder (not including the bases)? How does it compare to the other teams' cylinders?

    c. What is the height of the winning cylinder? How does it compare to the other teams' cylinders?

13.4 Volume of Submersed Objects versus Weight of Floating Objects

Class Activity 13U: Determining Volumes by Submersing in Water

For parts of this activity you will need a milliliter measuring cup, water, a centimeter ruler, and a good-sized lump of clay that still fits comfortably in your measuring cup. Use synthetic clay that does not dissolve in water. (Modeling dough dissolves in water.)

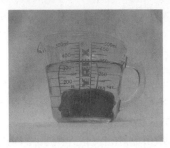

1. Form your lump of clay into a rectangular prism, and determine the volume of the clay in cubic centimeters by measuring the height, width, and length of the rectangular prism.

2. Pour water into your measuring cup and note the volume of water in milliliters. Predict what will happen to the water level when you submerse your clay prism in the water. Then test your prediction.

3. What if you subdivided your clay into several pieces or formed the clay into a different shape? Would the clay still displace the same amount of water when it is submersed?

Class Activity 13V:
Underwater Volume Problems

1. A container can hold 2 liters. Initially, the container is $\frac{1}{2}$ full of water. When an object is placed in the container, the object sinks to the bottom and the container becomes $\frac{2}{3}$ full. What is the volume of the object in cubic centimeters? Explain.

2. A tank in the shape of a rectangular prism is 50 cm tall, 80 cm long, and 30 cm wide. First, some rocks were placed at the bottom of the tank. Then 80 liters of water were poured into the tank. At that point, the tank was $\frac{3}{4}$ full. What is the total volume of the rocks in cubic meters? Explain.

3. A fish tank in the shape of a rectangular prism is 1 m long and 30 cm wide. The tank was $\frac{1}{2}$ full. Then 30 liters of water were poured in and the tank became $\frac{2}{3}$ full. How tall is the tank? Explain your reasoning.

Class Activity 13W: Floating versus Sinking: Archimedes's Principle

For this activity you will need a milliliter measuring cup, water, and modeling clay that does not dissolve in water. In part 3 you will need a scale for weighing. In part 4 you will need a small paper cup and several coins or other small, heavy objects that fit inside the cup.

1. Pour water into your measuring cup and note the volume of water in milliliters. Form your clay into a "boat" that will float. By how much does the water level rise when you float your clay boat? Does this increase in water level tell you the volume of the clay?

2. Predict what will happen to the water level when you sink your clay boat: Will the water level go up or will the water level go down? Sink your boat and see if your prediction was correct.

   Did the increase in water level in part 1 tell you the volume of the clay, or not? Explain.

3. Exactly how much water does a floating object displace? Do the following to find out:

   a. Weigh your clay boat from part 1.

   b. Weigh an amount of water that weighs as much as your clay boat.

   c. Float your clay boat in the measuring cup and record the water level.

   d. Remove your clay boat from the water and pour the water you measured in part (b) into the measuring cup. Compare the water level now to the water level in part (c). If you did everything correctly, these two water levels should be the same.

      This experiment illustrates **Archimedes's principle** that a floating object displaces an amount of water that weighs as much as the object.

4. Determine approximately how much a quarter weighs in grams by using Archimedes's principle. Observe how much the water level rises when you put several quarters in a small cup floating in water in a measuring cup.

5. Ships usually have markings on their sides to show how low or high the ship is floating in the water. Besides showing how low or high the ship is floating, what other information could the captain of the ship get by observing which mark is at the water line?

6. The Great Salt Lake in Utah and the Dead Sea in Israel and Jordan are lakes that have so much salt in them that people float in the water. (See Figure 13W.1) Use Archimedes's principle to explain why people float in these lakes. What is it about this salty water that causes people to float?

Figure 13W.1 Floating in the Dead Sea

Geometry of Motion and Change

14.1 Reflections, Translations, and Rotations

Class Activity 14A: Exploring Rotations

You will need scissors for this activity.

1. Cut out the large circle and the two copies of a shape on page 421.

2. Place one copy of the shape on one side of your circle. You will be rotating your circle by 180° (a half turn) about its center. But before you rotate your circle, try to visualize the final position and orientation of your shape. Place the second copy of the shape on the circle to show how you think the first shape will be oriented after you rotate the circle 180°.

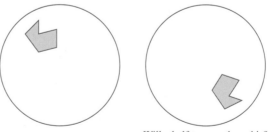

Will a half turn produce this?

3. Leave the first shape on the circle. Without changing the orientation of the second shape, move it to the side of the circle. Hold the center of the circle down with the tip of a pencil and rotate the circle 180° about its center. Did you correctly predict the final orientation of your shape? If so, the first and second shapes will be oriented in the same way.

4. Repeat the previous steps, but this time with your shape in a different orientation or in a different location on the circle. Keep repeating until you can accurately predict the final orientation of the shape after the circle is rotated.

5. Repeat the previous steps, but this time with a 90° rotation (a quarter turn), either clockwise or counterclockwise, instead of a 180° rotation.

Class Activity 14B: Exploring Reflections

You will need scissors, and reusable adhesive clay or paper clips, for this activity.

1. Cut out the large circle and the two copies of a shape on page 421. You may want to shade the backs of the shapes so that they look the same (more or less) on the front and back. Fold your circle in half to form a crease line that goes through the center of the circle.

2. Place one copy of the shape somewhere on the circle. You will be reflecting the shape across the crease line in the circle. But before you reflect the shape, try to visualize its final position and orientation. Place the second copy of the shape on the circle to show where you think the first shape will be located and how you think the first shape will be oriented after you reflect it across the line. Attach the second shape to the circle with adhesive clay or paper clips.

 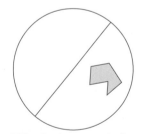

Will reflecting across the line
produce this?

3. Now reflect your first shape across the line by holding the shape in place, folding the circle along the line (with the shapes on the inside), and transferring the shape to the other side of the circle. Did you correctly predict the final position and orientation of your shape? If so, the two shapes will match one another exactly.

4. Repeat the previous steps, but this time with your shape in a different orientation or in a different location. Also, change the orientation of the crease line: Make it horizontal, vertical, and diagonal.

Class Activity 14C: Exploring Reflections with Geometer's Sketchpad

For this activity, you will need to use the drawing tools for drawing circles, line segments, lines, rays, and points in Geometer's Sketchpad. You will also need to select objects with the selection tool.

1. Draw a shape or design that is not symmetrical, such as the one shown in the next figure. Then, separately, draw a line, a line segment, or a ray. Select the line, line segment, or ray, and then choose *Mark Mirror* from the *Transform* menu.

2. Your next step will be to reflect your shape across your line. Before you continue, try to visualize the location and orientation of the reflected shape.

3. Select your shape, and then choose *Reflect* from the *Transform* menu. Geometer's Sketchpad shows you both the initial location of your shape and its final location after reflection across your marked line.

4. Move your original shape and your marked line around on the screen, and observe the new locations and orientations of the reflected shape. Be sure to change the direction of your marked line, too. Why does the final position of your shape turn out the way it does? Before you move your original shape or your marked line, try to visualize how the location and orientation of the reflected shape will change.

Class Activity 14D: Exploring Translations with Geometer's Sketchpad

For this activity, you will need to use the drawing tools for drawing circles, line segments, lines, rays, and points in Geometer's Sketchpad. You will also need to select objects with the selection tool.

1. Draw a shape or design that is not symmetrical, such as the one shown in the next figure. Then, separately, draw a line segment. Select the two endpoints of this line segment and choose *Mark Vector* from the *Transform* menu.

2. Your next step will be to translate your shape with the direction and distance specified by your line segment. Before you continue, try to visualize the location and orientation of the translated shape.

3. Select your shape, and then choose *Translate* from the *Transform* menu. Geometer's Sketchpad shows you both the initial location of your shape and its final location after translation by the distance and direction determined by your line segment.

4. Move your original shape around on the screen, and change the length and direction of your line segment. Why does the final position of your shape turn out the way it does? Before you move your original shape or your line segment, try to visualize how the location of the translated shape will change.

Class Activity 14E: Exploring Rotations with Geometer's Sketchpad

For this activity, you will need to use the tools for drawing circles, line segments, lines, rays, and points in Geometer's Sketchpad. You will also need to select objects with the selection tool.

Exploring rotations by a fixed angle:

1. Draw a shape or design that is not symmetrical, such as the one shown in the next figure. Then, separately, draw a single point. Select that point, and then choose *Mark Center* from the *Transform* menu.

2. Your next step will be to rotate your shape about your chosen point by an angle that you will specify. Before you continue, try to visualize the location and orientation of your shape after rotation.

3. Select your shape, and choose *Rotate* from the *Transform* menu. A dialog box will appear. Select *By fixed angle*, and enter any angle you wish in the appropriate place. (If the dialog box indicates that angles are being measured in radians, then choose *Preferences* from the *Display* menu, and change the angle unit to degrees using the pull-down menu.) Geometer's Sketchpad shows you both the initial location of your shape and its final location after rotation about the point you marked as center, by the angle you selected.

4. Move your original shape, and move the point that you marked as center around your screen. Observe the location and orientation of your rotated shape. Why does the final position of your shape turn out the way it does? Before you move your original shape or your marked center, try to visualize how the location and orientation of the rotated shape will change.

Exploring rotations by a marked angle:

1. Draw a shape or design that is not symmetrical, such as the one shown in the next figure. Then, separately, draw a single point. Select that point, then choose *Mark Center* from the *Transform* menu.

2. Make an angle by drawing two line segments that share an endpoint. Select the three endpoints so that the second point you select is the shared endpoint. Choose *Mark Angle* from the *Transform* menu.

3. Your next step will be to rotate your shape about your marked point, by your marked angle. Before you continue, try to visualize the location and orientation of your rotated shape.

4. Select your shape, and choose *Rotate* from the *Transform* menu. Geometer's Sketchpad shows you both the initial location of your shape and its final location after rotating about your marked point, by your marked angle.

5. Move your original shape and your marked center point around the screen. Why does the final position of your shape turn out the way it does? Before you move your original shape or your marked center, try to visualize how the location and orientation of your rotated shape will change.

6. Now move one of the endpoints of your marked angle. Why does the final position of your shape move the way it does? Before you move your marked angle, try to visualize how the location and orientation of the rotated shape will change.

Class Activity 14F: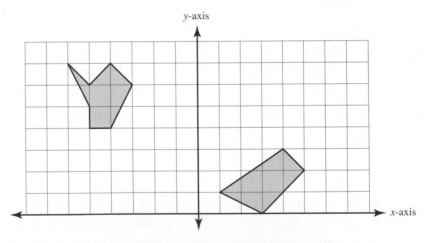
Reflections, Rotations, and Translations in a Coordinate Plane

1. Draw the result of translating the shaded shapes in the next figure according to the direction and the distance given by the arrow. Explain how you know where to draw your translated shapes. It may help you to consider the coordinates of the vertices of the shapes.

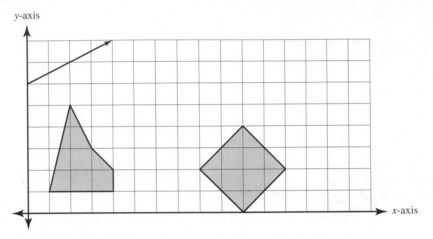

2. Draw the result of reflecting the shaded shapes in the next figure across the y-axis. Explain how you know where to draw your reflected shapes. It may help you to consider the coordinates of the vertices of the shapes.

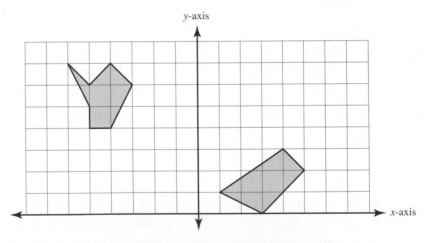

3. Draw the result of rotating the shaded shapes in the next figure by 180° around the origin, where the *x*- and *y*-axes meet. Explain how you know where to draw your rotated shapes. It may help you to consider the coordinates of the vertices of the shapes.

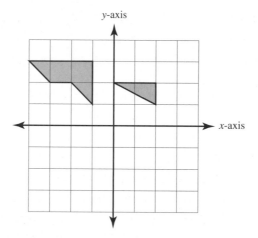

4. Draw the result of rotating the shaded shapes in the next figure by 90° counterclockwise around the origin, where the *x*- and *y*-axes meet. Explain how you know where to draw your rotated shapes. It may help you to consider the coordinates of the vertices of the shapes.

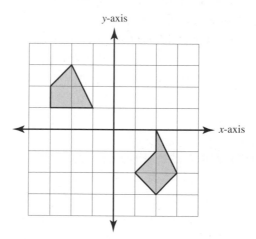

14.2 Symmetry

Class Activity 14G:
Checking for Symmetry

You will need scissors, and a toothpick or paper clip, for this activity.

Five small designs are shown in the next set of diagrams. Cut out two copies of each of these designs on pages 423 and 425. For each design, determine whether the design has reflection symmetry, and if so, what the lines of symmetry are; determine if the design has rotation symmetry, and if so, whether it has 2-fold, 3-fold, 4-fold, or other rotation symmetry; and determine whether the design has translation symmetry.

To determine whether a design has reflection symmetry, see if there is a line such that, when you fold the paper along the line, the portions of the design on either side of the fold line match one another.

To determine whether a design has rotation symmetry, put one copy of the design on top of another copy, so that when you hold the two pieces of paper up to a light, you see that the designs match one another. Poke a toothpick or paper clip through the two copies of the design. Then rotate the top copy of the design while keeping the bottom copy fixed. If you can rotate less than 360° and the designs match again, then the design has rotation symmetry. If you can rotate by that same amount n times in a row and the top design then moves back into its starting position, then the design has n-fold rotation symmetry.

To determine whether a design has translation symmetry, put one copy of the design on top of another copy, so that when you hold the two pieces of paper up to a light, you see that the designs match one another. Slide one copy of the design over the other copy. If the two copies of the design match again, then the design has translation symmetry. True translation symmetry can occur only with designs that are infinitely long, so you may need to imagine the design continuing on forever.

Class Activity 14H: Frieze Patterns

You will need scissors for this activity.

Seven different frieze patterns are shown next. Cut out two copies of each of these seven frieze patterns on pages 427, 429, 431, and 433 by cutting along the gray lines. Picture each of the seven frieze patterns repeating on an infinitely long strip of paper, continuing forever, forward and backward.

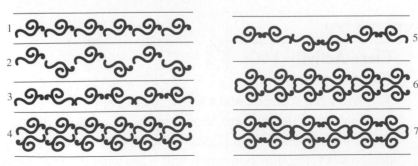

Show that each frieze pattern has translation symmetry. For each frieze pattern, determine whether the pattern has reflection symmetry and, if so, what the lines of symmetry are; determine whether the pattern has rotation symmetry and, if so, whether it has 2-fold, 3-fold, 4-fold, or other rotation symmetry; and determine whether the pattern has glide-reflection symmetry.

See the text or see Class Activity 14G to learn how to check for translation, rotation, and reflection symmetry.

To check for glide-reflection symmetry, put one copy of the pattern on top of another copy, so that when you hold the two pieces of paper up to a light, you see that the patterns match one another. Flip the top copy over, so that the two patterns are face to face. Slide one copy of the pattern over the other copy. If the two copies of the pattern can be made to match one another again, then the pattern has glide-reflection symmetry. As with translation symmetry, true glide-reflection symmetry can occur only with patterns that are infinitely long, so you will need to imagine the pattern continuing on forever.

Class Activity 14I: Traditional Quilt Designs

1. Complete the next four traditional quilt patch designs so that each one has both a horizontal and a vertical line of symmetry.

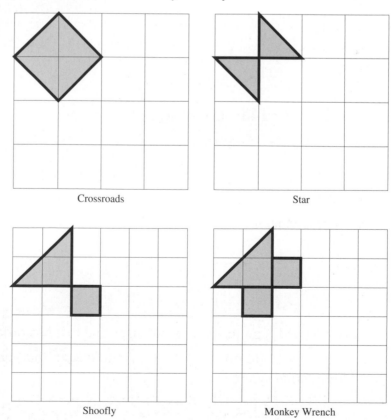

Crossroads

Star

Shoofly

Monkey Wrench

2. Complete the next four traditional quilt patch designs so that each one has 4-fold rotation symmetry.

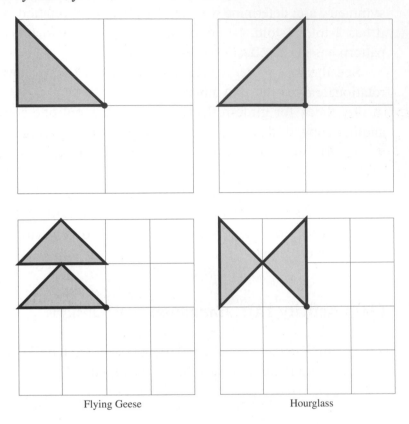

Flying Geese   Hourglass

Class Activity 14J: Creating Symmetrical Design with Geometer's Sketchpad

To do this activity, you need to rotate, reflect, and translate objects in Geometer's Sketchpad.

1. Start by making a shape that *does not* have symmetry, such as the following:

2. Create a design that uses your shape and that has reflection symmetry.

3. Create a finite portion of an infinite design that uses your shape and that has translation symmetry.

4. Create a design that uses your shape and has 6-fold rotation symmetry.

5. Now create a design that uses your shape and that has *both* 3-fold rotation symmetry *and* reflection symmetry. The design as a whole must have both types of symmetry. Describe how you created your design.

6. Create a finite portion of an infinite design that uses your shape and that has glide-reflection symmetry.

Class Activity 14K: Creating Symmetrical Designs (Alternate)

You will need graph paper for this activity.

1. On graph paper, draw a simple asymmetrical shape, such as this asymmetrical triangle.

2. By drawing copies of your shape, create a finite portion of an infinite design that has translation symmetry.

3. By drawing copies of your shape, create a design that has 4-fold rotation symmetry.

4. By drawing copies of your shape, create a design that has *both* 4-fold rotation symmetry *and* reflection symmetry. The design as a whole must have both types of symmetry simultaneously. Describe how you created your design.

5. By drawing copies of your shape, create a finite portion of an infinite design that has glide-reflection symmetry.

Class Activity 14L:
Creating Escher-Type Designs with Geometer's Sketchpad (for Fun)

To do this activity, you must rotate and translate objects in Geometer's Sketchpad.

Follow the instructions in Figure 14L.1 to create your own Escher-type design. Be sure to select the points, and not just the line segments, when you rotate and translate the various portions of the design. You will need some of those points to specify subsequent rotations or translations.

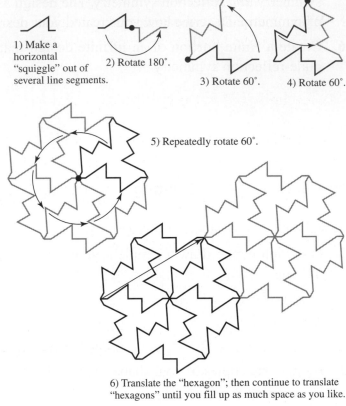

1) Make a horizontal "squiggle" out of several line segments.

2) Rotate 180°.

3) Rotate 60°.

4) Rotate 60°.

5) Repeatedly rotate 60°.

6) Translate the "hexagon"; then continue to translate "hexagons" until you fill up as much space as you like.

Figure 14L.1 How to make an Escher-type design

14.3 Congruence

Class Activity 14M:
Triangles and Quadrilaterals of Specified Side Lengths

You will need scissors, several straws, and some string for this activity.

1. Cut a 3-inch, a 4-inch, and a 5-inch piece of straw, and thread all three straw pieces onto a piece of string. Tie a knot so as to form a triangle from the three pieces of straw.

2. Now cut two 3-inch pieces of straw and two 4-inch pieces of straw, and thread all four straw pieces onto another piece of string in the following order: 3-inch, 4-inch, 3-inch, 4-inch. Tie a knot so as to form a quadrilateral from the four pieces of straw.

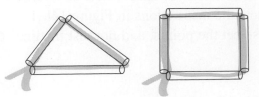

3. Compare your straw triangle and your straw quadrilateral. What is an obvious difference between them (other than the fact that the triangle is made of three pieces and the quadrilateral is made of four)?

4. When you made your triangle, if you had strung your three pieces of straw in a different order, would your triangle be different or not?

Class Activity 14N: Describing a Triangle

You will need a compass, protractor, and ruler for this activity.

For each of the following, draw a triangle that has vertices A, B, and C and has the given specifications. Think about whether any other such triangle will necessarily be congruent to yours or not. Then compare your triangle to a neighbor's. Are they congruent or not?

Triangle 1 Three side lengths are given:

From A to B is 6 cm.

From B to C is 7 cm.

From C to A is 8 cm.

Triangle 2 Two side lengths and the angle between them are given:

From A to B is 5 cm.

The angle at A is 40°.

From A to C is 7 cm.

Triangle 3 All three angles are given:

The angle at A is 20°.

The angle at B is 70°.

The angle at C is 90°.

Triangle 4 A side length and the angle at both ends are given:

The angle at A is 30°.

From A to B is 8 cm.

The angle at B is 45°.

Triangle 5 Two side lengths and an angle that is not between them are given:

The angle at A is 20°.

From A to B is 8 cm.

From B to C is 4 cm.

Class Activity 14O: Triangles with an Angle, a Side, and an Angle Specified

You will need a protractor and one or two straightedges or rulers for this activity.

1. Create a triangle that has AB (in the next figure) as one side, a 30° angle at A, and a 45° angle at B. Is there more than one way to do this? If so, compare the different triangles.

A ———————————— B

2. Create a triangle that has AB (in the next figure) as one side, a 100° angle at A, and a 30° angle at B. Is there more than one way to do this? If so, compare the different triangles.

A ———————————— B

3. Make up a problem like the previous two, but with different angles. Can you use any pair of angles, or is there some restriction on which pairs of angles you can specify at A and B in order to form a triangle? Explain.

A ———————————— B

Class Activity 14P:
Using Triangle Congruence Criteria

1. We defined a parallelogram to be a quadrilateral for which opposite sides are parallel. When we look at parallelograms, it appears that opposite sides also have the same length. Use a triangle congruence criterion and facts we studied previously about angles to explain why opposite sides of a parallelogram really must have the same length. In order to do so, consider the two triangles formed by the diagonal.

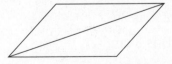

2. Here is an old-fashioned way to make a rectangular foundation for a house. Take a pair of identical pieces of wood for the length of the house and another pair of identical pieces of wood for the width of the house. Place the wood on the ground to show approximately where the foundation will go. The pieces of wood now form a quadrilateral whose opposite sides are the same length. Measure the two

diagonals of the quadrilateral, and keep adjusting the quadrilateral until the two diagonals are the same length. Explain why the quadrilateral must now be a rectangle. In other words, explain why the quadrilateral must have 4 right angles.

14.4 Similarity

Class Activity 14Q: Mathematical Similarity versus Similarity in Everyday Language

In mathematics, the terms *similar* and *similarity* have a much more specific meaning than they do in everyday language.

Examine the next shapes. In everyday language, we might say that all the shapes are similar. But mathematically, only the top two shapes on the right are similar to the original shape. How is the relationship of those two shapes to the original shape different from the relationship of the other two shapes to the original shape?

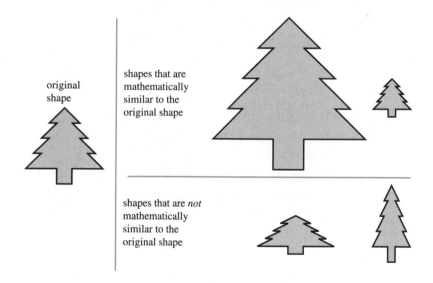

Class Activity 14R: A First Look at Solving Scaling Problems

You have a poster that is 2 feet wide and 4 feet long. The poster has a simple design on it that you would like to scale up and draw onto a larger poster. The larger poster is to be 6 feet wide. How long should the poster be?

Find as many different ways as you can to solve this poster-scaling problem. In each case, explain your reasoning.

Class Activity 14S: 🗿
Using the Scale Factor, Internal Factor, and Set Up a Proportion Method

1. Suppose that you have a postcard with an attractive picture on it and that you would like to scale up this picture and draw it onto paper that you can cut from a roll. The roll of paper is 20 inches wide, and you can cut the paper to virtually any length. If the postcard picture is 4 inches wide and 6 inches long, then how long should you cut the 20-inch-wide paper? Assume that the 4-inch side will become 20 inches long.

   Use three different methods to solve the postcard problem: the *scale factor* method, the *internal factor* method, and the *set up a proportion* method. In each case, explain why the method makes sense. Explain the first two methods in as concrete a way as you can, as if you were teaching fifth- or sixth-graders who know about multiplication and division, but who do not know about setting up proportions.

   Show how you can also apply the first two methods to the proportion you set up for the proportion method.

2. Decide whether the next problem is easier to solve with the scale factor method or with the internal factor method. Explain your answer.

   A stuffed-animal company wants to produce an enlarged version of a popular stuffed bunny. The original bunny is 6 inches wide and 11 inches tall. The enlarged bunny is to be 33 inches tall. How wide should the enlarged bunny be?

3. Decide whether the next problem is easier to solve with the scale factor method or with the internal factor method. Explain your answer.

   A toy company wants to produce a scale model of a car. The actual car is 6 feet wide and 12 feet long. The scale model of the car is to be $2\frac{1}{2}$ inches wide. How long should the scale model of the car be?

Class Activity 14T: A Common Misconception about Scaling

Johnny is working on the following problem:

    The picture on a poster that is 4 feet wide and 6 feet long is to be scaled down and drawn onto a small poster that is 1 foot wide. How long should the small poster be?

    Johnny solves the problem this way:

> One foot is 3 feet less than 4 feet, so the length of the small poster should also be 3 feet less than the length of the big poster. This means the small poster should be $6 - 3 = 3$ feet long.

Is Johnny's reasoning valid? Why or why not? If not, how might you convince Johnny that his reasoning is not correct? What would be a correct way to solve the problem in that case?

Class Activity 14U: Using Scaling to Understand Astronomical Distances

Ms. Frizzle's class has been studying planets and stars. Ms. Frizzle wants to help the students get a better sense of astronomical distances by scaling down these distances. The table that follows shows the distances in kilometers from the sun to the earth, the sun to Pluto, and the sun to Alpha Centauri. Alpha Centauri is one of the closest stars to the sun.

Heavenly Body	Approximate Distance from Sun
Earth	150 million km
Pluto	5.9 billion km
Alpha Centauri	38 trillion km

    If Ms. Frizzle represents the distance from the earth to the sun as 10 centimeters (about the width of a hand), then how should she represent the distance from Pluto to the sun? How should she represent the distance from Alpha Centauri to the sun? Explain your reasoning in such a way that fifth- or sixth-graders who understand multiplication and division, but who do not know about setting up proportions, might be able to understand.

    Will Ms. Frizzle be able to show these distances in her classroom? (Recall that 100 centimeters = 1 meter, and 1 meter is about 1 yard. One thousand meters is 1 kilometer, and 1 kilometer is about $\frac{6}{10}$ of a mile, so a little over half a mile.)

Class Activity 14V: More Scaling Problems

1. A large American flag can be 5 feet tall by 9 feet 6 inches wide. Suppose you want to make a scaled-down version of the flag. If the smaller flag is to be 2 feet tall, then how long should this smaller flag be? Give your answer in feet and inches.

2. A museum wants to put a scaled copy of one of its paintings onto a 3-inch-by-5-inch card. The painting is 42 inches by 65 inches. Explain why the copy of the painting can't fill the whole card without leaving blank spaces (i.e., explain why there will have to be a border). Recommend to the museum a size for the copy of the painting that will fit on a 3″ × 5″ card. Show your recommendation here in the rectangle, which is 3″ × 5″.

Class Activity 14W:
Measuring Distances by "Sighting"

To do this activity, you will need your own ruler and one or more yardsticks and tape measures that can be shared by the class.

This activity will help you understand how the theory of similar triangles is used in finding distances by surveying.

1. Stand a yardstick on end on the edge of a chalkboard, or tape the yardstick vertically to the wall.

2. Stand back, away from the yardstick, in a location where you can see the yardstick. Your goal is to find your distance to the yardstick. Guess or estimate this distance before you continue.

   Your guess of how far away the yardstick is:

3. Hold your ruler in front of you with an outstretched arm. Make the ruler vertical, so that it is parallel to the yardstick. Close one eye, and with your open eye, "sight" from the ruler to the yardstick. Use the ruler to determine how big the yardstick appears to be from your location.

   Record the apparent size of the yardstick here:

4. With your arm still stretched out in front of you, have a classmate measure the distance from your sighting eye to the ruler.

   Record the distance from your sighting eye to the ruler here:

5. Use the theory of similar triangles to determine your distance to the yardstick. Sketch your eye, the ruler, and the yardstick, showing the relevant similar triangles. (Your sketch does not need to be to scale.) Explain why the triangles are similar.

   Is your calculated distance close to your estimated distance? If not, which one seems to be faulty, and why?

6. Now move to a new location, and find your distance to the yardstick again with the same technique.

Class Activity 14X: Using a Shadow or a Mirror to Determine the Height of a Tree

This activity requires several tape measures that can be shared by the class. Part 2 requires a mirror.

How could you find the height of a tree, for example, without measuring it directly? This class activity provides two ways to do this with *similar triangles*.

First Method

Go outside and find a tree whose height you will measure. Before you continue, guess or estimate the height of the tree.

This method will work only if your tree is on level ground and casts a fully visible shadow. (So you need a sunny day.)

1. Measure the length of the shadow of the tree (from the base of the tree to the shadow of the tip of the tree).

2. Measure the height of a classmate, and measure the length of that person's shadow.

3. Sketch the two similar triangles in this situation. Explain why the triangles are similar. Use your similar triangles to find the height of the tree.

   Is your calculated height fairly close to your estimated height of the tree? If not, which one do you think is faulty? Why?

Second Method

Go outside and find a tree whose height you will measure. The tree should be on level ground for this method to work. Before you continue, guess or estimate the height of the tree.

1. Put a mirror on horizontal ground away from the tree. Stand back from the mirror at a location where you can look into the middle of the mirror and see the top of the tree (you will probably need to move around to find this location).

2. Record the following measurements:

   a. The distance from your feet to the middle of the mirror when you are looking into the middle of the mirror and can see the top of the tree.

   b. The distance from the ground to your eyes.

   c. The distance from the middle of the mirror to the base of the tree.

3. Sketch the two similar triangles in this situation. Explain why the triangles are similar. Use your similar triangles to find the height of the tree.

   Is your calculated height fairly close to your estimated height of the tree? If not, which one do you think is faulty? Why?

14.5 Areas, Volumes, and Scaling

Class Activity 14Y:
Areas and Volumes of Similar Boxes

You will need scissors and tape for this activity.

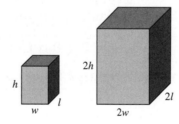

1. Cut out the patterns in Figures A.24A and A.25A on pages 449 and 451. Fold these patterns to make two boxes (rectangular prisms), but leave them untaped, so that you can still unfold them. One box will have width w, length l, and height h; and one box will have width $2w$, length $2l$, and height $2h$. So the big box is twice as wide, twice as long, and twice as high as the small box.

2. By working with the unfolded patterns of the two boxes, determine how the surface area of the big box compares with the surface area of the small box. Is the surface area of the big box twice as large, three times as large, and so on, as the surface area of the small box? Look and think carefully—the answer may not be what you first think it is. Explain clearly why your answer is correct.

3. Now tape up the small box. Tape up most of the large box, but leave an opening so that you can put the small box inside it. Determine how the volume of the big box compares with the volume of the small box. Is the volume of the big box twice as large, three times as large, and so on, as the volume of the small box? Once again, think carefully, and explain why your answer is correct.

4. What if there were an even bigger box whose width, length, and height were each three times the respective width, length, and height of the small box? How would the surface area of the bigger box compare with the surface area of the small box? Answer this question by thinking about how to make a pattern for the bigger box and determining how the pattern of the bigger box would compare with the pattern of the small box.

  How would the volume of the bigger box compare with the volume of the small box?

5. Now imagine a variety of bigger boxes. Fill in the first two empty columns in the next table with your previous results. Continue to fill in the remaining empty columns by extrapolating from your results.

Size of Big Box Compared with Small Box					
length, width, height	2 times	3 times	5 times	2.7 times	*k* times
surface area					
volume					

Class Activity 14Z: Areas and Volumes of Similar Cylinders

You will need scissors and tape for this activity.

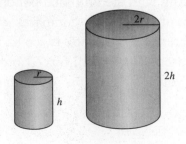

1. Cut out the patterns for cylinders, Figures A.26A and A.27A on pages 453 and 455. Use the patterns to make two cylinders, but don't glue or tape them because you will need to unfold them. The small cylinder has radius r and height h. The big cylinder has radius $2r$ and height $2h$, so the big cylinder has twice the radius and is twice as high as the small one.

2. How does the surface area of the large cylinder compare with the surface area of the small cylinder? Is it twice as large, three times as large, and so on? Use your patterns to get a feel for what the answer should be. Then give a clear and thorough explanation of your answer. To give a thorough explanation, you will have to do more than just physically compare the cylinders' patterns.

3. How does the volume of the large cylinder compare with the volume of the small cylinder? Is it twice as large, three times as large, and so forth? Tape up your patterns to form cylinders, and use the cylinders to get a feel for what the answer should be. Then give a clear and thorough explanation of your answer. To give a thorough explanation, you will have to do more than just physically compare the cylinders.

4. Now imagine a variety of bigger cylinders. Fill in the first empty column in the next table with your previous results. Continue to fill in the remaining empty columns by extrapolating from your results. Compare this table with the table in Problem 5 of the previous Class Activity.

Size of Big Cylinder Compared with Small Cylinder					
length, width, height	2 times	3 times	5 times	2.7 times	k times
surface area					
volume					

Class Activity 14AA: Determining Areas and Volumes of Scaled Objects

1. Compare your tables for part 5 of Class Activity 14Y and part 4 of Class Activity 14Z. Extrapolate from these results to answer the following questions: If someone made a Goodyear blimp that was 1.5 times as wide, 1.5 times as long, and 1.5 times as high as the current one, how much material would it take to

make the larger blimp compared with the current blimp? How much more gas would it take to fill this bigger Goodyear blimp, compared with the current one (at the same pressure)?

2. An adult alligator can be 15 feet long and weigh 475 pounds. Suppose that some excavated dinosaur bones indicate that the dinosaur was 30 feet long and was shaped roughly like an alligator. How much would you expect the dinosaur to have weighed?

alligator   dinosaur

3. Explain why we *can't* reason in either of the following two ways to solve part 2 of this activity:

   • Each foot of the alligator weighs 475 ÷ 15 = 31.6… pounds. So multiply that result by 30 to get the weight of the dinosaur as 950 pounds.

   • The dinosaur is twice as long as the alligator, so it should weigh twice as much, which is 950 pounds.

   What is wrong with those two ways of reasoning?

Class Activity 14BB: A Scaling Proof of the Pythagorean Theorem

This activity will help you use similar shapes to prove the Pythagorean theorem.

   Remember that the Pythagorean theorem says that for any right triangle with short sides of length a and b, and hypotenuse of length c,

$$a^2 + b^2 = c^2$$

1. Given any right triangle, such as the next triangle on the left, drop the perpendicular to the hypotenuse, as shown on the right.

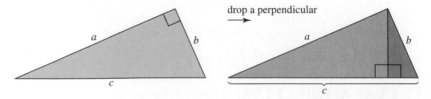

drop a perpendicular
→

   Use angles to explain why the two smaller right triangles on the right are similar to the original right triangle. (Do not use any actual measurements of angles, because the proof must be general—it must work for *any* initial right triangle.)

2. Now flip each of the three right triangles of part 1 over its hypotenuse, as shown. View each of the three right triangles as taking up a percentage of the area of the square formed on its hypotenuse. Why must each triangle take up the same percentage of its square?

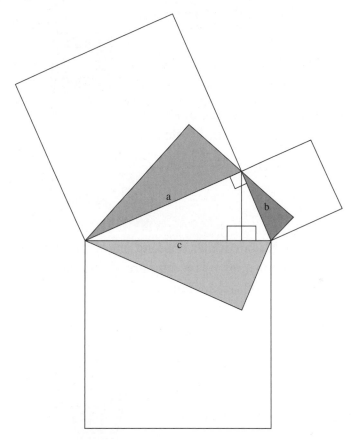

3. Let $P\%$ be the percentage of part 2. Express the areas of the three triangles in terms of $P\%$, and then explain why

$$P\% \cdot a^2 + P\% \cdot b^2 = P\% \cdot c^2$$

4. Use part 3 to explain why

$$a^2 + b^2 = c^2$$

thus proving the Pythagorean theorem.

Class Activity 14CC: Area and Volume Problem Solving

1. Explain in at least two different ways why the area of the next shaded region is 3 times the area of the unshaded square inside it. (State any assumptions you make about the shapes.)

2. How does the area of shaded region compare to the area of the unshaded region inside it? Explain. (State any assumptions you make about the shapes.)

3. A cup has a circular opening and a circular base. A cross-section of the cup and the dimensions of the cup are shown below. Determine the volume of the cup. Explain your reasoning.

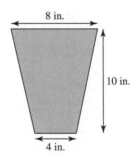

Statistics

15.1 Formulating Questions, Designing Investigations, and Gathering Data

Class Activity 15A: Challenges in Formulating Survey Questions

Lincoln Elementary School would like to add soup to its school lunch menu. The school staff decides to poll the students to learn about the soups they like. Compare the questions in 1 through 5. How might the data that the school would collect be different for the different questions? What are the advantages and disadvantages of each question?

1. What is your favorite soup?

2. If you had to pick a soup to eat right now, what soup would you pick?

3. Vote for one of the following soups you like to eat:

   - tomato

   - chicken noodle

   - vegetable

   - other

4. Circle all of the following soups you like to eat:

   - tomato

   - chicken noodle

   - vegetable

5. (Write your own question.)

Class Activity 15B: Choosing a Sample

A college newspaper wants to find out how the students at the college would answer a specific question of importance to the student body. There are too many students for the newspaper staff to ask them all. So the staff decides to choose a sample of students to ask. For each of the following ways that the newspaper staff could select a sample, discuss whether the sample is likely to be representative of the full student body or if there are reasons why the sample may not be representative.

   a. Ask their friends.

   b. Ask as many of their classmates as they can.

   c. Stand outside the buildings their classes are in and ask as many people as they can who come by.

   d. Stand outside the student union or other common meeting area, and try to pick people who they think are representative of the students at their institution to ask the question.

   e. Generate a list of random numbers between 1 and the number of students at the college. (Many calculators can generate random numbers; random numbers can also be generated on the Internet; go to *www.pearsonhighered.com/beckmann*.) Pick names out of the student phone book corresponding to the random numbers (e.g., for 123, pick the 123rd name), and contact that person by phone or by e-mail.

Class Activity 15C: Using Random Samples

   1. At a factory that produces computer chips, a batch of 5000 computer chips has just been produced. To check the quality of the computer chips, a random sample of 100 computer chips is selected to test for defects. Of these 100 chips, 3 were found to be defective. Based on these results, what is the best estimate you can give for the number of defective computer chips in the batch of 5000? Find several different ways to solve this problem, including ways that elementary school children might be able to develop.

2. Mr. Lawler had a bag filled with 160 plastic squares. The squares were identical, except that some were yellow and the rest were green. A student in Mr. Lawler's class randomly picked out 20 of the squares; 4 of the squares were yellow and the rest were green. Mr. Lawler asked his students to use this information to make their best scientific estimate for the total number of yellow squares that were in the bag. Mr. Lawler's students had several different ideas. For each of the following initial ideas, discuss the idea and describe how to use it to estimate the total number of yellow squares. Which ideas are related?

a.

20	20	20	20	20	20	20	20
↓	↓	↓	↓	↓	↓	↓	↓
4	4	4	4	4	4	4	4

b.

20	→	4
40	→	8
60	→	12
80	→	16
100	→	20
120	→	24
140	→	28
160	→	32

c. Of the 20 squares Taryn picked, $\frac{1}{5}$ were yellow.

yellow				

d. Taryn picked $\frac{1}{8}$ of the squares in the bag.

e.
$$\frac{4}{20} = \frac{8}{40} = \frac{12}{60} = \frac{16}{80} = \frac{20}{100} = \frac{24}{120} = \frac{28}{140} = \frac{32}{160}$$

f.

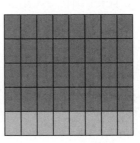

g.

$$\overset{\times 8}{\underset{\times 8}{\frac{4}{20} = \frac{x}{160}}}$$

h.

$$\times 5 \left(\frac{4}{20} = \frac{x}{160} \right) \times 5$$

Class Activity 15D: Using Random Samples to Estimate Population Size by Marking (Capture–Recapture)

You will need a bag filled with a large number (at least 100) of small, identical beans or other small objects that can be marked (such as small paper strips or beads that can be colored with a marker).

Pretend that the beans are fish in a lake. You will estimate the number of fish in the lake without counting them all by using a method called *capture–recapture.*

1. Go "fishing:" Pick between 20 and 50 "fish" out of your bag. Count the number of fish you caught, and label each fish with a distinctive mark. Then throw your fish back in the lake (the bag) and mix them thoroughly.

2. Go fishing again: Randomly pick about 50 fish out of your bag. Count the total number of fish you caught this time, and count how many of the fish are marked.

3. Use your counts from parts 1 and 2 to estimate the number of fish in your bag. Explain your reasoning.

4. When Ms. Wade used the method described in parts 1 through 3, she picked 30 fish at first, marked them, and put them back in the bag. Ms. Wade thoroughly mixed the fish in the bag and randomly picked out 40 fish. Of these 40 fish, 5 were marked. The children in Ms. Wade's class had several different ideas for how to determine the total number of fish in the bag. For each of the following initial ideas, discuss the idea and describe how to use the idea to determine approximately how many fish are in the bag. Which ideas are related?

a. 40   40   40   40   40   40
    ↓   ↓   ↓   ↓   ↓   ↓
    5   5   5   5   5   5

b. 40   →   5
    80   →   10
    120 →   15
    160 →   20
    200 →   25
    240 →   30

c. $\frac{1}{8}$ of the fish are marked.

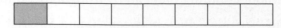

d. $\frac{1}{6}$ of the marked fish were chosen.

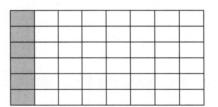

e. $\dfrac{5}{40} = \dfrac{10}{80} = \dfrac{15}{120} = \dfrac{20}{160} = \dfrac{25}{200} = \dfrac{30}{240}$

f.

g.

$$\overset{\times 6}{\frac{5}{40} = \frac{30}{x}}_{\times 6}$$

h. $\times 8 \left(\dfrac{5}{40} = \dfrac{30}{x} \right) \times 8$

15.2 Displaying Data and Interpreting Data Displays

Class Activity 15E: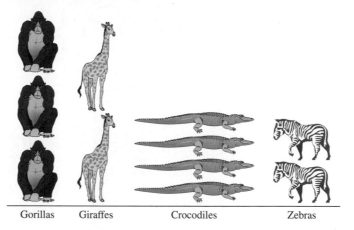
What Is Wrong with These Displays?

1. Ryan scooped some small plastic animals out of a tub, sorted them, and made a pictograph like the following:

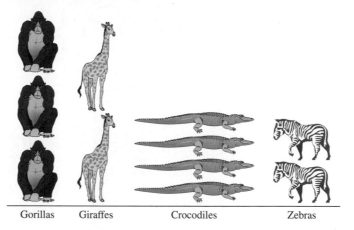

| Gorillas | Giraffes | Crocodiles | Zebras |

What is a problem with Ryan's pictograph?

2. What is wrong with the next data display? Show how to fix it.

Percent of children ages 7 to 10 meeting dietary recommendations of selected components of the Healthy Eating Index, 1994–96 average

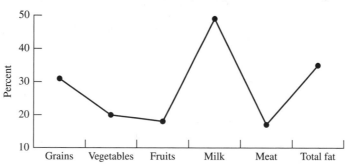

3. What is misleading about the next display of annual per capita carbon dioxide emissions in various countries? *Hints*: Think back to Section 14.5 on how scaling affects volume.

Annual CO_2 emissions per capita in metric tons

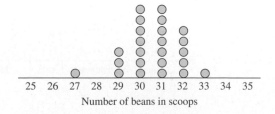

United States: 18.7   European Union: 8.0   China: 4.6

Class Activity 15F: What Is Wrong with the Interpretation of These Displays?

1. Students scooped dried beans out of a bag and counted the number of beans in the scoop. Each time, the number of beans in the scoop was recorded in the next dot plot.

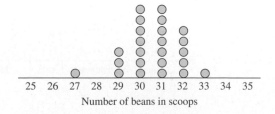

When a student was asked to make a list of the data that are displayed in the dot plot, the student responded thus:

$$1, 3, 7, 7, 5, 1$$

What is wrong with the student's response? What is a correct list of the data that are displayed in the dot plot? What do the student's numbers tell us?

2. Consider the next line graph about adolescents' smoking. Based on this display, would it be correct to say that the percentage of eighth-graders who reported smoking cigarettes daily in the previous 30 days was about twice as high in 1996 as it was in 1993? Why or why not?

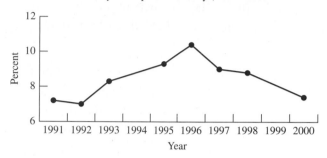

Percent of eighth-graders who reported smoking cigarettes daily in the previous 30 days, 1991–2000

3. Consider the next table on children's eating habits.

Food	Percent of 4–6-year-olds meeting the dietary recommendation for the food
Grains	27%
Vegetables	16%
Fruits	29%
Saturated fat	28%

Would it be appropriate to use a single pie graph, as shown here, to display this information? Explain your answer.

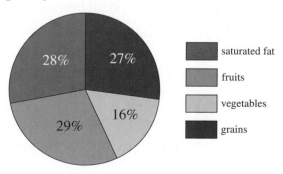

Class Activity 15G: Three Levels of Questions about Graphs

Recall that the three levels of graph comprehension discussed in the text are as follows:

Reading the data. This level of comprehension requires a literal reading of the graph. The reader simply "lifts" the facts explicitly stated in the graph, or the information found in the graph title and axes labels, directly from the graph. There is no interpretation at this level.

Reading between the data. This level of comprehension includes the interpretation and integration of the data in the graph. It requires the ability to compare quantities (e.g., greater than, tallest, smallest) and the use of other mathematical concepts and skills (e.g., addition, subtraction, multiplication, division) that allow the reader to combine and integrate data and identify the mathematical relationships expressed in the graph.

Reading beyond the data. This level of comprehension requires the reader to predict or infer from the data by tapping existing knowledge and knowledge developed from "reading the data" and "reading between the data" for information that is neither explicitly nor implicitly stated in the graph.

The following examples are questions at the different graph-reading levels. All questions are about a bar graph that shows the heights of children in a class ([3, p. 35]):

- What would be a good title for this graph? (Read between the data)
- How tall is (insert a name)? (Read the data)
- Who is the tallest of the students on the graph? (Read between the data)
- Who do you think is the oldest? Why? Can this be answered directly from the graph? (Read beyond the data)
- Who do you think has the smallest shoe size? Why? Can this be answered directly from the graph? (Read beyond the data)
- Who do you think weighs the least? Why? (Read beyond the data)

1. In your classroom you have a box with 100 small square tiles in it. The tiles are identical except that some are yellow and the rest are blue. Your students take turns picking 10 tiles out of the box without looking. Then they record the number of yellow squares (out of the 10) they picked on a sticky note and put the tiles back in the box. The class uses the sticky notes to make a dot plot on the chalkboard. It winds up looking like the one shown next (where each dot represents a sticky note).

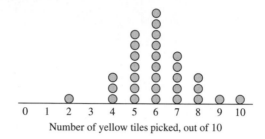

Number of yellow tiles picked, out of 10

   a. Write two "read the data" questions for the dot plot. Answer your questions.

   b. Write two "read between the data" questions for the dot plot. Answer your questions.

   c. Write two "read beyond the data" questions for the dot plot. Answer your questions (to the extent possible).

2. Consider the next two histograms, which are based on U.S. Census Bureau data from the 2000 census.

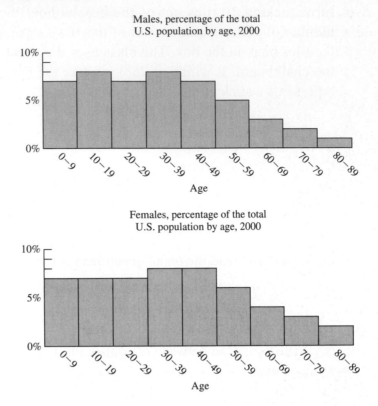

Write "read the data," "read between the data," and "read beyond the data" questions for the histograms. Questions may be suitable to ask separately about each histogram or may be about the two histograms together and how they compare. Answer your questions (to the extent possible).

Class Activity 15H: Display These Data about Pets

A class collected information about the pets they have at home, as shown in the next table.

Name	Pets at Home
Michelle	1 dog, 2 cats
Tyler	1 salamander, 2 snakes, 3 dogs
Antrice	hamster
Yoon-He	cat
Anne	none
Peter	2 dogs
Brandon	guinea pig
Brittany	1 dog, 1 cat

Name	Pets at Home
Orlando	none
Chelsey	2 dogs, 10 fish
Sarah	1 rabbit
Adam	none
Lauren	2 dogs
Letitia	3 cats
Jarvis	1 dog

1. Consider the following questions about pets:

   a. Are dogs our most popular pet?

   b. How many pets do most people have?

   c. How many people have more than one pet?

   d. Are most of our pets mammals?

   e. Write some other questions about their pets that may be of interest to students and that could be addressed by the data that were collected.

2. Make each of the following data displays and use them to answer the questions from part 1. Observe that different graphs will be helpful for answering different questions.

   a. A dot plot that shows how many students have 0 pets, 1 pet, 2 pets, 3 pets, and so on

   b. A bar graph that shows how the *students* in the class fall into categories depending on what kind of pet they have

   c. Another bar graph like the one in part (b), except pick the categories in a different way this time

   d. A bar graph that shows how the *pets* of students in the class fall into categories.

Class Activity 15I: Investigating Small Bags of Candies

For this activity, each person, pair, or small group in the class needs a small bag of multi-colored candies. All bags should be of the same size and consist of the same type of candy. Bags should not be opened until after completion of the first part of this activity.

1. Do not open your bag of candy yet! Write a list of questions that the class as a whole could investigate by gathering and displaying data about the candies.

2. Open your bag of candy (but do not eat it yet!) and display data about your candies in two significantly different ways. For each display, write and answer questions at the three different graph-reading levels.

3. Together with the whole class, collect and display data about the bags of candies in order to answer some of the questions the class posed in part 1.

Class Activity 15J: The Length of a Pendulum and the Time It Takes to Swing

A fifth-grader's science fair project[1] investigated the relationship between the length of a pendulum and the time it takes the pendulum to swing back and forth. The student made a pendulum by tying a heavy washer to a string and attaching the string to the top of a triangular frame, as pictured. The

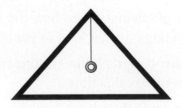

---

[1]Thanks to Arianna Kazez for the data and information about the project.

length of the string could be varied. The next table and scatterplot show how long it took the pendulum to swing back and forth 10 times for various lengths of the string. (Several measurements were taken and averaged.)

length of string in inches	time of 10 swings in seconds
1	2.61
2	2.97
3	3.04
4	3.41
5	3.96
6	4.13
7	4.22
8	4.5
9	4.64
10	5.13
11	5.32
12	5.56
13	5.62
14	5.87

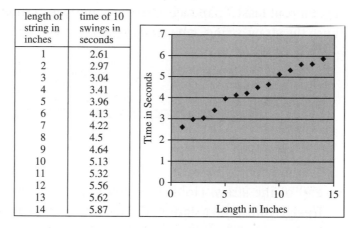

1. Write one or two questions about the scatterplot for each of the three graph-reading levels. Answer each question (to the extent possible).

2. Arianna used her science fair data to predict how long it would take a pendulum with 100 inches of string to swing back and forth 10 times. She started by observing that for every 4 inches of string it takes 1 second longer. Explain how to use this observation to determine approximately how long it might take a 100-inch pendulum to swing back and forth 10 times.*

3. Arianna used her science fair data to predict how long a string she would need so that one swing would take 1 second (like a grandfather clock). She started by observing that for every 4 inches of string it takes 1 second longer. She also used the fact that a 14-inch pendulum took 5.87 seconds for 10 swings. Arianna knew she needed to get to 10 seconds. Explain how to use these ideas to determine approximately how long a string is needed so that one swing will take 1 second.*

---

*This provides a good initial estimate, but according to physical theories, the estimate won't be fully correct.

Class Activity 15K: Balancing a Mobile

For this activity, each person, pair, or small group in the class needs a drinking straw, string, tape, at least 7 paper clips of the same size, a ruler, and graph paper. Participants will use the straw, string, tape, and paper clips to make a simple mobile.

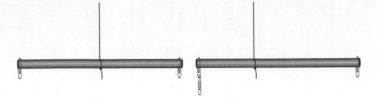

1. Tie one end of the string snugly around the straw. Tape one paper clip to each end of the straw. Hold the other end of the string so that your mobile hangs freely. Adjust the location of the string along the straw so that the straw balances horizontally. The string should now be centered on the straw, as in the picture, on the left. Measure the distance on the straw from the string to each end.

2. Repeatedly add one more paper clip to one side of the straw (but not to the other side). Every time you add a paper clip, adjust the string so that the straw balances horizontally. Each time, measure the distance on the straw from the string to the end that has multiple paper clips, and record your data.

3. Make a graphical display of your data from part 2. (Use graph paper.)

4. Write and answer several questions at each of the three different graph-reading levels about your graphical display in part 3.

15.3 The Center of Data: Mean, Median, and Mode

Class Activity 15L: The Mean as "Making Even" or "Leveling Out"

In this class activity you will use physical objects to help you see the mean as "making groups even." This point of view can be useful in calculations involving means. You will need a collection of 16 small objects such as snap-together cubes or blocks for this activity.

1. Using blocks, snap cubes, or other small objects, make towers with the following number of objects in the towers, using a different color for each tower:

2,   5,   4,   1

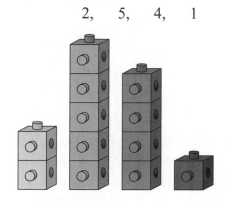

Determine the mean of the list numbers 2, 5, 4, 1 by "leveling out" the block towers, or making them even. That is, redistribute the blocks among your block towers until all 4 towers have the same number of blocks in them. This common number of blocks in each of the 4 towers is the mean of the list 2, 5, 4, 1.

2. Use the process of making block towers even in order to determine the means of each of the lists of numbers shown. In some cases you may have to imagine cutting your blocks into smaller pieces.

List 1:   1,   3,   3,   2,   1

List 2:   6,   3,   2,   5

List 3:   2,   3,   4,   3,   4

List 4:   2,   3,   1,   5

3. To calculate the mean of a list of numbers *numerically,* we add the numbers and divide the sum by the number of numbers in the list. So, to calculate the mean of the list 2, 5, 4, 1, we calculate

$$(2 + 5 + 4 + 1) \div 4$$

Interpret the *numerical* process for calculating a mean in terms of 4 block towers built of 2 blocks, 5 blocks, 4 blocks, and 1 block. When we add the numbers, what does that correspond to with the blocks? When we divide by 4, what does that correspond to with the blocks?

Explain why the process of determining a mean physically by making block towers even must give us the same answer as the numerical procedure for calculating the mean.

Class Activity 15M: Solving Problems about the Mean

1. Suppose you have made 3 block towers: one 3 blocks tall, one 6 blocks tall, and one 2 blocks tall. Describe some ways to make 2 more towers so that there is an average of 4 blocks in all 5 towers. Explain your reasoning.

2. If you run 3 miles every day for 5 days, how many miles will you need to run on the sixth day in order to have run an average of 4 miles per day over the 6 days? Solve this problem in two different ways, and explain your solutions.

3. The mean of 3 numbers is 37. A fourth number, 41, is included in the list. What is the mean of the 4 numbers? Explain your reasoning.

4. Explain how you can quickly calculate the average of the following list of test scores without adding the numbers:

81,   78,   79,   82

5. If you run an average of 3 miles a day over 1 week and an average of 4 miles a day over the next 2 weeks, what is your average daily run distance over that 3-week period?

   Before you solve this problem, explain why it makes sense that your average daily run distance over the 3-week period is *not* just the average of 3 and 4, namely, 3.5. Should your average daily run distance over the 3 weeks be greater than 3.5 or less than 3.5? Explain how to answer this without a precise calculation.

   Now determine the exact average daily run distance over the 3-week period. Explain your solution.

Class Activity 15N: The Mean as "Balance Point"

1. For each of the next data sets:

   • Make a dot plot of the data on the given axis.

   • Calculate the mean of the data.

   • Verify that the mean agrees with the location of the given fulcrum.

   • Answer this question: does the dot plot look like it would balance at the fulcrum (assuming the axis on which the data is plotted is weightless)?

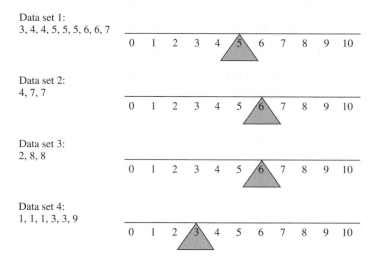

Data set 1:
3, 4, 4, 5, 5, 5, 6, 6, 7

Data set 2:
4, 7, 7

Data set 3:
2, 8, 8

Data set 4:
1, 1, 1, 3, 3, 9

2. For each of the next dot plots, guess the approximate location of the mean by thinking about where the balance point for the data would be. Then check how close your guess was by calculating the mean.

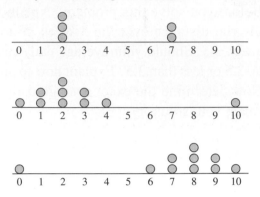

Class Activity 15O: Same Median, Different Mean

In most cases, the median of a list of numbers is not the same as its mean. In this activity, you will alter a data set to keep the same median, but vary the mean.

The pennies along the axis at the top of Figure 15O.1 are arranged to represent the following data set:

4,   5,   5,   6,   6,   6,   7,   7,   8

Arrange real pennies (or other small objects) along the number line at the bottom of Figure 15O.1 to represent the same data set.

1. Rearrange your pennies so that they represent new lists of numbers that still have median 6, but have means *less than* 6. To help you do this, think about the mean as the balance point. Draw pictures of your penny arrangements.

2. Rearrange your pennies so that they represent new lists of numbers that still have median 6, but have means *greater than* 6. To help you do this, think about the mean as the balance point. Draw pictures of your penny arrangements.

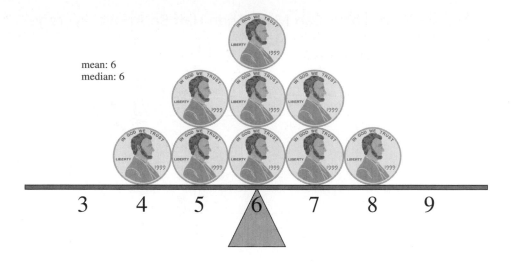

mean: 6
median: 6

3   4   5   6   7   8   9

3   4   5   6   7   8   9

Show data sets with the same median, different means.

Figure 15O.1 Same medians, different means

Class Activity 15P: Can More Than Half Be Above Average?

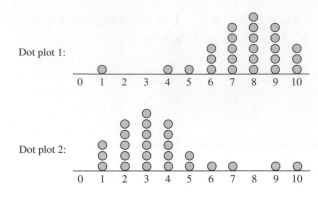

Dot plot 1:

Dot plot 2:

1. For each of the dot plots shown, decide which is greater: the median or the mean of the data. Explain how you can tell without calculating the mean.

2. A teacher gives a test to a class of 20 students.

   Is it possible that 90% of the class scores above average? If so, give an example of test scores for which this is the case. If not, explain why not.

   Is it possible that 90% of the class scores below average? If so, give an example of test scores for which this is the case. If not, explain why not.

3. A radio program describes a fictional town in which "all the children are above average." In what sense is it possible that all the children are above average? In what sense is it not possible that all the children are above average?

Class Activity 15Q: Errors with the Mean and the Median

1. When Eddie was asked to determine the mean of the data shown in the next dot plot he calculated thus:

$$1 + 2 + 4 + 2 + 1 = 10, \quad 10 \div 5 = 2$$

Eddie concluded that the mean is 2. What error did Eddie make? Why do you think Eddie calculated the way he did?

2. Discuss the misconceptions about the median that the student work below shows.

Median   5, 5, 6, 6, 6, 3, 4, 5, 4, 5, 5, 6, 4, 7, 5, 5, 5, 4, 6, 5
error 1:
                                    ↑
                              Median: 5

_____

What kind of tree should we plant in front of the school?

Median
errors 2 and 3:

9 ⌐
8 ⊢
7 ⊢
6 ⊢
5 ⊢   1, 2, 4, 6, 9
4 ⊢   ↑
3 ⊢   Median: oak
2 ⊢
1 ⊢
0 └
     Maple   Dogwood   Oak   Sycamore   Pine
              ↑
        Median: dogwood

15.4 The Distribution of Data

Class Activity 15R: What Does the Shape of a Data Distribution Tell about the Data?

1. Examine histograms 1, 2, and 3 on the next page and observe the different shapes these distributions take.

   - The shape of histogram 1 is called *skewed to the right* because the histogram has a long tail extending to the right.

   - The shape of histogram 2 is called *bimodal* because the histogram has two peaks.

   - The shape of histogram 3 is called *symmetric* because the histogram is approximately symmetrical.

   Histogram 1 is based on data on actual household incomes in the United States in 2007 provided by the Current Population Survey from the U.S. Census Bureau. The histogram could be continued to the right, but less than 2% of households had incomes over $250,000. Histograms 2 and 3 are for hypothetical countries A and B, which have different income distributions than the U.S. income distribution.

2. Discuss what the shapes of histograms 1, 2, and 3 tell you about household income in the United States versus in the hypothetical countries A and B. What do you learn from the shape of the histograms that you wouldn't be able to tell just from the medians and means of the data?

3. Discuss how each country could use the histograms to argue that its economic situation is better than at least one of the other two countries.

4. Write at least three questions about the graphs, including at least one question at each of the three levels of graph comprehension discussed in Section 15.2. Answer your questions.

Histogram 1 Distribution of household income in the United States in 2007 (approximate)

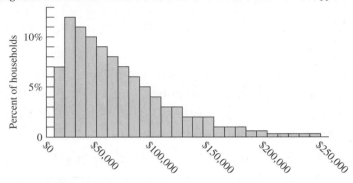

Histogram 2 Distribution of household income in hypothetical country A

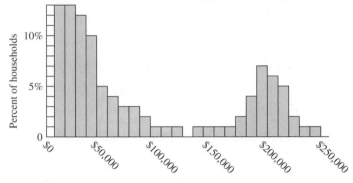

Histogram 3 Distribution of household income in hypothetical country B

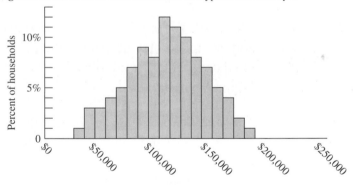

Class Activity 15S: Distributions of Random Samples

For this activity, you will need a large collection of small objects (200 or so) in a bag. The objects should be identical, except that they should come in two different colors: 40% in one color and the remaining 60% in another color. The objects could be poker chips, small squares, small cubes, or even small slips of paper. Think of the objects as representing a group of voters. The 40% in one color represent yes votes and the 60% in the other color represent no votes.

1. Pick random samples of 10 from the bag. Each time you pick a random sample of 10, determine the percentage of yes votes and plot this percent on a dot plot. But before you start picking these random samples, make a dot plot at the top of the next page to predict what your actual dot plot will look like approximately. Assume that you will plot about 20 dots.

   • Why do you think your dot plot might turn out that way?

   • How do you think the fact that 40% of the votes in the bag are yes votes might be reflected in the dot plot?

   • What kind of shape do you predict your dot plot will have?

2. Now pick about 20 random samples of 10 objects from the bag. Each time you pick a random sample of 10, determine the percentage of yes votes and plot this percentage in a dot plot in the middle of the next page. Compare your results with your predictions in part 1.

3. If possible, join your data with other people's data to form a dot plot with more dots. Do you see the fact that 40% of the votes in the bag are yes votes reflected in the dot plot? If so, how? What kind of shape does the dot plot have?

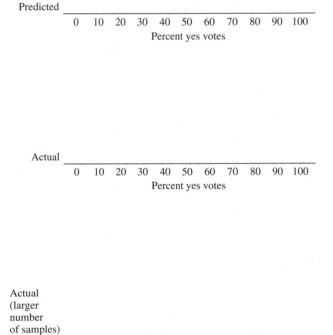

Predicted
0   10   20   30   40   50   60   70   80   90   100
Percent yes votes

Actual
0   10   20   30   40   50   60   70   80   90   100
Percent yes votes

Actual
(larger
number
of samples)
0   10   20   30   40   50   60   70   80   90   100
Percent yes votes

4. Compare the two histograms on the next page. The first histogram shows the percent of yes votes in 200 samples of 100 taken from a population of 1,000,000 in which 40% of the population votes yes. The second histogram shows the percent of yes votes in 200 samples of 1000 taken from the same population.

   Compare the way the data are distributed in each of these histograms and compare these histograms with your dot plots in parts 2 and 3.

   How is the fact that 40% of the population votes yes reflected in these histograms?

   What do the histograms indicate about using samples of 100 versus samples of 1000 to predict the outcome of an election?

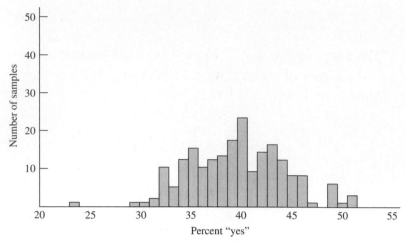

Percent of yes votes in **samples of 100** taken from 1,000,000 voters in which 40% vote yes.

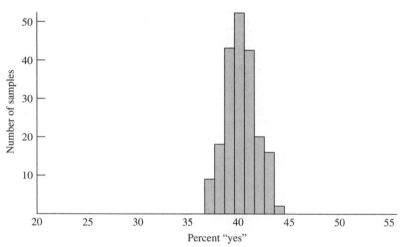

Percent of yes votes in **samples of 1000** taken from 1,000,000 voters in which 40% vote yes.

5. What if we made a histogram like the ones above by using the same population, but by picking 200 samples of 500 (instead of 200 samples of 100 or 1000)? How do you think this histogram would compare with the ones above? What if samples of 2000 were used?

Class Activity 15T: Comparing Distributions: Mercury in Fish

The next two histograms display hypothetical data about amounts of mercury found in 100 samples of each of two different types of fish. Mercury levels above 1.00 parts per million are considered hazardous.

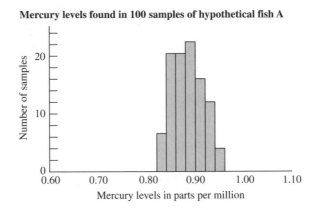

Mercury levels found in 100 samples of hypothetical fish A

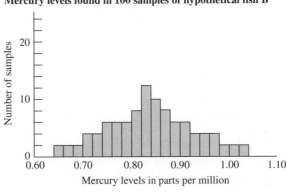

Mercury levels found in 100 samples of hypothetical fish B

1. Discuss how the two distributions compare and what this tells you about the mercury levels in the two types of fish. In your discussion, take the following into account: mean levels of mercury in each type of fish, and the hazardous level of 1.00 parts per million.

2. In comparing the two types of fish, if you hadn't been given the histograms, would it be adequate just to have the means of the amount of mercury in the samples, or is it useful to know additional information about the data?

Class Activity 15U: Determining Percentiles

1. Determine the 25th, 50th, and 75th percentiles for each of the hypothetical test data shown in the following:

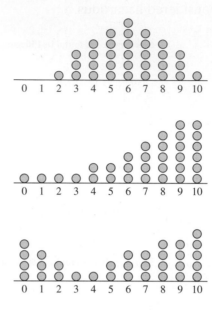

2. Suppose you only had the percentiles for each of the 3 data sets from part 1 and you didn't have the dot plots. Discuss what you could tell about how the 3 data sets are distributed. Can you tell which data set is most tightly clustered and which are more dispersed?

Class Activity 15V: Box Plots

1. Make box plots for the 3 dot plots that follow.

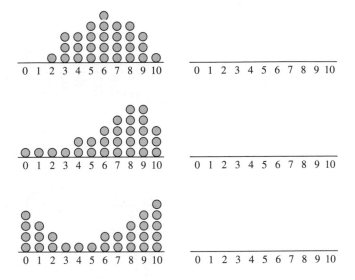

2. Suppose you had the box plots from part 1, but you didn't have the dot plots. Discuss what you could tell about how the 3 data sets are distributed.

Class Activity 15W: Percentiles versus Percent Correct

1. Determine the 75th percentile for each set of hypothetical test data in the next 3 dot plots.

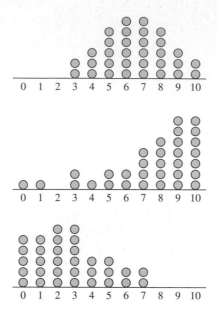

2. Discuss: On a test, is the 75th percentile the same as 75% correct?

3. Mrs. Smith makes an appointment to talk to her son Johnny's teacher. Johnny has been getting As in math, but on the standardized test he took, he was at the 80th percentile. Mrs. Smith is concerned that this means Johnny is really doing B work in math, not A work. If you were Johnny's teacher, what could you tell Mrs. Smith?

Probability

16.1 Basic Principles of Probability

Class Activity 16A: Probabilities with Spinners

1. Many children's games use "spinners." You can make a simple spinner by placing the tip of a pencil through a paper clip and holding the pencil so that its tip is at the center of the circle as shown. The paper clip should spin freely around the pencil tip.

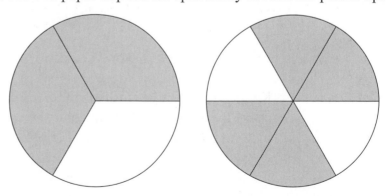

This problem is similar to a problem in an activity book for grades 1–3; see [6]:

Compare the two spinners shown above. For which spinner is a paper clip most likely to point into a shaded region? Explain your answer.

2. Compare the next two spinners. For which spinner is the paper clip that spins around a pencil point held at the indicated center point most likely to land in a shaded region? Explain your answer.

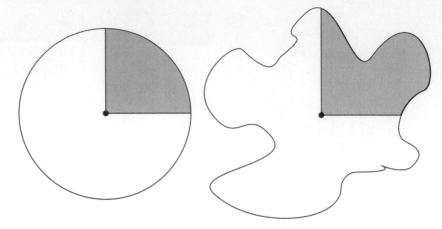

3. Draw a 4-color spinner (red, green, yellow, blue) such that

   • landing on green is twice as likely as landing on red;

   • landing on yellow is equally likely as landing on green;

   • landing on blue is more likely than landing on yellow.

   Determine the probabilities of landing on each of the colors on your spinner and explain your reasoning.

       Could someone else make a different spinner with different probabilities?

Class Activity 16B: Some Probability Misconceptions

1. Kevin has a bag that is filled with 2 red balls and 1 white ball. Kevin says that because there are two different colors he could pick from the bag, the probability of picking the red ball is $\frac{1}{2}$. Is this correct?

2. A family math night at school features the following game. There are two opaque bags, each containing red blocks and yellow blocks. Bag 1 contains 2 red blocks and 4 yellow blocks. Bag 2 contains 4 red blocks and 16 yellow blocks. To play the game, you pick a bag and then you pick a block out of the bag without looking. You win a prize if you pick a red block. Eva thinks she should pick from

bag 2 because it has more red blocks than bag 1. Is Eva more likely to pick a red block if she picks from bag 2 than from bag 1? Why or why not?

3. The probability of winning a game is $\frac{3}{1000}$. Does this mean that if you play the game 1000 times, you will win 3 times? If not, what does the probability of $\frac{3}{1000}$ stand for?

Class Activity 16C: Using Experimental Probability to Make Predictions

A family math night at school includes the following activity. A bag is filled with 10 small counting bears that are identical except that 4 are yellow and the rest are blue. A sign next to the bag gives instructions for the activity:

Win a prize if you guess the correct number of yellow bears in the bag! There are 10 bears in the bag. Some are yellow and the rest are blue. Here's what you do:

- Reach into the bag, mix well, and pick out a bear.
- Get a sticky note that is the same color as your bear, write your name and your guess on the note and add your note to the others of the same color.
- Put your bear back in the bag, and mix well.

The sticky notes will be organized into columns of 10, so it will be easy to count up how many of each there are.

1. How will students be able to use the results of this activity to estimate the number of yellow bears in the box?

2. What do you expect will happen as the night goes on and more and more bears are picked?

3. Discuss any additions or modifications you would like to make to the activity if you were going to use it for math night at your school.

Class Activity 16D: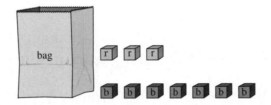
Experimental versus Theoretical Probability: Picking Cubes from a Bag

Each person (or small group) will need an opaque bag, 3 red cubes, 7 blue cubes, and a sticky note. In this activity you will compare experimental and theoretical probabilities of picking a red cube from a bag containing 3 red and 7 blue cubes.

1. Put the 10 cubes in the bag, mix them up, and randomly pick a cube from the bag without looking. Record the color of the cube, and put the cube back in the bag. Repeat until you have picked 10 cubes. Record the number or red cubes you picked on your sticky note. Calculate the experimental probability of picking a red cube based on your 10 picks. Is it the same as the theoretical probability of picking red?

2. Now work with a large group (e.g., the whole class). Collect the sticky notes of part 1 from the full group. Determine the total number of reds picked and the total number of picks among the large group. Use these results to determine the experimental probability of picking a red cube obtained by the large group. Compare this experimental probability with the theoretical probability of picking red.

3. Use the sticky notes of part 1 to create a dot plot. How is the fact that there are 3 red cubes and 7 blue cubes in the bag reflected in the dot plot?

Class Activity 16E: If You Flip 10 Pennies, Should Half Come Up Heads?

You will need a bag, 10 pennies or 2-color counters, and some sticky notes for this activity.

1. Make a guess: What do you think the probability is of getting exactly 5 heads on 10 pennies when you dump the 10 pennies out of a bag?

2. Put the 10 pennies in the bag, shake them up, and dump them out. Record the number of heads on a sticky note. Repeat this for a total of 10 times, using a new sticky note each time. Out of these 10 tries, how many times did you get 5 heads? Therefore, what is the experimental probability of getting 5 heads based on your 10 trials?

3. Now work with a large group (e.g., the whole class). Collect the whole group's data on the sticky notes from part 2. Find a way to display these data so that you can see how often the whole group got 5 heads and other numbers of heads.

4. Is the probability of getting exactly 5 heads from 10 coins 50%? What does your data display from part 3 suggest?

16.2 Counting the Number of Outcomes

Class Activity 16F: How Many Keys Are There?

Have you ever wondered: how can millions of *different* car keys be produced, even though car keys are not very big? Keys are manufactured to be distinct from one another by the way they are notched. Car keys have intricate notching. For simplicity, in this activity let's consider only simple keys that are notched on one side.

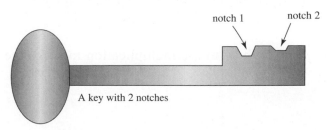

notch 1   notch 2

A key with 2 notches

1. Suppose a simple type of key is to be made with 2 notches, and that each notch can be one of 3 depths: deep, medium, or shallow. How many different keys can be made this way? Explain.

2. Explain how to use multiplication to solve the problem in part 1 if you haven't already.

3. Now suppose the key is to be made with 4 notches, and each notch can be one of 3 depths: deep, medium, or shallow. How many keys can be made this way? Explain.

4. Now suppose the key is to be made with 10 notches, and each notch can be one of 5 depths. How many keys can be made this way? Explain.

Class Activity 16G: Counting Outcomes: Independent versus Dependent

1. How many 3-letter security codes can be made from the 4 letters A, B, C, D? For example, BAB and ABB are two such codes, and DAC is another. Explain.

2. How many 3-letter security codes can be made from the 4 letters A, B, C, D without using a letter twice? For example, BAC and ADB are two such codes. Explain.

3. Explain how to use multiplication to solve the problem in part 2 if you haven't already.

4. Contrast how you use multiplication to solve the problems in parts 1 and 2 and explain the distinction.

16.3 Calculating Probabilities in Multi-Stage Experiments

Class Activity 16H: Number Cube Rolling Game

Maya, James, Kaitlyn, and Juan are playing a game in which they take turns rolling a pair of number cubes. Each child has chosen a "special number" between 2 and 12, and each child receives 8 points whenever the total number of dots on the two number cubes is their special number. (They receive their points regardless of who rolled the number cubes. Their teacher picked 8 points so that the children would practice counting by 8s.)

- Maya's special number is 7.
- James's special number is 10.
- Kaitlyn's special number is 12.
- Juan's special number is 4.

The first person to get to 100 points or more wins. The children have played several times, each time using the same special numbers. They notice that Maya wins most of the time. They are wondering why.

1. Roll a pair of number cubes many times, and record the total number of dots each time. Display your data so that you can compare how many times each possible number between 2 and 12 has occurred. What do you notice?

2. Draw an array showing all possible outcomes on each number cube when a pair of number cubes are rolled. (Think of the pair as *number cube 1* and *number cube 2*.)

   a. For which outcomes is the total number of dots 7? 10? 12? 4?

   b. What is the probability of getting 7 total dots on a roll of two number cubes? What is the probability of getting 10 total dots on a roll of two number cubes? What about for 12 and 4?

   c. Is it surprising that Maya kept winning?

Class Activity 16I:
Picking Two Marbles from a Bag of 1 Black and 3 Red Marbles

You will need an opaque bag, 3 red marbles, and 1 black marble for this activity. Put the marbles in the bag.

If you reach in without looking and randomly pick out 2 marbles, what is the probability that 1 of the 2 marbles you pick is black? You will study this question in this activity.

1. Before you continue, make a guess: What do you think the probability of picking the black marble is when you randomly pick 2 marbles out of the 4 marbles (3 red, 1 black) in the bag?

2. Pick 2 marbles out of the bag. Repeat this many times, recording what you pick each time. What fraction of the times did you pick the black marble?

3. Now calculate the probability theoretically, using a tree diagram. For the purpose of computing the probability, think of first picking one marble, then (without putting this marble back in the bag) picking a second marble. From this point of view, draw a tree diagram that will show all possible outcomes for picking the two marbles. But draw this tree diagram in a special way, *so that all outcomes shown by your tree diagram are equally likely.*

   Hints: The first stage of the tree should show all possible outcomes for your first pick. Remember that all branches you show should be equally likely. In the second stage, the branches you draw should depend on what happened in the first stage. For instance, if the first pick was the black marble, then the second pick must be one of the three red marbles.

   a. How many total outcomes for picking 2 marbles, 1 at a time, out of the bag of 4 (3 red, 1 black) does your tree diagram show?

   b. In how many outcomes is the black marble picked (on 1 of the 2 picks)?

   c. Use your answers to parts 3 (a) and (b) and the basic principles of probability to calculate the probability of picking the black marble when you pick 2 marbles out of a bag filled with 1 black and 3 red marbles.

4. Why was it important to draw the tree diagram so that all outcomes were equally likely?

5. Here's another method for calculating the probability of picking the black marble when you pick 2 marbles out of a bag filled with 1 black and 3 red marbles:

   a. How many unordered pairs of marbles can be made from the 4 marbles in the bag?

   b. How many of those pairs of marbles in part (a) contain the black marble? (Use your common sense.)

   c. Use parts a and b and basic principles of probability to determine the probability of picking the black marble when you pick 2 marbles out of a bag containing 1 black and 3 red marbles.

6. Compare your answers to parts 3a and 5a, and compare your answers to 3b and 5b. How and why are they different?

Class Activity 16J: More Probability Misconceptions

1. Simone has been flipping a coin and has just flipped 5 heads in a row. Simone says that because she has just gotten so many heads, she is more likely to get tails than heads the next time she flips. Is Simone correct? What is the probability that Simone's next flip will be a tail? Does the answer depend on what the previous flips were?

2. Let's say you flip 2 coins simultaneously. There are 3 possible outcomes: Both are heads, both are tails, or one is heads and the other is tails. Does this mean that the probability of getting one head and one tail is $\frac{1}{3}$?

Class Activity 16K: Expected Earnings from the Fall Festival

Ms. Wilkins is planning a game for her school's fall festival. She will put 2 red, 3 yellow, and 10 green plastic bears in an opaque bag. (The bears are identical except for their color.) To play the game, a contestant will pick 2 bears from the bag, one at a time, without putting the first bear back before picking the second bear. Contestants will not be able to see into the bag, so their choices are random. To win a prize, the contestant must pick a green bear first and then a red bear. The school is expecting about 300 people to play the game. Each person will pay 50 cents to play the game. Winners receive a prize that costs the school $2.

1. How many prizes should Ms. Wilkins expect to give out? Explain.

2. How much money (net) should the school expect to make from Ms. Wilkins's game? Explain.

16.4 Using Fraction Arithmetic to Calculate Probabilities

Class Activity 16L:

Using the Meaning of Fraction Multiplication to Calculate a Probability

Use the circle in Figure 16L.1, a pencil, and a paper clip to make a spinner as follows: Put the pencil through the paper clip, and put the point of the pencil on the center of the circle. The paper clip will now be able to spin freely around the circle.

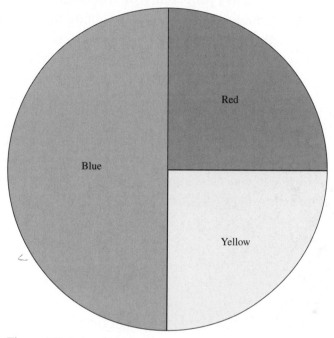

Figure 16L.1 A spinner

This rectangle represents many pairs of spins.

To win a game, Jill needs to spin a blue followed by a red in her next 2 spins.

1. What do you think Jill's probability of winning is? (Make a guess.)

2. Carry out the experiment of spinning the spinner twice in a row 20 times. (In other words, spin the spinner 40 times, but each experiment consists of 2 spins.) Out of those 20 times, how often does Jill win? What fraction of 20 does this represent? Is this close to your guess in part 1?

3. Calculate Jill's probability of winning theoretically as follows: Imagine that Jill carries out the experiment of spinning the spinner twice in a row many times. In the ideal, what fraction of those times should the first spin be blue? _____ Show this by shading the rectangle on the previous page.

   In the ideal, what fraction of those times when the first spin is blue should the second spin be red? _____ Show this by further shading the rectangle on the previous page.

   In the ideal, what fraction of pairs of spins should Jill spin first a blue and then a red? Therefore, what is Jill's probability of winning? _____ Explain how you can determine this fraction from the shading of the rectangle and from the meaning of fraction multiplication. Compare your answer with parts 1 and 2.

Class Activity 16M: Using Fraction Multiplication and Addition to Calculate a Probability

A paper clip, an opaque bag, and blue, red, and green tiles would be helpful.

A game consists of spinning the spinner in Figure 16L.1 and then picking a small tile from a bag containing 1 blue tile, 3 red tiles, and 1 green tile. (All tiles are identical except for color, and the person picking a tile cannot see into the bag, so the choice of a tile is random.) To win the game, a contestant must pick the same color tile that the spinner landed on. So a contestant wins from either a blue spin followed by a blue tile or a red spin followed by a red tile.

1. Make a guess: What do you think the probability of winning the game is?

2. If the materials are available, play the game a number of times. Record the number of times you play the game (each game consists of both a spin *and* a pick from the bag), and record the number of times you win. What fraction of the time did you win? How does this compare with your guess in part 1?

3. To calculate the (theoretical) probability of winning the game, imagine playing the game many times. Answer the next questions in order to determine the probability of winning the game.

   a. In the ideal, what fraction of the time should the spin be blue? _____ Show this by shading the rectangle below.

      In the ideal, what fraction of those times when the spin is blue should the tile that is chosen be blue? _____ Show this by further shading the rectangle below.

      Therefore, in the ideal, what fraction of the time is the spin blue and the tile blue? _____ Explain how you can determine this fraction from the shading of the rectangle and from the meaning of fraction multiplication.

   b. In the ideal, what fraction of the time should the spin be red? _____ Show this by shading the rectangle below.

      In the ideal, what fraction of those times when the spin is red should the tile that is chosen be red? _____ Show this by further shading the rectangle below.

      Therefore, in the ideal, what fraction of the time is the spin red and the tile red? _____ Explain how you can determine this fraction from the shading of the rectangle and from the meaning of fraction multiplication.

   c. In the ideal, what fraction of the time should you win the game, and therefore, what is the probability of winning the game? Explain why you can calculate this answer by multiplying and adding fractions. Compare your answer with parts 1 and 2.

This rectangle represents playing the game many times.

Bibliography

[1] George W. Bright. Helping elementary- and middle-grades preservice teachers understand and develop mathematical reasoning. In *Developing Mathematical Reasoning in Grades K–12*, pages 256–269. National Council of Teachers of Mathematics, 1999.

[2] T. P. Carpenter, E. Fennema, M. L. Franke, S. B. Empson, and L. W. Levi. *Children's Mathematics: Cognitively Guided Instruction*. Heinemann, Portsmouth, NH, 1999.

[3] Frances Curcio. *Developing Data-Graph Comprehension in Grades K–8*. National Council of Teachers of Mathematics, 2d ed., 2001.

[4] K. C. Fuson. Developing mathematical power in whole number operations. In J. Kilpatrick, W. G. Martin, and D. Schifter, eds. *A Research Companion to Principles and Standards for School Mathematics*. Reston, VA, NCTM, 2003.

[5] K. C. Fuson, S. T. Smith, and A. M. Lo Cicero. Supporting First Graders' Ten-Structured Thinking in Urban Classrooms. *Journal for Research in Mathematics Education*, vol. 28, Issue 6, pages 738–766, 1997.

[6] Graham Jones and Carol Thornton. *Data, Chance, and Probability, Grades 1–3 Activity Book*. Learning Resources, 1992.

[7] Edward Manfre, James Moser, Joanne Lobato, and Lorna Morrow. *Heath Mathematics Connections*. D. C. Heath and Company, 1994.

[8] National Council of Teachers of Mathematics. *Navigating through Algebra in Pre-Kindergarten–Grade 2*. National Council of Teachers of Mathematics, 2001.

[9] National Research Council. *Adding It Up: Helping Children Learn Mathematics*. J. Kilpatrick, J. Swafford, and B. Findell, eds. Mathematics Learning Study Committee, Center for Education, Division of Behavioral and Social Sciences and Education. National Academy Press, Washington, DC, 2001.

[10] A. M. O'Reilley. Understanding teaching/teaching for understanding. In Deborah Schifter, ed., *What's Happening in Math Class?*, vol. 2: Reconstructing Professional Identities, pages 65–73. Teachers College Press, 1996.

[11] Dav Pilkey. *Captain Underpants and the Attack of the Talking Toilets*. Scholastic, 1999.

[12] Singapore Curriculum Planning and Development Division, Ministry of Education. *Primary Mathematics Workbook*, vol. 1A–6B. Times Media Private Limited, Singapore, 3d ed., 2000. Available at *http://www.singapore-math.com*

[13] K. Stacey. Traveling the Road to Expertise: A Longitudinal Study of Learning. In Chick, H. L. and Vincent, J. L. eds. *Proceedings of the 29th Conference of the International Group for the Psychology of Mathematics Education*, vol. 1, pp. 19–36. PME, Melbourne, 2005.

[14] V. Steinle, K. Stacey, and D. Chambers. *Teaching and Learning about Decimals* [CD-ROM]: Department of Science and Mathematics Education, The University of Melbourne, 2002. Online sample at *http://extranet.edfac.unimelb.edu.au/DSME/decimals/*

Index

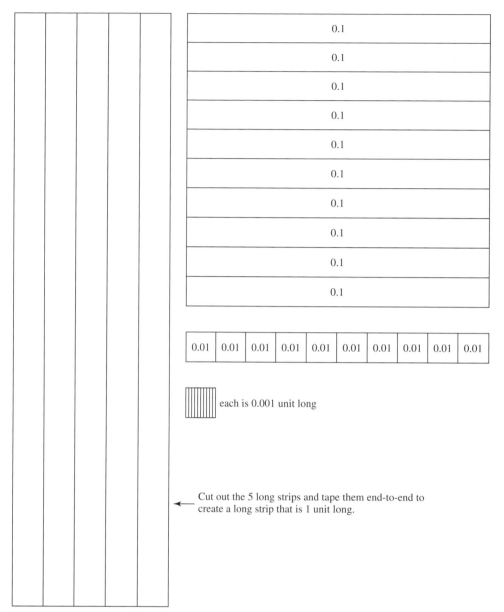

Figure A.1 Use these strips to represent decimals as lengths in Class Activity 1F on page 8

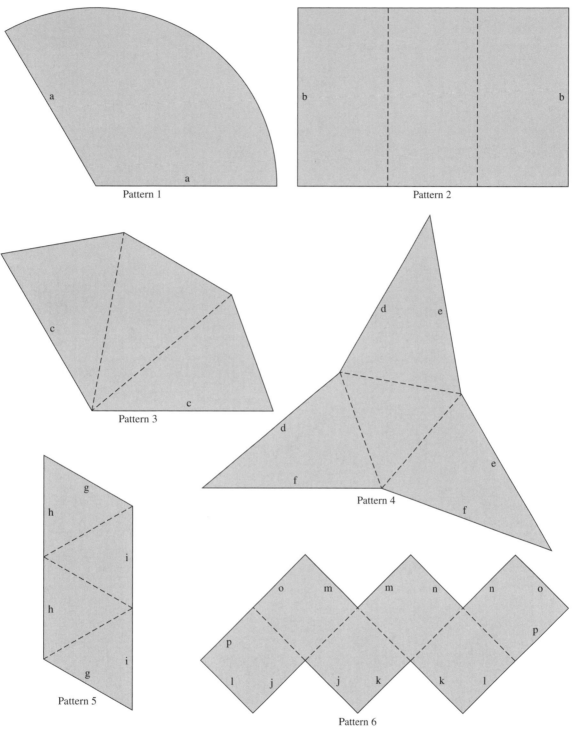

Pattern 1

Pattern 2

Pattern 3

Pattern 4

Pattern 5

Pattern 6

Figure A.9 Patterns for shapes for Class Activity 13G on page 314

Figure A.10 For Class Activity 13H on page 315

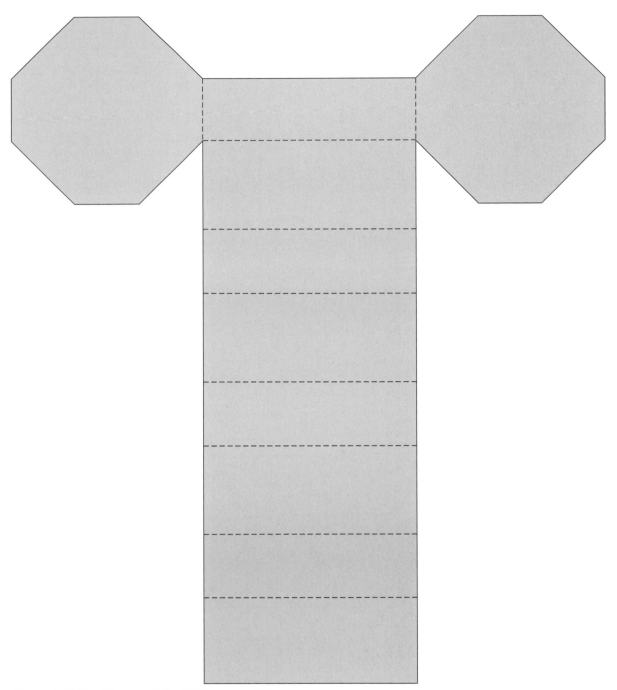

Figure A.11 For Class Activity 13H on page 315

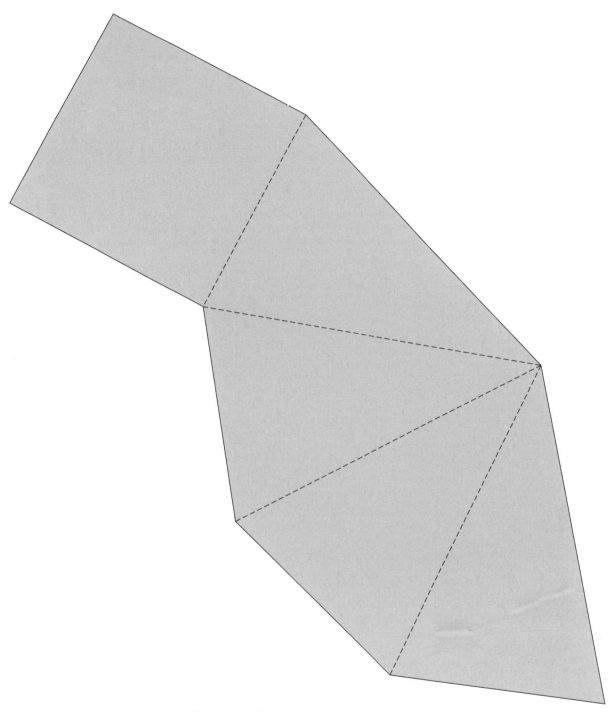

Figure A.12 For Class Activity 13H on page 315

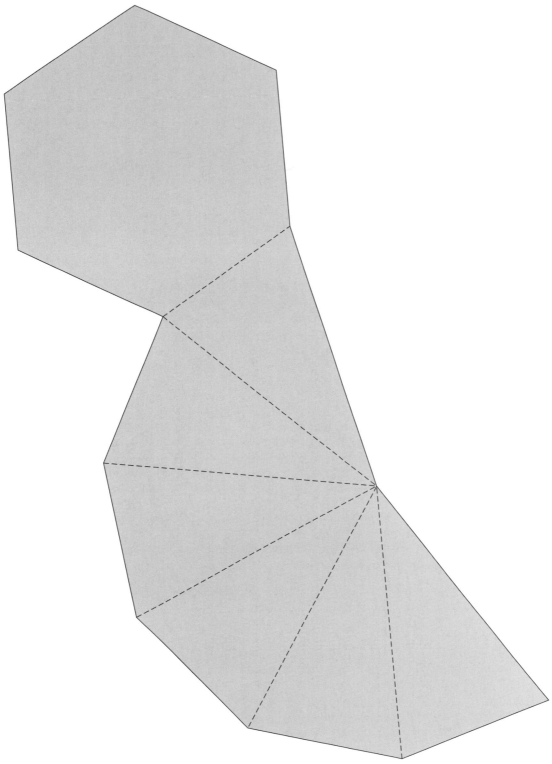

Figure A.13 For Class Activity 13H on page 315

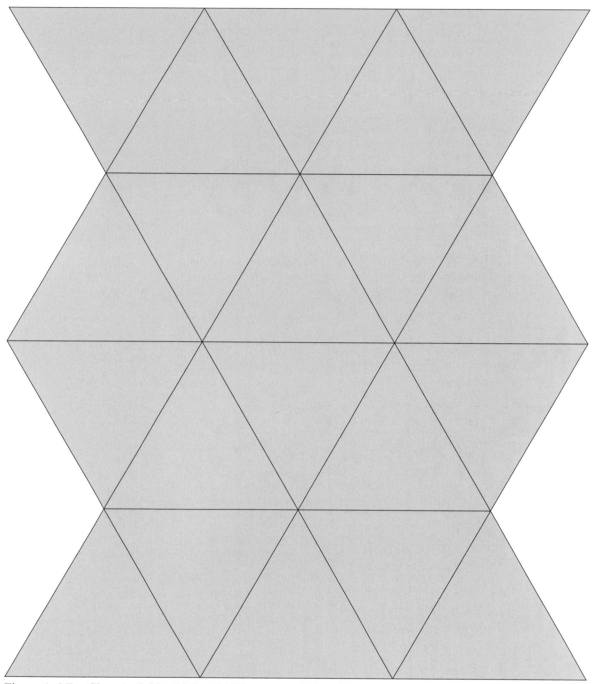

Figure A.6 For Class Activities 13C and 13E on pages 310 and 311

Figure A.7 For Class Activity 13E on page 311

Figure A.8 For Class Activity 13E on page 311

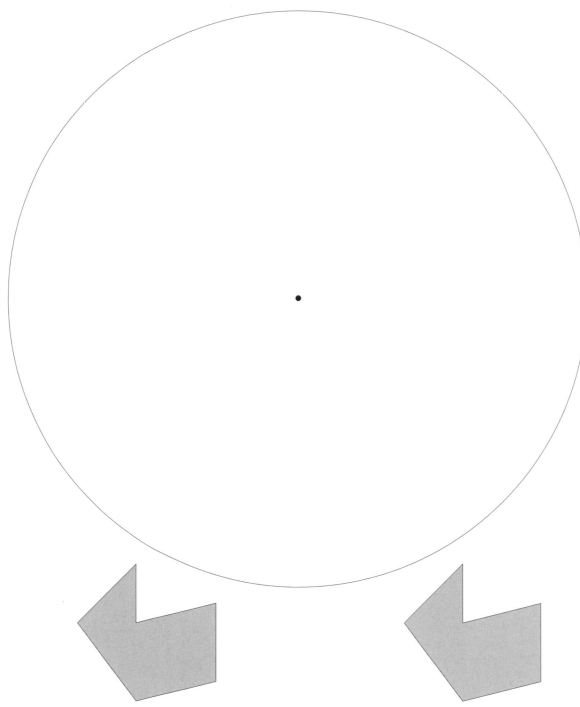

Figure A.20 A circle and two shapes for Class Activities 14A and 14B on pages 329 and 330

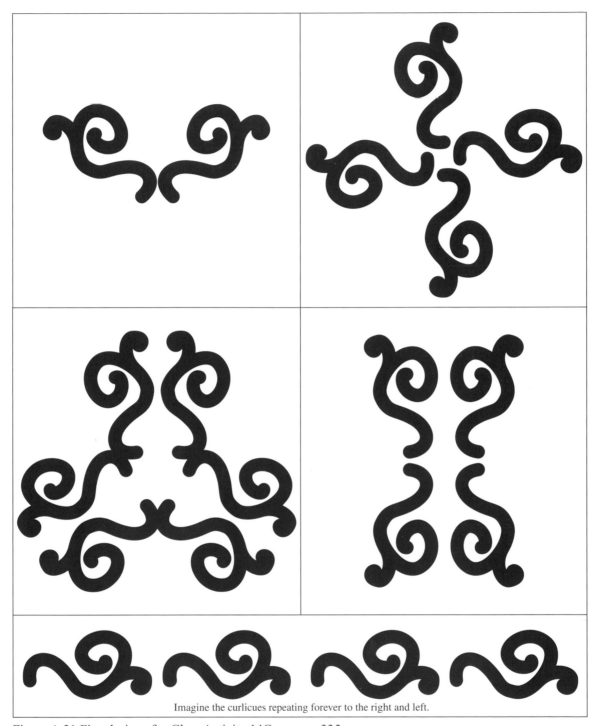

Imagine the curlicues repeating forever to the right and left.

Figure A.21 Five designs for Class Activity 14G on page 335

Imagine the curlicues repeating forever to the right and left.

Figure A.22 Second copy of five designs for Class Activity 14G on page 335

Figure A.23 Four frieze patterns for Class Activity 14H on page 336

Figure A.24 Copy of four frieze patterns for Class Activity 14H on page 336

Figure A.25 Three frieze patterns for Class Activity 14H on page 336

Figure A.26 Copy of three frieze patterns for Class Activity 14H on page 336

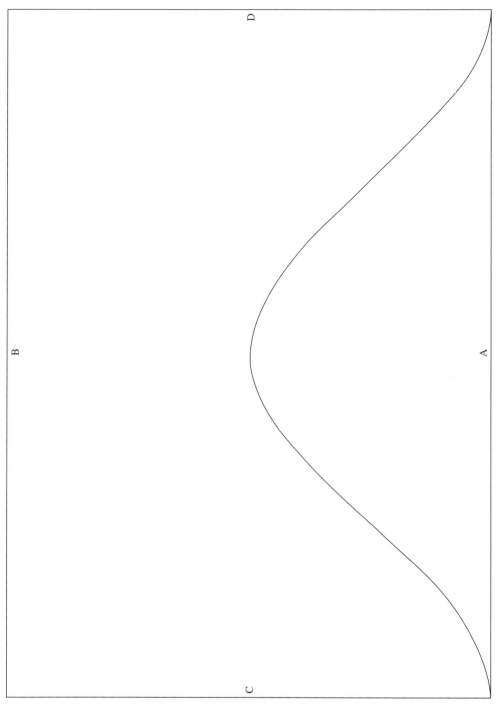

Figure A.21 To cut out for Class Activity 11C on page 272

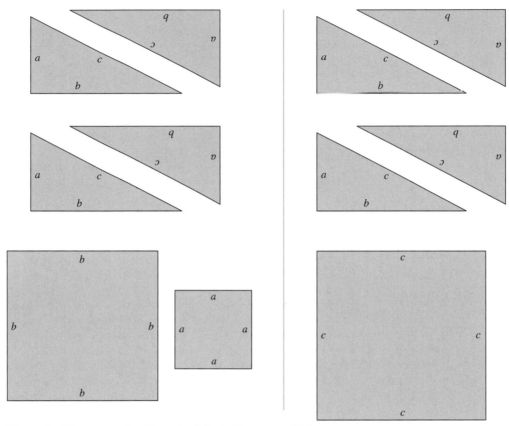

Figure A.5 To cut out for Class Activity 12Z on page 305

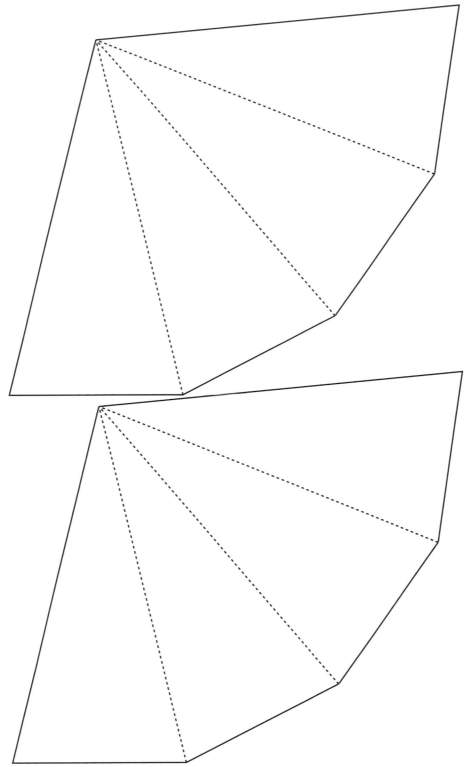

Figure A.15 Pyramid patterns for Class Activity 13P on page 322

Pattern for Class Activity 13P on page 322.

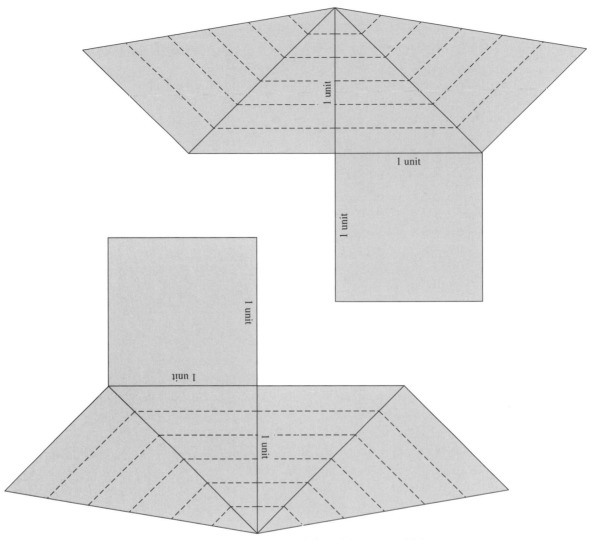

Figure A.16 Patterns for oblique pyramids for Class Activity 13Q on Page 322

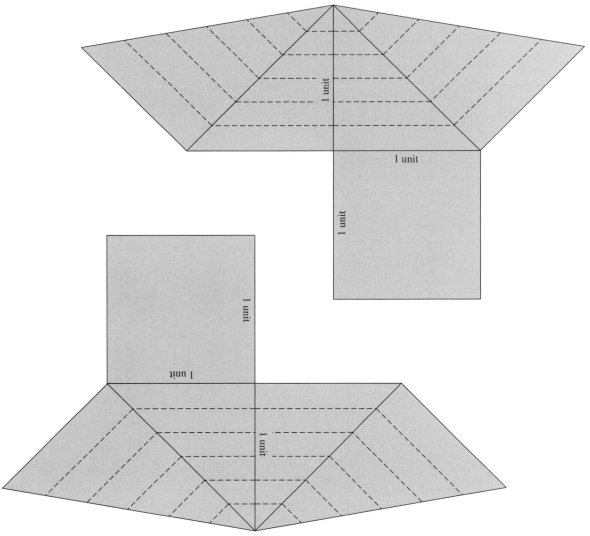

Figure A.17 Patterns for oblique pyramids for Class Activity 13Q on page 322

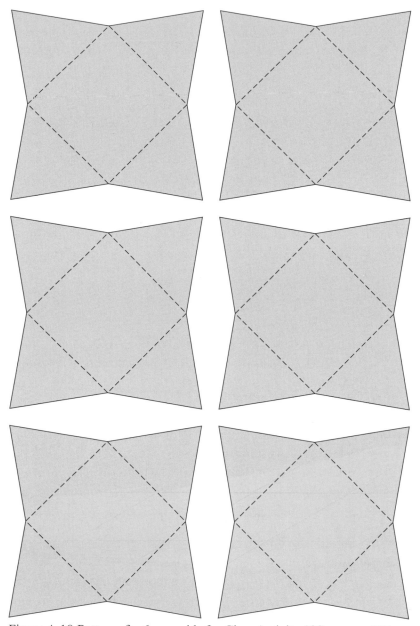

Figure A.18 Patterns for 6 pyramids for Class Activity 13S on page 324

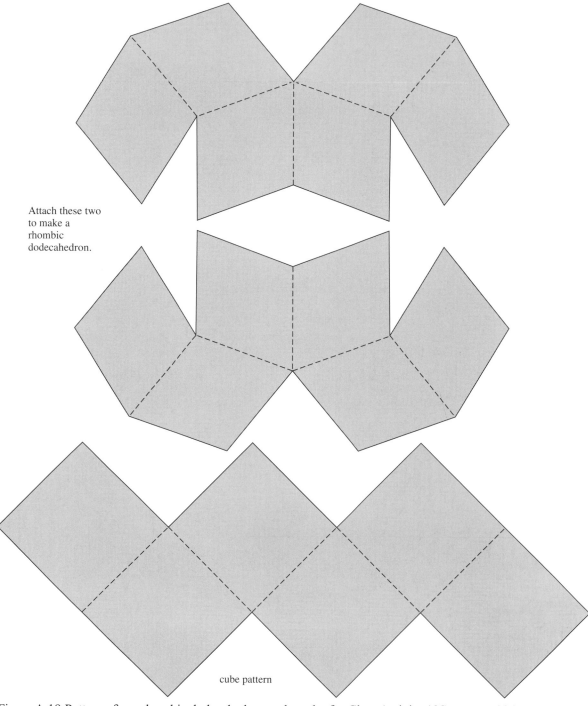

Attach these two to make a rhombic dodecahedron.

cube pattern

Figure A.19 Patterns for a rhombic dodecahedron and a cube for Class Activity 13S on page 324

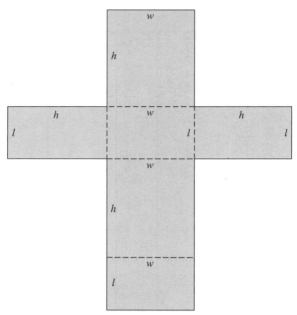

Figure A.27 A pattern for a small box for Class
Activity 14Y on page 349

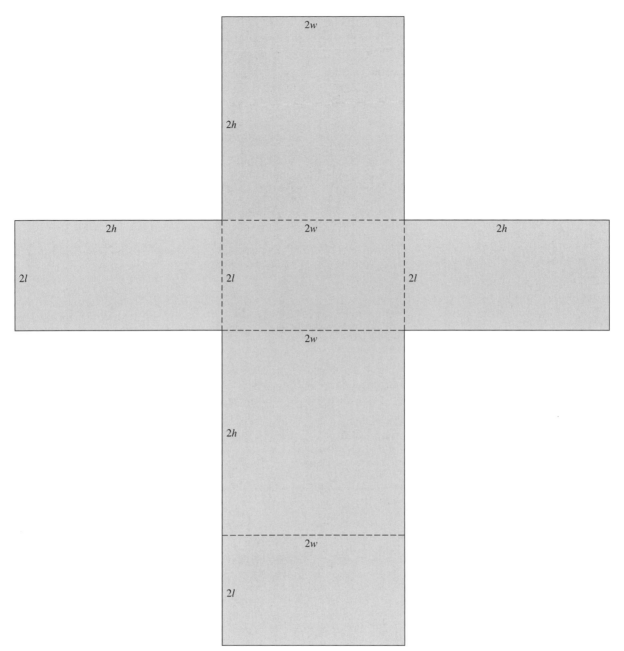

Figure A.28 A pattern for a big box for Class Activity 14Y on page 349

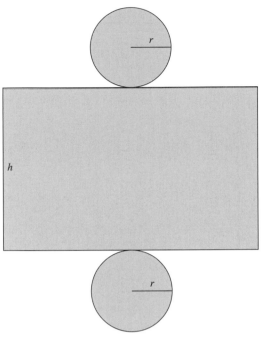

Figure A.29 A pattern for a small cylinder for
Class Activity 14Z on page 350

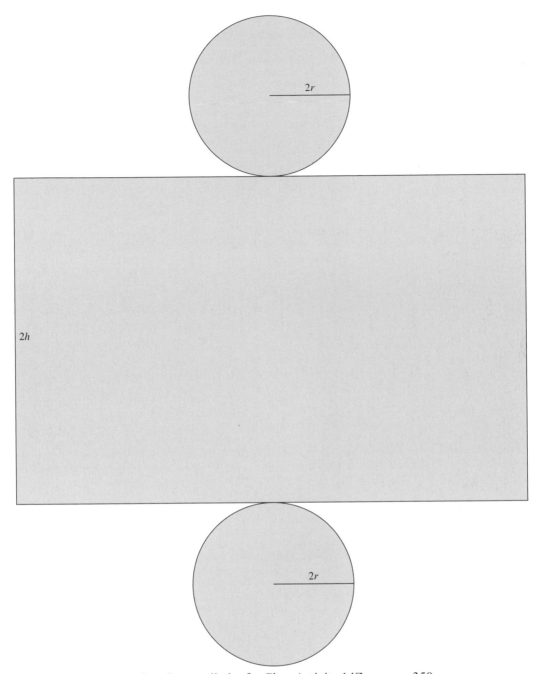

Figure A.30 A pattern for a large cylinder for Class Activity 14Z on page 350

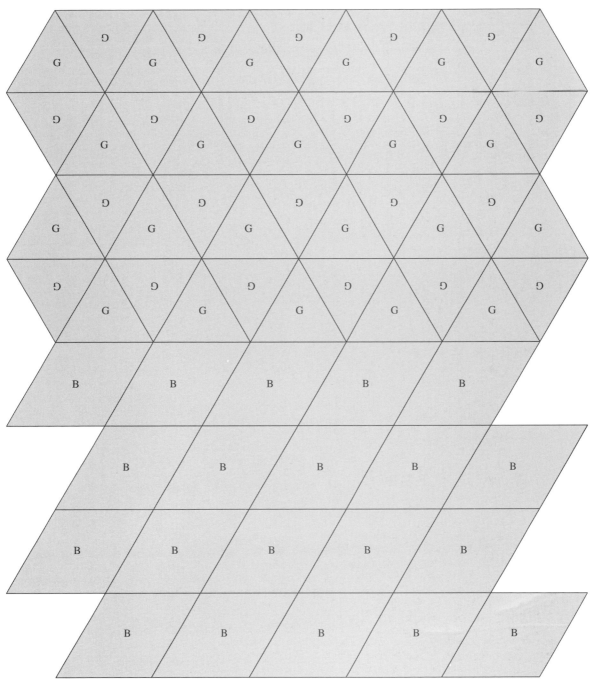

Figure A.2 Pattern tiles for Class Activity 8V on page 180

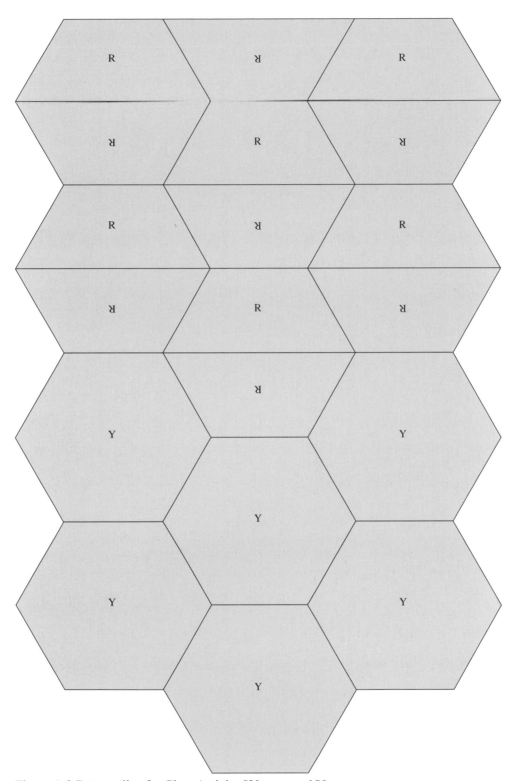

Figure A.3 Pattern tiles for Class Activity 8V on page 180

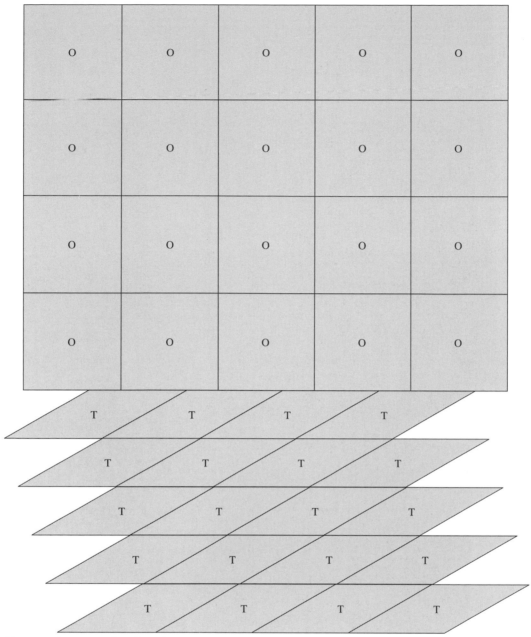

Figure A.4 Pattern tiles for Class Activity 8V on page 180